An Unknown Woman

An Unknown Woman

A Journey to Self-discovery
by Alice Koller

HOLT, RINEHART AND WINSTON
NEW YORK

An Unknown Woman

I

The October morning sunlight pours against my reflection in the bathroom mirror of a New York apartment which isn't mine. My makeup has ceased to be a subterfuge: it looks thick and caked, even though I carefully rub off all but the barest cover for my skin. Two long lines are being etched on either side of my mouth. Semicircles are beginning to form under my eyes. My thirty-seven years haven't been visible until now. I can no longer conceal them.

Yet I must. If I look thirty-seven, I have to explain why it took so long to get my Ph.D. But if I can pass as ten years younger, I'm a brilliant young scholar, and the easy excuse for why I'm not teaching at a good college is that it takes a little while to settle in. But I haven't even decided whether I want to teach. If I said that out loud, someone would ask why I went so far in philosophy. And I don't know.

Twenty-seven without a husband: I can smile and murmur, "I've been too busy working for my degree." Thirty-seven with a trail of men I try not to remember: I have to say stupid things about why I never married.

I stare into the mirror. I don't have a life: I'm just using up a number of days somehow. There is no *reason* for me to be here. No plan formulated at some point in the past has led me to this void that is my day, every day. No obligation to anyone requires me to live in this apartment, or in this city. I don't live anywhere: I perch. Four months in New York, three in Cambridge as though I hadn't fled it. Two months in Berkeley, four in Santa Barbara. Boston. New York again. I despise my little busy-work job, and yet I don't try to find something else. I try, instead, to turn it into a permanent connection:

I must be certain of my income, at least. I must have something certain in all this flux: no career, no home, no man.

I shake my head and bend over the washstand. My hands grip the sides of the basin for support. I couldn't answer Ed's question last month: "What sustained you through all those years of getting your Ph.D.?" It was his tone that made me understand the question. Ed, not seen for the dozen years since we were students at the University of Chicago, now a successful editor, speaking as though being sustained is something people have the right to expect. As though it's a normal and healthy part of the ordinary course of things for people to support one another's plans and expectations. But support is something to be begged for, isn't it? Or to be bought with wit and smiles and entertaining conversation and lies of perhaps only the palest gray? But even the sustaining I bought from Dr. Kant at twenty-five dollars an hour was to be had only two or three times a week. Where was the support that was supposed to have been free?

My stomach sustained me. But there's no stomach left now. I'm tired, from the inside out. Tired of perpetually having to fight for everything: degree, men, jobs, money. Tired of running after things that always elude me.

It has to stop. Can't I just stop, right now, and try to figure out what I'm doing? What I should be doing?

If I could only go away somewhere. Somewhere quiet, without traffic or factories. Somewhere where I can be really alone, so that I don't have to be pleasant to people all day long, so that I don't even have to see other faces when I walk outside my door. Somewhere where I don't have to do anything but think all day long.

With what? I have no money. Familiar terminal.

Suddenly I stand quite still and listen to the echoes of my sentence: "I have no money." Something about it is trying to get through to me. I always say I have no money. It's true, of course. I've never had enough money to do anything but feed and shelter myself: I'm still in debt for my education and for Dr. Kant.

Well, *would* I go somewhere to think if I had the money? Is it only the money that's stopping me?

All right, I'll *get* the money. I'll add up what my expenses will be for, say, another month. I'll see how much of what I owe needs to be paid now. Then I'll save the whole rest of my salary.

I sit down on the edge of the tub, trembling. I have a goal that is my own. A goal: a focus for the long minutes of my day. I will get money, and then I will go away.

Each day I look through the *Times* classified section under "Houses to Rent." There are phone numbers in Connecticut, on Long Island, in upper New York State, in Pennsylvania, but owners want too much rent, or too much security against damage, or too long a lease.

I open the *Saturday Review* to its classified section. There is a house available near Montego Bay for someone who wants to do some beachcombing; the rent is announced as "low"; there are two rooms. I try to imagine which two rooms they are.

I turn the page. There is a house at the far end of Nantucket, "totally private but not isolated." I consider it briefly. Nantucket is really very far away. From what? There *is* no place from which other places are too far away. Still, an island would be like voluntarily imprisoning myself. No, I'll keep on looking.

A week stumbles by without anything becoming clearer: where to go, or when. I get to work early Monday morning and look for the ad for the house on Nantucket. I read it again and again:

Siasconset, Nantucket—Fully furnished, heated year-round house. 5 rooms, 2 baths, fireplace, modern kitchen. Beautiful view overlooking moors. Totally private but not isolated. Garage, but car unnecessary. Will rent till June to writer, artist, at fraction summer rental. References.

A lot of rooms: it will be expensive. But "fraction summer rental": there are large fractions and small fractions. It's very, very far away. An island: it could be hard to get away from.

No. It's impossible. But it's my only lead.

I phone the person who ran the ad. No, the house is not yet taken. Am I busy for lunch? She and her husband can meet me and we can all talk about it. I hang up. Something close to excitement swoops from my belly to my throat, and I close my lips, smiling, to hold it in.

They give me one day to make up my mind about their house. The expenses are the easiest part. With what I've saved, and with my final salary check, I can last a lean four months.

Four months: time, real elbow-room time.

And quiet. During the winter there's almost no one at the eastern end of the island.

So: alone. Exactly what I was looking for. Not only alone in a whole house of my own, but alone outdoors, too.

I lie on my bed trying to picture it all, and then suddenly I know I'll have to have a dog. To warn me about strangers. To take walks with me. Yes, that makes it all fit together.

I telephone the owners to say I'll take their house. When I hang up, I write a check for four months' rent and water, and then I look for the little black book whose dated pages I so frequently leave blank. October 18. Today. The thirty-first will be my last day of work. I'll head for Boston on November 1, buy a dog at the Angell Memorial Shelter, and be on my way to Nantucket that Sunday. Two weeks and two days from now.

I go to bed early. It lets me quickly cross out the first of the fourteen days that I still have to get through in New York. But sleep is as bashful as though this were one more night in the old life, and I lie trying to imagine what is to come, until the whole building is quiet around me.

My last day in New York I stare the dawn into my room, and then I wander out into the kitchen to make the morning pot of coffee. In some span of time that seems too soon, the whole household is awake. Laurel is dressed and ready to leave for work.

"Timmie." She stops me in the hall. "Good luck." We put our arms around each other. "Write. Let me know how you're doing."

"Yes. Thank you, Laurel. You were very good to put me up so long."

"Good-bye, Timmie. Alice. I wish you hard thinking." She is gone. I head back to my room to begin tying off all the little ends that have so loosely connected me to this apartment, this city, this job. I finish packing, put on my coat, and catch the bus to the midtown garage where my car is being serviced.

Some small sense of release begins within me as I drive uptown to load my car, and it waits in abeyance even when I swing out to the Hudson River Drive. As I pass the second toll barrier and settle into a steady sixty-five miles an hour, I feel closer to the road with the added weight of luggage and five cartons of belongings. The sky is overcast all afternoon. Eighty miles outside of Boston the rain begins. Great sheets of water are thrown at my windshield, and the slowly moving wipers become an impediment to my vision. Something unexpectedly presses my right foot all the way down on the accelerator: it is the realization that I am now cut free of daily ties. I laugh out loud. I drive through the rain and the dark faster than I've ever driven under good road conditions. I want the feeling of my freedom, and I can know its size by flaunting my own cowardice at this speed.

I smile all the way to June's familiar street in Cambridge.

2

I awaken on the sagging couch in the living room of the Cambridge apartment in which I began and completed the writing of my doctoral dissertation. Three years ago. The glass doors that open directly outside are still covered by the lengths of fabric that I hung from floor to ceiling, the play of orange, red, and brilliant pink somewhat less crisp now. The floor end of the fabric is still unhemmed, its unraveled threads floating on vagrant drafts. The chair I sold to June when she moved in is here. The long high counter separating off the kitchen from the rest of the room still serves all the purposes it served for me: eating, writing, drinking, bill paying, letter reading, thinking, something solid to cry against. June has changed the kitchen curtains; I try now to remember what they used to be. I lie with the covers forming a sheath for my body, knowing that my first movement to get out of bed will make me catch my breath from shock at the cold. The same useless gas burner is still the only source of heat for the room, even though it heats only that corner of that end of the room where it sputters. Sometimes I lighted the oven, throwing its door wide open for extra warmth. But I didn't dare, nor does June, let either appliance burn throughout the night. Nor will there be hot water until twenty minutes after I strike a match to light the gas. It makes for a lot of obstacles to getting out of bed in the morning. And when these things are merely the first things in the day, so that the whole of it lies curled up, waiting to roll in on you inch by slow inch until midnight comes again, it is some miracle to marvel at abstractly, now and evermore, that for five hundred mornings I did indeed get out of bed in this apartment.

The thing to do is get out of bed roaring, as paratroopers do when they begin their fall, to get out at it before it gets in at you. But June lies asleep in the bedroom, one thin wall away, with her young son

Richard, and I do not repay her hospitality by startling her awake. I am up, across the room, lighting the gas, into the bathroom, and dressing, all in one connected motion. I fool myself to believe that I can be silent, for I hear June as she now hears me. I hurry to leave the unheatable bathroom and find her, wrapped in a robe, sitting on a high stool at the counter, smoking quietly. The corners of her mouth are always upturned: to show off the lovely high cheekbones, or to prevent the age lines from forming? The resulting look is that of an untouchable cameo. We trade comical remarks about the morning flight to the water heater, and then I make the coffee while she awakens Richard and starts to turn the handle of her day.

I wait for the coffee to percolate and think of what it is for me to be in Cambridge and in this apartment, patent symbols of the ring I never-endingly traverse. This room: I waited and wept for Jim, and then for Mike, and then for Marvin here. Wouldn't only a fool be standing in it now? This town: every street carries some shadow of unfinished business, or of business finished beyond the boundaries of endurance. Three days, four at most, and then I catch the boat to Nantucket. Two hundred people to avoid between here and Boston, all but a dozen of them within a few minutes' walk from here in Harvard Square. I cover my face with my hands. It is only seven o'clock in the morning.

Each time I come away from Angell Memorial Animal Shelter, I am more certain that my dog will be a German shepherd. And male, I think. I want him to be smart and lively. And protective.

Five visits are fruitless.

Marie. Marie, the practical, the efficient, the problem solver, will have an idea about where to find a dog.

I drive out to Marblehead to visit her and Lincoln in the eighteen rooms of the house they bought six months ago. Their unpaved private road demands caution in navigating it, and as I turn off my ignition I wonder whether I'll stay an hour or overnight.

"Alice." Marie's smile, somehow wry and patient at the same time, is by now her shorthand for wondering how I could have lived so long and still be so dumb. "Here are the local papers. There's the phone. That drawer—no, the one on the left—has pencils and paper. Linc and I are just going out for groceries. Get to it."

I look through the classified ads. Two phone numbers are busy. At the third an old man answers. Yes, he has one shepherd left: male. Seventy-five dollars.

"Suppose I don't take his papers. Would he be less expensive?"

The man is silent a few seconds. Sixty dollars if I don't take papers. Not much of a help.

I write down the directions for getting to his house, and when I hang up I scribble some figures. Sixty for the dog leaves fifty in my wallet. Three hundred and fifty in the bank for Nantucket itself. A very lean four months indeed.

Marie insists on coming with me. "You can't manage a puppy that's probably never been in a car before, and also drive at night. Now you wait."

I bite back my words. My dog is waiting for me: not yet seen, but mine.

We cover the back seat and floor of her car with newspapers. She is tired and irritable, but trying to be pleasant.

Twenty minutes beyond Salem we find the road leading to the small house in the woods.

In the cluttered living room the heavily powdered wife of the very fat old man sits next to me. The couch we share borders the kitchen, where every surface is covered with the remains of food or dirty dishes. The man heaves himself out of his chair to get the puppy. We wait.

All at once a golden-tan-and-gray mass of energy flies through the doorway, makes two full circles of the living room, finds the pathway between the furniture into the kitchen, and heads for the open garbage pail near the sink. The man reaches down to pick him up and walks toward me, holding the pup under one arm. I see the lively face for the first time, and then the man sets the pup on my lap. Instantly he's on the floor again, and now the woman catches him to give him back to me. I touch him lightly. He trembles, sniffing my hands, my coat, my slacks. I can neither speak nor take my eyes off him.

The man goes outside again and in moments returns with the puppy's sire. Immediately the pup leaps to the floor and makes swift circles of the room, twice, three times. The older dog watches him quietly and, as the pup passes him for another round, opens his jaws without warning and takes the puppy's head in his mouth. I catch my breath. He lays the puppy on its side on the floor, still holding the little head, and then the puppy is quiet. Slowly the large dog opens his mouth and releases the puppy but keeps his head very close. The puppy lifts an awkward paw in feeble protest, but the sire starts to bring his mouth around the head again, and the paw falls back to the puppy's side.

The woman gets up to bring the puppy to me one more time. We've been here fifteen minutes and I haven't yet bought him. Marie: "Do you like him, Alice?"

"I don't know. I think so. He's probably okay." Nothing in me moves out to say: "Yes, I want him." Each of those words is too strong for me. But here in this suffocatingly small room sit two bizarre people whose business it is to sell me this puppy, this very one. I can't think it over; we can't come again. I have to take this puppy now.

I say it very low: "I'll take him." I write the check. I own a dog.

The woman tells me what to feed him, how to keep him clean. She holds the puppy while Marie and I settle into the car, then she hands him to me. He's on my lap, on the floor, on the seat now, whimpering.

"Just talk to him while you ride along," the woman calls to me through the window.

In the darkness of the car I start to pet him, my dog. He shakes and trembles and looks straight ahead. I talk to him, but the talking is words of no account, to let him know he's safe, and mine. He doesn't care. Saliva starts to pour from his mouth. My coat is soon soaked from it, but he doesn't get sick. I stroke him to calm him. What is he leaving behind? What, for that matter, is he going to?

I have begun my journey.

We leave the pantry lights on for the puppy, cover the floor with newspapers, and close the kitchen door behind us.

In bed, I think what to name him. I won't name him after someone. How, then? A name from something close to me. Something from philosophy.

An hour passes as I wander back through thirteen years of the erratic study that, at a cost I still don't know, has given me my Ph.D. I try out names of philosophers. I test philosophical terms. In the dark I smile.

And then something of what lies waiting for me on Nantucket slowly begins to serve as a filter for my thoughts. There will be no fellow philosophers to grin with recognition when I speak my puppy's name. There will be no one except me to whom this name will mean anything. This name will have to be only for me. I must make it a name that will somehow say what I'm going to do on Nantucket, as it will remind me later what I did there. And what will that be? This puppy will be my only contact with anything living. He's the only creature I'll be talking to. Words. Discourse.

Logos.

I open my eyes and turn to lie on my back, staring into the dark. I say "Logos" over and over. This is the name. Logos: the rational principle of the universe; the Word; reasoned discourse. The puppy's name is Logos.

An unfamiliar excitement begins in my stomach. I lie for long minutes trying to understand what it is, but I fall asleep before I have the matter even formulated.

The instant I awaken I know that something new is in my life. The puppy. I open the door, but from downstairs comes no sound. I fly into my clothes, and still buttoning, still zipping, I creep down the stairs and quietly open the kitchen door. Linc squats on the floor, petting the puppy. "Why, he's beautiful!" Linc looks up at me and smiles hugely.

The puppy takes an uncertain step toward me, sniffs, and then remembers me, kissing half my cheek as I stoop and reach out to hold him. Until this moment I've hung back from him: he's too small; suppose he's not intelligent; do I even like him? But from this moment, he starts to become mine.

Late in the morning I have the house to myself. I get down on the dining-room floor to teach the puppy his name. For the next hour we're absorbed in one another's tumbling. When I hear Marie's car in the driveway, I make one last test: "Logos!" He comes flying to my arms, and I hold him close for a minute before I stand up.

I keep him with me through the entire day of errands, packing, and good-byes.

3

I'm awake before the alarm goes off, and I dress quickly, thinking of the beautiful puppy, now mine, downstairs. I lift the shade: yesterday's gale winds off Marblehead haven't abated. Most of the night I lay listening to the heavy rain. But I'm going today anyway. The ferry *must* leave for Nantucket.

At the kitchen door Logos greets me, leaping up and uttering little cries until I kneel matching our heights. This lovely, clumsy pup: my untried companion and protector. I muffle my laughter: I want to be gone before anyone is awake. But Linc enters the kitchen while I'm making coffee and we share a hurried breakfast.

In the rain he helps me load the last luggage into the car's back seat, the bucket seat next to me saved for Logos. I suddenly remember that the car-sickness pill the vet gave me needs thirty minutes to take effect. I thrust it down the puppy's throat. My fault if he's afraid for the first half-hour.

Sunday morning, nearing seven o'clock, traffic into Boston is light. I talk to Logos to reassure him. He remains worried: about the noise, our unceasing movement, the other rushing cars, perhaps even about my driving.

All at once I see him rocking lightly back and forth on the edge of the front seat. I hold my breath. What new problem is he preparing for me? Nimbly he springs down to the floor. I talk to him rapidly, but he steps in front of the gearshift and sits squarely on my right foot. The car leaps forward. I try to lift my foot to remove his warm weight but his bulk immobilizes my instep. I resist the urge to slip my foot out from under his body: his thirty pounds would land on the accelerator pedal and we'd be at top speed immediately. I swear abundantly at Logos and at the cars in lanes on either side of me. With all my strength, I raise my right foot high enough off the pedal to slow us down slightly. The car on my right forges ahead, clearing the road for me to pull over to the side.

"Now, listen." I pause. The tender, terrified face looks up at me. Our two days together give me no leverage with him: neither affection, nor habit, nor training links him yet to me. He has no reason to listen. I shape some old towels into a nest on his side of the car.

Logos trembles quietly. No soothing words of mine can stop him. It's too soon to give him another pill, and although I sympathize with him to the limits of my ignorance of what to do for him, I pick up speed once again.

Near Falmouth, I turn southwest at the sign WOODS HOLE—4 MILES.

What am I doing here on this desolate road, speeding to catch a boat to an island?

Next to me Logos implores the trip to end. I touch his head lightly.

I am closed off into myself and no one but me can ever help me get out.

I climb the narrow stairway to the enclosed top deck of the ferry, Logos padding after me, his ears pasted back against his head to obliterate the sound and feeling of the engines' deep throbbing.

The New York Times lies open in front of the man standing next to me at the coffee bar. Leaning on his elbows, he turns his head onto his right shoulder and watches Logos without speaking. When he looks up at me, I see that his eyes are pale blue. He's tired, or still drunk. But his voice is even. "How did you teach him to go up stairs so young?"

Is it something to be taught? "I just walked up and he followed me."

A steaming cup of coffee and a plate of English muffins are placed on the counter for the man, but he turns his attention to Logos again. "We have a two-year-old collie who won't go up stairs. I think it's because she's frightened of coming down."

We.

I suddenly remember how bad my skin looks up close. Twenty-five years of evading strong light, especially when a man is near, battles with a fragile half-morning's start on shedding pretenses. And wins. I turn my face down into the shadow of the counter as Logos rests his head on my foot.

The counterman wants my order. I murmur, "Coffee. Black."

"Anything else?"

I want the man next to me to know that my life is like his, that he and I have in common some bits of our way of moving through our days: that kind of breakfast, that newspaper, that manner of dressing, that casualness, that way of talking without prelude. No. What am I doing? Who is this man to me? Why do I have to show him who I am, how I live, what is mine? This is what I'm going to Nantucket to tear away. Do I start only when I land there?

"Just coffee."

My new stand abruptly transforms the man into someone apart from me. What is there about him that makes me so sure he's drunk or just beginning to sober up? The whites of his eyes are streaked with red, but it's something else that involves the whole aspect of him. He tosses some coins onto the counter to pay for his food. Half the coins fall to the floor, not by accident, but from his lack of coordination. There. I neutralize him by considering him an object for an intellectual exercise.

The motors start up. An unfamiliar excitement in me expands toward their reverberations. This is going to be new. This is the beginning of something I haven't yet done. Yes, I will try. I will.

I head for one of the deserted tables nearby, far enough away from the bar so that if I sit facing the water I can temporarily believe Logos and I are here alone. I reach into the leather double-pouch that serves as a purse and general carrier, and pull out the new notebook.

Scribbling on the fresh page of the journal, my pen moves far more slowly than the words come. Ed's question returns to me again: "What sustained you during all those years of getting the degree?" When I leave Nantucket, I may know. Now I can say only: blind pride, together with a constant and ignorant heedlessness of the consequences of my acts and of the passage of time. Even saying I ignored them assumes that I knew what the consequences were but was tossing them aside. But I didn't know, and I still don't.

I'm going now to a place where no one knows me. In this place I'll tear away all the sham and all the acting. If anything at all is left, it will at least be mine. No one else's standards will guide me. No one else's reasons.

"Thirty minutes to Nantucket." An attendant, passing my table to inform me, reaches down to pet Logos. I have been making myself ready for the silence that is to come, but all day—on the dock at Woods Hole and here—I have been surprised by the amount of attention I, a stranger, receive simply because I'm on the other end of a leash that holds a beautiful puppy. Not only will Logos be my contact with the living by his very presence: he'll also keep me in touch with people.

I feel that I'm about to burst a prison. Nothing except my own will-lessness can prevent it. The life that is beginning now is the one that will make sense of all the other ones. The only thing left for me to do now is to understand all the things I've done up to now. Can I write? And do I want to? Who is part of me? Is anyone?

A motor stopped a while back, a buzzer sounds, we're passing reefs, and soon we land. It's two o'clock in the afternoon, November 11, 1962.

4

I follow the caretaker's car six slow miles. The straight road, empty of houses, stretches ahead. The bleakness of the land matches the gray day, the green of the trees the only color anywhere. The woods thin into moors covered with bristly shrubs. The sky is vast. A low house breaks into the flat perspective, then another.

Something round and silver-gray looms high in the air: a water tower. We turn left into the road on whose corner it stands. On its side of the street sit three houses, two close together, the third farther down. On the other side of the street, there is nothing, only moor. No, there is one house, just one, and Mr. Santos is turning into its driveway. I like it on sight: lawns, setting, privacy. My own gray house.

I tighten my hold on the wheel: the gravel road is badly rutted. I pull into the driveway beside Mr. Santos' car, and Logos and I pile out and into the house.

Mr. Santos explains where things are. I've never had a house to myself before (power supply? main water valve? thermostat?).

"Sure you don't need any help unloading your car?"

"No. Thank you for meeting me. And for opening the house."

I call Logos to me as Santos' car backs out the driveway, and I close the door.

"Logos!" I shout. "This is our home!" Together we fill the kitchen. I fly into the living room: windows almost everywhere, a fireplace, furniture better than I had tried not to hope for.

This is where we live.

Each time I unload a carton or suitcase from the car, Logos is close on my heels. I get the hang of opening doors, my arms full, while try- ing not to step on him or to drop anything on his head. The final time out of the house I cross the lawn to open the garage door. He is between my heels. I try to persuade him to stay sitting on the lawn while I drive the car into the garage, but he, too swiftly for me to stop, leaps onto the car floor, over the pedals, and takes up a station on the floor of the passenger's side. He sits and faces me as pert and ready for a drive as though he hadn't spent every minute on the trip here trying to get out. And then, awed, I understand: he prefers the hated car *with* me to the possibility of being somewhere without me.

I walk restlessly through the living room from corners to middle to doorway, cartons still sealed on the floor. The room is not yet mine. This dining table at the room's side entrance: wrong for me. It will be my desk. I drag it across the room to the bay of windows that looks out onto the moor. Bookshelves are now directly behind where I'll write. Fireplace chairs get shuffled closer this way. Couch against the wall to give more walking area.

While I stop to survey the newly enlarged room, Logos approaches each piece of furniture with a slow crouching motion, equally ready for flight or attack in case the motionless object he sniffs becomes a moving thing. I have a comic in my house.

I begin to unpack. Books here. Files there. Typewriter on the desk. I look out across the moor. The sun is falling toward the horizon, making manifest the enormous sky. I hurry to finish so that I can watch the sunset in peace.

The thought arrests me, my blue enamel coffeepot in my hand. Whose rule am I following that it speaks to me with so much urgency: Finish unpacking, because you've started it. Finish (whatever) because you've started it. My mother: "You can't start the new book until you finish the one you're reading," and so I bent my head over the last fifty pages, at that instant hating the book that had lost my interest anyway. At seven I was too unsophisticated simply to turn the pages slowly, feigning reading, and so I finished the book, reading every word. Thirty years later, I'm still obeying. Why did I finish the book? She told me to. Why shall I finish unpacking? I try to think of an answer.

A feeble desire dances into the empty space: I'd like a drink. But I hesitate over the boxes. The faint wish fleshes into a full image: I'd like to sit with a drink, watching the sunset. Didn't I come here to see what I am when I divest myself of everyone else's rules?

I turn away from the boxes abruptly. Where is the bottle of bourbon I bought in Cambridge? Good Mr. Santos: the ice trays are full. Back through the living room, where the open cartons don't roar at me at all, and up the stairs. The highly waxed wooden steps are steep, and Logos slips and claws his way up after me.

I move a wicker rocker close to the bedroom window, and then pull a stubby table toward me. Logos, exhausted from following my every movement and from the drugged trip, flops onto the floor beside me and instantly falls asleep. I take one long swallow of my drink and lean back in the silence to watch the great rumbling clouds pour into one another above the sunset that now reddens the whole horizon. Like the sky in the opening scenes of *Great Expectations*. My diploma says I am that: *femina optimae spei,* a woman of great expectations. Then what am I doing alone in this strange room overlooking a moor?

Oh, I am *tired*. From the trip here. From the whole ten days of battering through obstacles since I left New York.

What can I do here? How do I know that coming here will let me understand who I am and what I want, when two dozen years of trying so many other ways in so many other places have failed?

I don't now. The answer is: I don't know at all.

The sun is down. A narrow band of brilliance outlines the edge of the moor. From this second-floor window, so few objects jut up into the sky that the sunset has no competitor for my attention. The horizon is uninterrupted by high buildings or moving steamships or bridges or looping expressways. The line of the ground here is low and flat, overarched by the sky that forms the frame for the sunset to dominate the land.

My drink is gone. Logos must be hungry.

We are ready for bed early. Logos ignores the corner of the room I covered with the newspapers I found downstairs. He curls comfortably on a needlepoint rug, trying to keep awake to check on me. How do I let him know that the papers are for him? One more thing I don't know. I climb into the high iron bedstead. I have time only to notice that its mattress slopes in toward the center, and then one deep sigh.

I wake up abruptly without knowing why, and then as quickly I know.

"Logos! Damn you! That's what the newspapers are for." I drag him downstairs, smack his rear, and shove him outside. I ransack all the closets for mops and pails and old cloths. Suddenly I realize that Logos might run away, and I rush to open the back door to look for him. He sits quietly on the stoop, looking up at me uncertainly. I restrain myself from petting him and let him in.

Bucket and mops in either hand, halfway up the stairs I start to laugh. Here am I, at three o'clock in the morning, trying to find cleaning equipment in an unfamiliar house for a mess on some needlepoint rugs that are not mine. There at the top of the stairs stands

a four-month-old puppy who is mine, happy now to see me laughing. A pair of loners, one of whom is housebroken, one not.
I sleep wakefully through the night.

5

The light washing against the pale window shades arouses me. With a full heave of my body, I turn my face into the crook of my arm, trying to hide from the assault on my eyes. When I lift my head a few inches, I find a puppy staring into my face.

I race him downstairs and outside. My coat over my robe over nothing at all, I look up into the gray sky and shudder in the cold air. I can begin today. I want to have breakfast, walk over to my desk, and start. But we need food. A vet to tell me more about how to take care of Logos. Arrange about the phone. Get things into drawers and closets. My mail: there should be a check.

I coax Logos to come inside.

Earrings, necklaces, bracelets, and other decorations go into the bottom drawer of the bedroom bureau. All makeup goes into the medicine chest. What will I look like now that no one I know will see me? Can I dress without following anyone else's rules? I stand in the bedroom trying to let myself reach for whatever clothes come to hand, trying to make myself not care how I look.

I'm fighting to break out of the pattern of what I've been doing for, my God, twenty-four years. A quarter of a century, a third of a lifetime. I haven't got twenty-four years to undo the pattern slowly: I have to smash its hold as fast as I can. Each thing I do during the course of a day is something I've been told to do, or taught to do. I have to replace all of it with what I choose to do. I have to learn how to choose one thing over another, one way of doing something over another way. That means I have to want one thing, or one way, more than another.

My stomach tightens. Want one thing more than another? What will I use as a criterion? I don't know. I know only that I have to uproot all of the old while I'm learning what I want. Tear out every habit, every way of responding to people or to things. Or to ideas.

Look at it without mercy and ask: Is this mine? Mine as the specific human being that I am. Do I do the things I do because I'm Alice Koller? Or do I do them for reasons that I don't yet know?

I've arrived at this outermost edge of my life by my own actions. Where I am is thoroughly unacceptable. Therefore, I must stop doing what I've been doing. And I can't stop doing it until I know what I do.

So I'll wear something if it's clean and will keep me warm. I'll try not to think whether it fits or is without patches or holes or is too long or too short. Except: the color will matter. I'll play with colors in all sorts of ways, but some I will not have together. I'm sure of my sense of color.

So soon. It's my first clear judgment, *my* judgment. A very tiny step I take. How will knowing that I trust my eye for color take me to knowing how I want to live my life? The chasm stretches beneath me.

I fasten the leash onto Logos' collar before I open the outside door. Are there cars here? Bicycles? Children, old people, fishermen? Once I get organized, I'll look up the two or three people whose names I collected in New York. Or will I? They'll say, "What do you do?"

Logos drags me across the lawn and into the road before I find the strength to resist his unexpected pull. I seek out a dry path through all the deep puddles, and although I hang on to the leash, Logos chooses our direction. At the water tower on the corner, I haul him back toward me and stand for a moment, unsure of my route to the post office.

There isn't a car to be seen. Or a person. I turn left; east, I hope, toward the sea. At the first corner, far down the street, two boys are running with a dog. In the opposite direction, a long block away, some men fix a roof. The wind muffles their hammering. The boys and dog sound muted, too. I cross the street, and the sounds disappear behind me. Half a dozen steps farther, I slowly come to a stop. I listen. There are no sounds of living things. The wind. A familiar dull roar which I suppose is the sea. But otherwise, silence.

I start to walk again, examining the houses we pass. Shingled, every one. Gray from the weather, differing only in size and in the color of the trim. No, there someone has stained the shingles a pale green. Who lives in these houses? And where are they now?

In two blocks, I turn right onto a narrow street. At its end is the post office. I try the door on the near side of the little frame building.

Locked. As is the door on the far side. I shade my eyes to peer through the glass. No movement, no person, no light.

Perhaps it's a holiday. Why else are there no people where there are perfectly good buildings? It's not real. An apprehensiveness catches me up, and I fight to grasp some element of reasonableness. I tell myself the date: November 12, Monday. Wait. November 11, Veterans Day. Fell on Sunday, celebrated on Monday. So it *is* a real post office.

No mail means no food, either. Or phone. So all the things that stand in the way of my beginning remain to botch up tomorrow. No point in going back to the house so fast.

The sea stretches before us at the bottom of a cobblestoned street so steep that Logos and I can't stop ourselves from running down it. Our momentum carries us onto the sand, I breathless and laughing. I unsnap Logos' leash. He flies ahead of me, stopping every few yards to smell something deep beneath the surface.

The tide is coming in, hitting the shore and bouncing high. Logos skips, a true skip, as we get close to the water. Who ever heard of a dog skipping? His delight thanks me. He is ahead of me, behind me, to my left, then running straight toward the surf. He digs with half a dozen incredibly swift motions of his paws, sticks his nose down deep into the hole, and then runs off, stopping abruptly ten feet ahead to repeat his action. He forgets I'm here, glorying in the vast new playground.

Gray water against gray sky. The shore is unendingly long, behind me and ahead as well. The sand is wet and packed, so that my feet move more or less on top instead of sinking in. I smell the air, then look out across the water to nothing at all.

The shores that I've lived on or walked along or sought out: the beaches of Marblehead; the dunes at Provincetown; the southern unfashionable strip of Malibu; the Cambridge bank of the Charles River; the beach at Carpinteria; East Beach in Santa Barbara; the beach at Goleta; the walk along the Neckar in Heidelberg; the view from the little park behind Notre Dame where the Seine stretches in two or three directions; Lake Michigan from Chicago's Near North beach; the beach on the ocean side of San Francisco; the bay at Sausalito. I don't want to be on the water, but merely to look at it from shore. Only the ride on the Staten Island ferry is tame enough for me.

All those walks along all that water, alone or with all those different people, at night in the cold, or at dawn and sunrise, or late afternoon and sunset: when something intolerable is in my life, I head for the water. It leavens me in some way. Some middlemost part of me is soothed and silenced by it. As now.

The air is unexpectedly soft and warm. The smell and look and sound of the ocean shore is so familiar that in these few minutes of being near it again I know how much a part of my days here it will become. But it's a seduction: I think of the hours at Malibu I used to spend walking on the sand, feeding the gulls, watching the waves roll in, even in the rain. It may keep me from what I've come here to do.

I move up onto drier sand. Logos lags far behind me. At a chain barrier hung between thick low posts, I see a path away from the sand. I wait for Logos and together we scramble along the street that curves upward at a treacherous angle. I remember to snap the leash onto Logos' collar. We wander past boarded-up houses and houses crowding each other on narrow streets, unpaved or cobblestoned. We reach a perfectly paved road. Where does it go? Blocks away to my left the water tower intrudes its fat head upward. I've come full circle.

Almost in front of my house, two running boys and a dog come toward us. The dog is large and white, somewhat Saint Bernard. I keep an eye on Logos, who cowers between my ankles. Both boys stop to pet him. One of them runs on, the other stays.

"Is your dog friendly?" I ask him.

"He's not my dog," says the boy. "I have a retriever."

Caught in the Fallacy of Many Questions by a boy on the edge of a moor. "Well, what's this one's name?"

The boy starts after his companion. Ten feet away he calls back his answer: "Saint."

Saint stays to sniff the new inhabitant. I stoop to console Logos. "Go home, Saint," I say firmly, and turn to walk into my driveway. Logos is as far ahead of me as the leash permits.

I reach for my journal and record the events of arriving on Nantucket, of the walk this morning, the extraordinary silence. I'll write two things while I'm here. The journal, which I'll keep on the desk: for saying what happens here, outside. The other pages will come out of the typewriter: whatever I can exact from my memory, whatever I can force myself to fit together.

Writing in the journal can make up for not having anyone to talk to. It even has certain advantages over talking. I don't have to wonder whether what I'm saying gets through. There have been so few people to whom all my words penetrated: two, three. George, most of all: I still remember what it was like. Stan: I tell myself that I remember it, but it was very long ago; suppose I don't remember it the way it was? Well, I don't have either one of them. Etel: we understand what we haven't yet said or what lies buried in what we say; odder still, because English isn't her native tongue. Or George's, either.

"Not Russian, no," he said. I was guessing at the barest trace of his accent. "Ukrainian. They're different languages."

His English was without flaw.

"We left when I was two." He considered me briefly, then spoke in that upward flipping tone he saved for special subjects that I had early learned I was not to press. "They told my mother thirty minutes before the train left Kiev that she could take one thing, and she took me."

But George is gone. And Stan.

And when Etel and I talked in Berkeley last winter, I came to see that ours is a friendship for long distance, in small doses. So there's no one to talk to that way anymore.

The sun comes out in time to set. I get up from my desk to play with the puppy. In the east a brilliant white outlines the clouds from below: the moon is about to rise. The puppy is quiet at my feet. A full moon rises. So here's my entertainment: the sky at moonrise and sunset. And the water, from the shore.

I feed Logos and take him outside. The air is mild. There is no wind. Last night the wind sang through the long hours I watched. The moon is high and lights the grounds with a light I never saw before. How could I never have seen moonlight before? I know. Here there are no lights outdoors, streetlights or car lights or traffic lights or the lights from houses; nothing competes with this light. It freely shows me the moor, the water tower, the houses farther down the street, the clump of trees behind the garden.

Suddenly I hear the sharp crack of wood. A man? An animal? I hurry Logos into the house, turn off the indoor lights, and go to each window to look outside, my heart still pounding. How did I forget that isolation can also be a hazard? Logos is puzzled by the new game. Ten minutes go by, and although I hear nothing, I don't turn on the lights again. I reach down to stroke the puppy, amused that my main reason for buying him was to have him protect me.

I arrange some rugs for him in the downstairs bathroom, cover the floor with newspaper, lead him to his new bed, pet him quietly to sleep, and quickly leave the room, closing the door behind me. I stand outside the door for a moment, and then start up the stairs. Immediate barking and crying. I get into bed, curling under the covers, and hope the noise downstairs will soon cease. In time it does.

But all at once a great pounding begins. It takes me a moment to figure it out: Logos is throwing himself against the door to break it down. I fly downstairs and throw open the bathroom door. A small body forcefully hurtles against me. Logos licks my face, my hands, his paws on my shoulder, head buried in my lap, moaning, crying, ecstatic at our reunion. The display dazzles me, and I spend long minutes holding him, quieting him. I know I can't have him upstairs. The needlepoint rugs aren't mine.

But maybe I don't have to confine him so thoroughly. The L-shaped hall outside the bathroom has a linoleum floor. I'll leave the rugs in the bathroom, put the papers in the hall, and close the hall door instead of the bathroom door. I start toward the hall door, but Logos, wary of my tricks, is ahead of me and into the living room, hiding behind chairs, under the desk, scampering out of the way as I reach for him. Behind the couch he traps himself, and I fish him out by the tail. I carry his wriggling thirty pounds to his rug bed, petting him asleep one more time. This time I stay until his chest moves regularly up and down, and then I tiptoe out, closing the hall door behind me.

I sleep for several hours before the furious pounding awakens me. Angry and out of ideas, I shout to be heard: "Be quiet!" He doesn't know what "quiet" means, but he hears me, and that's enough to tell him that I haven't deserted him. Silence from downstairs. I cover myself, and then it all begins again. The body now sounds bigger, hurled against the door; there is clawing (new) and yelping, barking, crying. I think awhile. I go downstairs. The joy that greets me is even greater, although I feel a certain grimness as I accept it.

In between three or four of these performances, I sleep.

Shivering in my robe, I take Logos outside to a morning wind so strong that it blows him backward as he heads for the field grass on the other side of the garage. I'm cranky from sleeplessness, and when we go inside, I settle him on a cotton rug at the bottom of the stairs, where he is pleased to fall asleep. I crawl upstairs and do so too. An hour and a half later I wake up and remember that I had been up before but went back to bed.

I smile. I've torn away another rule and put one of my own in its place: to go to sleep when I'm tired.

"My name is Philip Morris, if you'll believe it." The postmaster extends his hand for me to shake through the small window opening. A neighborly face. "I had a German shepherd for twelve years. Lost him just a little while ago."

"I'm sorry."

During the winter, mail is available only at the post office. It comes by boat. When there's a boat. By the time it gets sorted in Nantucket and driven out to Siasconset, and by the time Mr. Morris and his part-time helper do the local sorting, it's three-thirty. After three-thirty I may ask for mail.

Mr. Morris talks as he watches Logos nose his way from the door at one end of the public area to the door at the other. "I've been postmaster here for thirty-three years. Retiring January first to go to a little house we have in Florida." I inspect the colored photo he holds out for me to see.

I thank him, as much for his pleasantness as for his information, and gather up my letters.

"We were beginning to wonder when you'd get here," he calls after me as I open the door.

Outside, flicking through the stack of mail, I hear his words: "We were beginning to wonder." No friend of mine was concerned at my coming here: one more wild and dramatic thing I was doing. But all the while, ever since I wrote from New York to ask the postmaster here to hold my mail until I arrived, someone I didn't know was watching for me. I'm suddenly ill at ease to be treated as though I'm part of the world of human interconnectedness.

I was wrong: the puppy hasn't made his peace with the car. He runs out of my reach, battling the heavy wind that rushes against him. I catch him and carry him in my arms. My body slants, walking toward the car. The wind is another presence, demanding my attention. Logos, ears back, coils into himself on the passenger seat. I back out of the driveway, up the road, and onto that undeviating, long, marsh-bordered, then pine-bordered, road leading to Nantucket. I talk to Logos to calm him. Or to calm myself. I push the accelerator down to the floor to counteract the fierce pressure coming at us from the side, but the speedometer reads only 40 miles per hour. I hold the wheel tightly, working hard for each of the five miles of straightaway.

Now here's a traffic circle. I turn off it to the right, wondering whether I'm correctly retracing the route Mr. Santos led me along two days ago. In a quarter of a mile I come to a stop at one edge of the town square. I did it.

Three shelves for bread in the grocery store stand empty. A sign reads NO BOAT TODAY. I'm on an island: it's another kind of life.

I pack the grocery bags into the car, tell Logos I'll be back, and cross the street to the hardware store.

A bell clangs when I close the door behind me. The smell of nuts and bolts and grease and nails and turpentine and tools and the thousand small things I used to help my father sell wraps around me, and I stand still. The crowded aisles are arranged in no apparent order. Toward the back of the store I see a counter, its free surface large enough only to write up a sales slip, the rest covered by clusters of inexpensive sorts of things that you always forget to buy unless you see them in front of you while you're waiting for a clerk. Daddy tempted customers that way, too. The clerk wears a zippered sweater and knows where each thing in the clutter is. As Daddy did. I think of the slow irrevocable atrophying of my father's brain. Daddy had that same patience as he'd listen to someone describe some nonworking piece of plumbing. While the customer was still searching through his pockets for the slip of paper on which he had scribbled the dimensions of something, Daddy would have placed exactly the unit he needed on the counter before him.

Another clerk appears from the rear of the store. "Pet things," I say. He leads me to a heretofore hidden area, shelves filled with collars, leashes, baskets, balls, combs, brushes for every size of dog there is. What do I want? My father well again. "I want a ball for my dog." I take two, and a rubber mouse.

I find the change. I am too slow. I have to hurry from this store, or cry before I reach the door.

In the car I squeak the mouse for Logos before I can turn the ignition key.

The wind becomes a tailwind on the drive home, and then once again takes up its more terrifying position from the side. Logos senses the overbearing presence and tries to find a secure footing. He moves from floor to seat to my lap and back to the floor again. I prepare to intercept a move onto my foot on the accelerator. I can neither calm him nor make him settle in one position. He's too frightened to hear me. I become angry, more so for being afraid that the car may flip over. I'm losing control, of the car and of myself. No one told me about such winds. Will it be like this for the whole time I'm here?

The battle with the wind intensifies when we get out of the car, I with packages in my arms, Logos with only thirty pounds to pit against its power. The screaming sounds of the wind add to my darkening mood, and even the puppy knows that all is not well as he comes to sit quietly near me on the couch.

I am irritated in the extreme. How did this happen? Yesterday was lovely, alone with Logos all day, except for the carpenters and boys I saw on our walk. But then this morning when I read the mail, every letter jolted against me. And all the stores and people and stopping and starting ever since. And now the wind: it flies around the house as though it's looking for an entrance.

I cannot shake off the sense of fragmentation.

6

The wind is so monstrous this morning that Logos refuses to move from the doorway when I want to let him out. I fume at the wind for interfering with my plans for housebreaking him, and we go back inside. Twice before noon he tries to go out into the heavy wind. Twice I clean up after him.

He does take time. I think of what his food bill will be, and how large he'll grow, and what a problem he may become wherever I might live later. But he gives me my freedom: I'm not afraid to be here alone at night. That has to cost something.

Lying against the fender of the fireplace I've closed off, Logos lifts one heavy eyelid to make sure I won't move from my chair, then lowers it, heaves a deep sigh, and, sleeping, guards me.

I think of a way to start: I'll use the letters I've saved. If I can't see what I do, I can surely see what other people think I do or am, or thought I did or was. It will come through, not just in what they say about me, but in their manner. I'll be able to see what I thought I wanted to do when I was writing to them, and how I managed to muddy it all up.

I reach for the packages of old letters. How shall I sort them? I begin by years: all the letters from 1962, then from 1961, as far back as they go. Bad idea: so few of them are dated that I have to read too much of each letter to discover when it was written. How else then?

I'll sort them by person. If I can't get a year-by-year view of how I looked to all the people who wrote to me, I can get a person-by-person view. That will show me the scope of each relationship. And that might teach me more than the record of my changes over the years.

I take up a handful of letters. Quickly I see this as a job for the floor. A pile for Isabel. One for Mimi. Daddy. Mike.

I get up from my knees and stand staring at the batches of paper. There's no one unitary Me standing here: I'm portioned out into each of these persons that I've written to. I reach for a letter: George's. I read half a page. His words bring back what it was like to know him last year in Cambridge. Now another: Randall. And I'm different by the ten years that preceded knowing George. Did one Me know both men? Is the later one Me? Or is the earlier one truer somehow? And how does that Me relate to all these little paper islands?

The sense of being splintered backs me against my desk, and then I run out of the room to escape it. I enter the kitchen and reheat the coffee, to be performing some action in the present. The past wants to swallow me up, spread out on the rug as it is. I have to find some handle on it that will let me push it away from me but still let me study it to see it for what it is.

I take the coffee back to the living room. Logos wanders across the littered floor and circles the spot he chooses for his nest on top of it all. I persuade him to settle elsewhere for the rest of his nap.

I must impose some order on all the letters. I write down the name of the author of each stack and try to remember what years our correspondence covered. The list is long: I count seventy-five names. Idly I put a mark next to the names of people with whom I'm still in some sort of touch. One I cross out after including it; two or three will come to an end soon; ten remain.

My eyes run through the full list over and over, seeking some way into it. I can reread one person's letters each day, starting with the longest ago and coming up to the present.

The only letter I've kept from Mimi is dated 1947. I first knew her in the sixth grade. That was 1936. I must remember not to let my stomach sink at how far back this will take me. After "Mimi" I write "1." And Isabel, through high school and beyond, gets "2."

At "21" I stop, exhausted. It will do for a beginning.

I lean back in my chair, listening to the howling of the battering wind. Can Logos make it to the post office with me? For that matter, can I? But we can take the car. I smile at myself. Out here I want to walk wherever I go. But today a natural force prohibits me from using my natural locomotion, and it takes me several minutes to realize that I have some man-made defense against it.

The jingle of my keys puts Logos immediately on the alert.

The shattered feeling of the afternoon remains with me through the evening. The unceasing shrieking of the wind intensifies it. I turn on my radio, moving the selector slowly across the whole range of possible stations. A musical phrase floats into the room and I stop to hear what it might be. It's gone with a gasp and a roar. All the way around the FM dial I find only silence or static. I switch to the AM band: football scores from Providence. I endure them to the end for the sake of what might come next. An answer-and-win program. I keep turning the dial and am rewarded by some unmistakable Handel. I take a few seconds to clear the station, and then a spurt of interference blankets the announcement of the music to be played next. Nameless it comes, and I welcome it into the room, lying down on the couch to listen. Logos sits in front of the radio, head cocked to one side, trying to understand how this blue box, silent since our arrival, has surprisingly come alive. The volume decreases while I'm settling a pillow under my head, and then gradually the sound fades away. I wait, expecting it to return, then go to the radio to see whether I can tempt it back again. Neither CBC, nor Providence, nor any other sound of human life. I snap it off and go to my journal to outline the past two days. From time to time I get up to try the radio again, but even the nearby AM stations, if they come in at all, fade within a few minutes.

It occurs to me that I'm very tired, and that on Nantucket we are at sea.

Near midnight I lie listening to the wind, feeling my bed shaking with the whole house. I can neither stop the wind nor go elsewhere. I try to think of something strong enough to absorb my attention. The *Journal of Philosophy* arrived today. The Philosophical Association meets in New York after Christmas, discussing some of the things that interest George. Will I go? Will he? And will it matter by then?

The wailing increases. I must know what's happening. Who, at midnight, can tell me? I pick up the telephone. Fire? Police? I put it down again, and then as quickly pick it up and dial the operator. "Is there a weather bureau here?"

"No, we don't have a special number for weather information."

"Operator, somebody must know something about this wind. Will you help me find out?"

"Wait a minute, dear." I spend the seconds while she dials reflecting on the meaninglessness of her "dear." Yet not meaningless: she heard my fear, and that made her drop her stereotyped response.

A man's voice speaks in my ear. "Nantucket Airport."

I grin to thank the operator. "Can you give me a weather report?"

He laughs. "Wind. At fifty miles an hour."

"Yes, I know. When is it going to stop?"

"No sign of stopping. We haven't had a plane land in twenty-four hours."

I need to know more. "Listen. I live in Siasconset and I'm here alone. The house has been shaking for the last two hours. It sounds as though the roof is about to be blown off. Will you tell me what to do?"

"Miss, I live out there myself. The wind is pretty bad tonight, but I don't think my house will blow away before I get home. You go to sleep. You're safe. You call me again later if it'll make you feel better."

I hold the receiver away from me and look at it for a brief instant. The pinpoint of sound coming out of this black object that is small enough to hold in one hand is my only connection with humankind on this top floor of a house on the edge of a moor near the tip of an island thirty miles out at sea. "Thank you. I may do that. Good night."

For an hour I try to sleep, and then I go downstairs to the puppy. To comfort him or to have him comfort me. I pet him to sleep again, then stay with him a long time, reluctant to part from his living warmth.

I decide to bring my blankets and pillow downstairs to sleep on the couch, closer to the ground. I open the hall door between Logos and me, filling the space with chairs and pillows to prevent his coming through. He's content to sleep on his bed of rugs in the downstairs bath so long as I leave this door open. He has figured out that if I go upstairs, I have to come down again eventually, and he can wait. It's when the door is closed that he thinks I may sneak out on him.

Lying on the couch in the black room, I fancy I perceive a difference in the wind's tonality. Down here there's more bass, less modulation, whereas upstairs the corners and peaks of the roof invite whistling cadenzas that seem a prelude to a resolution sufficient to roar the house away.

Each morning Logos leaps, wriggles, yelps, and plasters my face with kisses when he first sees me. I find myself inventing new endearments. The simple repetition of his name isn't sufficient to last through the minutes that all the loving takes.

The howling does not stop: the wind is even stronger. When I try to go outside with Logos, I must force the door open, my back up against it, one leg wedged in the doorjamb for leverage. Logos slips out through the small opening I make, takes two steps onto the lawn, and then stands there, head down into the wind, trying to oppose his strength to that of the unseen demon. He presses forward a few steps at a time, only to be blown backward an equal distance, but he fights his way to the protecting bushes on the other side of the garage. When he returns to me, the wind is at his back and he almost flies.

I call the telephone company to ask them to bill the phone in my name and to remove the downstairs extension. The clerk wants certain information about me: Where am I employed?

"I'm not employed."

There is an extraordinarily short pause, and then: "I see. Shall we put down that you receive private income?"

Glorious. Who would have guessed that the telephone company divides human beings into these two categories? "Let us put that down."

I sigh my way into my clothes, thinking apprehensively of the drive to Nantucket in the unfailing wind.

We are barely across the threshold of the veterinarian's office when Logos sinks to the floor, his ears back. The vet reaches down to swing him up onto the table, pats him briefly on the head, and begins to ask me questions about the puppy's age and weight. He turns to his desk to write the information on a card. A sudden clank: Logos has leaped to the floor and stands at the door begging to be let out. This time I stand close to him at the table while the vet gives him the first of two distemper shots.

"I'd like to know what books I can read to learn how to take care of him."

The man fumbles through a stack of dusty magazines, and then suggests there might be something at the library. "Bring the puppy back in two weeks for the second shot. How long will you be on Nantucket?"

I tell him that I'm not sure. His slapdash attitude puzzles me. I must keep Logos healthy and away from him.

"You writing a book here?"

It's easier to say yes. He tells me that Sterling Hayden is writing a book here too.

I open the door. Logos' eagerness to get out carries him to the far end of the leash. He pulls me forward, straining against his own collar, choking but free.

My fifth day here, and I'm still scattering my time on little things. I seem to welcome these distractions. Like now: waiting till six-thirty to pick up the newspapers the grocery store promised me. But that's two and a half hours away.

I'm evading what I came here to do.

I could write. Not the day's events, but the people I saw. I try to draw a ring of words around the vet, but I remember him only as pudgy and dark. Will I be able to describe the look of people? They started to look alike some time back: new people either remind me of people I already know or else I can't remember their faces. Like the druggist today who knew exactly how to scratch Logos: he reminds me of Dick, and that lets me write down that he's tall and thin, with an easy way of talking. Like Marvin. But then Marvin always reminded me of Dick.

The sun, yellow-orange, comes out of the gray sky almost at the horizon. In a few minutes it will set. Will the wind die down then, or increase?

So this is how a person enters a town. You locate the post office and the grocery, and then one by one the little services. And then you're here, connected.

The sun is down; the wind is not.

Odd about not missing people. What do I need people for? To understand my words, to present a novel point of view on the world, to tell me funny stories, to share warm things, to give me some applause. But when every contact with people becomes a bruise and a shock (this must be how George sees the world), then the way I now spend my day is the easiest and the best way for me to live. On my way here, I tested all the lines connecting me with people and found them ready to be cut. If indeed the lines weren't already cut before I tried them. So back there I leave nothing and no one. I may as well be here, alone, where there's no one to seek, as to be somewhere else where I might begin to hope again.

I awaken to the unmistakable silence of no wind and to blazing sunshine.

"Logos!" I throw on my robe in my race down the stairs, and fling away the barrier at the hall door to hug the puppy as my share of the joyous greeting. This morning I can push open the door with my fingertips. Logos tentatively puts forth his nose, takes an unsteady step outside, and then leaps onto the lawn, misses his footing, rolls on his back, and comes to rest, nose between the tips of his paws, chin flat on the ground. Instantly he's up again, speeding twice around the house, while I stand amazed by the softness of the air, the unclouded blue of the sky, the perfect stillness.

During breakfast I briefly consider getting down to work, but I long to stretch my legs on a good walk, to exhaust Logos by running, to approach the sea by some new path. The immense red-and-white body of the lighthouse is partly visible from my yard. It looks far enough away to fulfill all those requirements. New things cry to be done in this new weather, and Logos finds my plan absolutely crackerjack.

The hardened ruts of the unpaved road turn walking into leapfrogging to avoid a twisted ankle. Soon there are only fields on either side of us. I slip around the chain barrier at the end of our road and pass some wooden sheds. What do they store? In a few strides I recognize the kind of terrain: we are at the farthest edges of a golf course. Yards of fairway spread out around us. I try to keep Logos away from the greens, beautifully cropped even in November.

Thursday evenings and Sunday mornings I caddied for my father. Nine holes on Thursdays, because that's all there was left of the summertime light after he closed the hardware store; eighteen holes on Sundays, because then we could be out on the first tee as the sun was rising. I think for the hundredth time how curious it is that I never played golf, never did more than take an experimental swing with a club, never asked to be taught, through four years and more of twice a summer week. I'd stand quietly as he swung at each teeing-off place or wherever the ball landed on the fairway; I'd search for the lost balls, sometimes finding other people's along with his, and he'd examine them, looking around to see whose they might be, so that whether he'd claim them would depend upon the time of day, whether there were people playing behind us, and the condition of the ball; I'd hold my breath and stand respectfully still on each putting green. I don't remember that we talked very much, walking all those miles together. There was a certain candy bar that he'd buy for me after we finished the day's round; it tasted particularly good on Sundays, because I was eating it before lunch.

Here's a wide circular bench to sit on. A good place to wait for someone: you can see in all directions easily. Logos leaves me to romp up the clubhouse steps where two telephone repairmen stop their work to play with him. I go over to collect him. We talk of Logos and of their dogs and of the cessation of the wind. When I call Logos to come away with me, I realize that the telephone company has provided me with almost my only human contacts in three days.

The lighthouse is even more massive up close. Large signs say GOVERNMENT PROPERTY, NO VISITORS. But the gate of the fenced enclosure is open and I walk in. Logos, nose to the ground, is picking up ravishing new scents. There is no one to be seen.

I stand at the base of the lighthouse, hoping to be permitted to go in, despite the signs. Close by are two houses. I decide which one of them might contain someone awake, and start up the stairway. Before I can knock, I hear a baby cry inside and I come away. We walk back toward the entrance, and then a strange sound stops me: slapping, hollow, but familiar, somehow. I stand listening, and then I know: the flag whipping against the breeze. It's the only sound I can hear, aside from the sea.

A paved road leads away from the light. We cross the lawn of someone's splendid vacant house and walk toward the edge of a very high bluff. The view of the sea and its shore is all the more spectacular for being unpeopled. To my left, the lighthouse at the very tip of the island, high above the water; to my right, house after empty house, and long wooden stairways leading from the bluff down the dunes to the sea.

The puppy trots three steps, lies down to rest, drags himself up, then flops gratefully down each time I stop to look. Well, let's stop then and have one full long look at the gloss of the sun on the waves, at the pattern of the water and its green clarity today against the shore and sky.

We walk home very slowly by the shortest route.

7

Now I have to begin. I sit in front of my typewriter, aware of this moment as the center around which all of my preparations have swirled. I'm here to understand myself, deliberately to turn myself open to my own view. I know, as I sit here, what I must have known for many years: that I can recognize what's true about myself when I see it. It's whatever I find myself refusing to admit, whatever I say no to very fast. That blanket admission right at the start may save me a lot of time. May save me, period. I'm using that "no" to protect myself from something. What? I'll find out. I'll write down everything I can remember, so that I can see the full extent of it, pick out some patterns in what I've been denying for so long.

So that's first: to get it all written, no matter how ugly.

But I know now, too, that all the years I made myself sit over philosophy books, examine philosophers' reasoning, set out my own reasoning for a teacher to examine—all that accumulated discipline can now be shaped into the one tool I need: to be able to say with perfect care whatever I want to say. I can push my saying to the point of saying what I mean.

What else do I know, now as I begin? That what's accessible to me through these letters can give me only a part of what I'm trying to find. After all, there are so few of them, and the record they offer, itself schematic, begins only since my graduation from high school. It's what came before high school that I so often find difficult to remember.

When I have only one letter or only a few from some one person, I'll try to fit together whatever else I can force myself to remember. I won't hold myself to any order. It will be best if I keep my fingers on the typewriter keys and write while I think.

Am I writing out rules to follow? I think not. I want only to let myself write as clearly as I can what I think or remember or am reminded of, or what I in that moment understand.

I search for Mimi's one letter and, reading it, begin. I cover three pages with single-spaced typing, swinging a wide circle that encompasses Mimi, her father, her mother, her house, the boys she knew. It's not what I want to be saying. I want to come to a focus on Mimi and me.

I begin again. This time I write of the evening we sat under a streetlight halfway between our houses, planning how I could go to acting school. Mimi supplied a sorority sister to meet me in Chicago, but more: she encouraged the hope that I could act. From my parents I needed permission and money. It was just before my seventeenth birthday. When they asked me what I wanted for a present, I told them to sit down, because I had a plan. I told them I'd pay for the first quarter's expenses at Goodman Theatre with money I had saved from my summer job, but if I liked it, would they pay for the rest of the year? The usual screaming battle with my mother. She gave in, grudgingly, only because Mimi's involvement made me respectable. Daddy, listening quietly, asked me whether I was sure it was something I wanted to do, and promised me his help. He never would have told me what it cost him, but she, for years afterward, reminded me of the amount he borrowed from his brother.

And yet, the very week I was to leave, I almost didn't go because Bob, whom I had loved *in absentia* during most of my senior year, was due home on army furlough. Mimi said, "You come with me and talk to this friend of my mother's. She's very smart. Let's tell her about it and see what she says." And what that nameless, faceless lady said was, "Go to school. You're too young to think of getting married, and you've given me little evidence to believe that Bob is thinking of anything serious with you. Anyway, if you're not here, and he really wants to see you, he'll go to Chicago. You have to go to acting school, if that's what really interests you." Compare the woman in the dean's office at the University of Chicago three years later who said, "Stay and learn," when I wanted to leave after that year or less. "What value will you be to the world without any education or training of any significant sort? You'll be able to do something if you learn something; otherwise, likely not." Did I stay longer than another quarter, even after her advice? I don't think so. "Stay and see how you like it," said Mimi toward the end of that first quarter at Goodman, and so when I returned for the second quarter, I was given a small part in a play, and then on the basis of that, the bitchy Miriam in *Guest in the House*. "Stay," says Weck now, thinking I'm still in New York. But there has to be a Where to stay and a What to do. "Stay," I decided to myself after the first savage year at Radcliffe; I decided it one morning lying in the sun in Weck's yard. But did I decide so fast because I wanted to be at the pier in New

York to see Stan off for Salzburg, or did I decide because of something I wanted to do? Oh, idiot: you wanted to see Stanley; you've never known what you *wanted* to do. "Stay. Why don't you?" said Dr. Kant about my entry job at Houghton Mifflin. "Until you have something else, or until you see better whether you like it." But I left because I didn't want to sign another lease with the fool who was my landlady, and because the situation with Jack, my good-friend-turned-lover, had taken a difficult turn. So I stepped off the edge of the world for the ho-humth time, and the morning I had to go to New York (I think of it now and thought of it then as *having* to go, even though I was the one who had decided to go) I started to cry and found it very hard to stop crying, and Jack stopped by and put his arms around me, and held me close, trying to comfort me both as a lover and as a friend. "Stay in New York and take the job with Knopf," said Dr. Kant, and it was one of the few times he was aghast at something I had done. "Have you told them already, and is it too late for you to change your mind by writing them?" And yes, it was too late. And why didn't I stay in New York? Because I wanted to be in Cambridge with George. Three months seemed to be the limit I could tolerate anything, and then I wanted to run; and only sometimes could someone else's wisdom make me stay: Mimi's was one. For the rest, I was going somewhere else because a man was there, or because he wasn't. I could never decide an issue concerning the course of my life in terms of how it affected *me*. Whether I was capable of seeing the consequences of my action, they never seriously entered my plans. I knew only one thing: I was unhappy there (wherever it was) and I could only hope that at least I'd leave this unhappiness behind if I left there (wherever it was).

Logos tries to scramble into my lap, to force his nose between my stupid wet face and the right arm that cradles it on my desk. He licks my mouth, my chin, and then finds a trickle somewhere on my neck, but that's too far away from my eyes, and it's to these he turns with a strength he doesn't yet know. I smile, wondering what he thinks he's doing.

"Sweet puppy," I say, and rub his ears. He turns his back to me for equal treatment. I break out of my mood. "Sweet puppy, do you want to go for a walk?"

He turns his head sharply to look back at me. Something in that sounds familiar, but I haven't moved from my chair, so he isn't sure.

"We could go for a walk."

He runs across the room, then stops abruptly, paws spread on the floor at an irregular angle from his body, ready to flee. I chase him to the kitchen, and when I open the outside door, his standing start carries him to the farthest edge of our lawn.

I awaken to the second straight windless morning, securely possessing nine perfect hours of sleep. I try to remember the last time I slept so uninterruptedly and long. A year ago, the weekend I drove alone from Santa Barbara to Berkeley to see Stan, most of the 350 miles by dark after a Friday's teaching. I turn on my side to throw off the sudden presence of that painful meeting at midnight ("But we were becoming close again in Berkeley." "Alice, I saw you because you were there."), the sleepless hours afterward in the hotel I found at 4 A.M., the whole Saturday in San Rafael where Etel tried to make me climb out of that despair that was my mourning for my loss of Stan. I slept finally, for the first time in two days, and I awakened twelve hours later at seven o'clock Sunday morning. And because the air smelled of the woods surrounding Etel's little house, and because it was silent without the noises of even a small city, and because I hadn't yet remembered the agony I had just passed through and the dreariness that lay ahead, I stretched each limb that morning, grateful for the gift of sleep, even as now. But the case is the same, and I must not forget it: everything preceding Nantucket has been a horror, and may be so again, if there is an again, unless I force out all the truth there is in me.

From Berkeley there was a 350-mile drive back to my ill-paid job, to things I *had* to do. Here there's nothing I have to do; there's only what I choose to do, once I learn how to choose.

A tail is thumping against the landing at the bottom of the stairway.

"Logos!" Invited, he flies up the steep stairs, and we have that breathtaking, vital encounter that unfailingly begins my new days.

Over coffee I try to work out a schedule. Walk to the ocean in the morning to give Logos a run after a long night? Or go in the afternoon, and pick up the mail on the way home? Or both? How long can I stay writing at one time?

The sunlight gets me outside in spite of myself, onto our rutted road, turning right at the unkempt field. Logos, trotting ahead of me off the leash, leaps over a low fence and sniffs his way to some compelling spot. He surprises me by jumping. Is that simply something that a pup can do? I wait for him, leash in hand, thinking how funny we must have looked our first day here, I being pulled through the streets on the other end of a leash from a puppy. How could I know there was nothing to leash him from? No cars on the streets. No people, except children playing.

Six days ago. And all I know so far is that color is important to me and that a lot of people have tried for a lot of years to make me responsible for my own life. But I seem to find that responsibility unendurable, like being underwater without enough air. And whenever I can find some way to break that pressure, I come up for air, screaming. Like a baby at its first gasp. And then, as if propelled by what I've just inhaled, I skitter in an almost random direction until the burst of energy gives out. And then I light, again at random, and stay, for almost no reason, until I sink below the surface. And then I do the whole thing over again.

Logos leaps back over the fence onto the unpaved road, and we head slowly for the ocean.

But I can't just stay at one of those unplanned stopping-places. Staying for discipline's sake isn't something I can do. Yet I did (I wonder how) finish my dissertation. Dr. Kant was the continuity that kept me at my desk in between the Tuesdays and Fridays of seeing him. He even asked me to call him at home to let him know that I had passed the oral exam on my thesis. And so when his wife answered the phone, and asked who was calling, I said, almost gargling the words in my excitement, "Dr. Koller." He came to the phone immediately, laughing, warm, praising me, wanting to know the details. He was my family for those few minutes: my family, my friend, my teacher. My doctor: "See you Friday. I'm very glad for you, Alice." Killed last March in an auto accident. Gone.

No. I can't stay, just to stay, just to learn how to stay. There has to be a reason to stay somewhere. What reasons are there?

We reach a grassy lot, the edge of which drops abruptly down to the dunes. The tide is out. Even from this distance I can see wet sand contrasted against the dry, where the water never reaches. I walk parallel to the water, still on the bluff. The first house shows no signs of habitation. I walk closer and am surer. I step onto the porch. Through the windows, I see furniture draped in white. Stray mothballs on the floor to keep mice away. Some magazines. Nothing living. The house next door is larger, separated from this one only by connecting lawns, but rendered private by high shrubs near its windows. I stand, my back to the ocean, looking at the line of big, old, empty houses. Who keeps them so well? When I face the water, I see the view these houses have: unbroken by trees or other houses or wharves or warehouses. From their lawns, particularly from their second stories, there is only the ocean. I think of the photographer's line in *Philadelphia Story:* "There is no prettier sight in this pretty, pretty world than the sight of the privileged classes enjoying their privileges." Except that I'm not of the privileged class. And yet, glory to them all, they've vacated this entire end of the island for the winter. And all of this space and light and air and sea and sand are mine to walk along and look at and feel, morning or night, for all the time I'm here.

They've even built long flights of wooden steps down to the dunes. Logos starts down one of the stairways, then stops with only two paws on the first step. His body points downward, the front end unmoving on the step, the rear part scrambling for footing on the ground next to me. I imagine descending the steep flight on all fours, head first, and instinctively I retreat. As does he. But the sand lures him and he tries again. And draws back, whimpering. And then in one burst of bravery, he scrambles down the entire long flight, and when he hits the sand he leaps, straight-legged, then lands, shoving his nose into the sand, and digs. And then he's off, running toward the water.

No one's on the beach. I look up at the line of houses. No one on the path. No one even in a boat out on the water. No one. No one. Where the sand is dry, the footing is difficult. I sink in at each step. I hurry closer to the water, where the sand is wet at its edge. I stand inhaling the air, one last deep breath telling me I've arrived at some destination.

I date the page for my second try with the letters. Mimi brought back unexpected connections yesterday. Should I even bother about what method I use, so long as I get it all down?

All at once I'm in the horrifying circle that I've never resolved. It began in Cambridge at election time, the fall of 1954, I think. I was walking toward the Square, when suddenly a candidate's truck carrying a loudspeaker system drove slowly by, playing music that I to this day can't remember, that I couldn't remember five minutes after having heard it, but that brought back such a flood of pain that I almost cried out standing on the street. I started to run after the truck (what *is* that music?) but it was gone. I felt as though my whole body had just been battered. I could barely control the sounds that tried to escape my throat. The music made me think of a merry-go-round; maybe it *was* merry-go-round music.

The only merry-go-round I can remember is the one I couldn't go on the day I first menstruated. My mother and I were standing watching the other kids riding the horsies, when her friend who had driven us to the picnic asked her why I wasn't riding. My mother told her why. I hated her for telling, I hated the whole business, and I vowed I would never do *that* again. I don't remember that day as being one of such raw dread that the mere sound of the same tinkly music in Cambridge years later could tap such powerful roots of memory. It was the quality of the music, not the melody, that caught me. The thing about the sound wasn't only the tinniness, which I've just remembered, but the fact that the music stopped for a while between playings. Sometimes when the music stopped the ride would be over. The horses would slow down, and— No, that's not it. The music stopped while we were still riding, and then it would start again, and somewhere in the middle of that second playing, the horses would stop. So that you always got on or got off to the playing of music. I am now feeling very anxious and tight in my throat and almost on the verge of tears. What am I remembering? No answer.

Try Mimi again. I seem to be looking for what the memory of her sets off in my own memory. Yet originally I was looking for what sorts of relationships I had had with people throughout my life. Or rather: how they saw me, how I must have looked to them. What I want to know, thinking of Mimi, is what she saw of me that will shed light on me, because during the years I knew her, I must have solidified my idea of wanting to be an actress. Did we simply ask one another a long time ago what we wanted to be, and then help one another forward our projects? Did we ever ask: Is that what you really want to do? or How do you know that's what you want to do? or *Can* you do that thing? or When you're doing it, do you like it?

How did I know I wanted to be an actress, anyway? Did I know it, or was it just that people kept telling me I had a good voice? The grade-school carnival at which Eugene (I've just remembered his name) and I alternated as masters of ceremonies. In between the afternoon and the evening performances in the gym, everyone except me and the custodians left the building. No one questioned my right to wander along the corridor, in and out of familiar classrooms converted for the day to sideshows. I was behind the scenes for the first time. At age eleven I knew what a theater looked like under houselights.

I was taken for elocution lessons because my upper lip didn't meet my lower lip when I talked. Miss Eloise Something had me reciting things to keep bringing my lip down. There were also tap-dancing lessons. I'm sure I showed no talent for either, nor would those tenth-rate ladies have recognized it anyway. But at no time did anyone give me a hint that any of this was supposed to be fun or exciting. They were simply things that had to be practiced at home; that was all I knew. My mother wouldn't let me show her my new steps until the old ones were perfect.

I started saying, "Hey, look what I can do!" when Pat and Laurel and I had our apartment in Chicago. One or the other of them would listen or watch and laugh at the right time. I don't remember anyone ever laughing when I was a little girl. I was twenty-two before I knew what "fun" meant. I remember asking Pat's friend Liz just as we were driving up to a turnpike tollbooth. She said, "Look, I'll show you what fun is," and instead of stopping she slowed down only enough to let her coin drop into the tollkeeper's palm, and then she accelerated, and she said, "See, that's fun." If I have to use only a single idea to characterize my growing up, it's that I had the feeling that everything had to be paid for, nothing was free.

On the way to the post office, Logos' tail comes up for the first time. Instead of hanging down and curving inward between his hind legs, it swings from side to side, and he holds it high. I take this as a sign that he's stopped being frightened of the new surroundings. I no longer even carry his leash.

Mr. Morris makes a small crying sound in his throat to catch Logos' attention. The puppy's beautiful head cocks to one side, his ears quivering, straining to collect every clue about the source of the sound. "Shepherds make that sound," Mr. Morris tells me. "Mine did, to get my attention. Are you a writer?"

The question silences me. I think about it. "Yes," I say, smiling good-bye, and go out the door with my mail. Next time I'll have to have written something. No one can conceive that I could be here without being occupied in some familiar way. In the winter, at least.

Logos tears ahead as soon as we curve toward the water.

I think of the half-dozen closely typed pages lying on my desk, surprising myself with how much I remember of details: names of people not thought of for twenty years, clothes I used to wear. How does all this come back to me? I haven't been able to trust my memory for years, and yet here, doing this, my memory opens up like a door that I never knew existed. Before now, I forgot so many things. And then when I noticed that I was forgetting happenings of the immediate past, I suspected that I was showing early signs of inheriting my father's brain disease. Even if there's no organic basis, does that make my forgetting less terrible? I close my eyes and hold my stomach to think of the exams I first failed ten years ago. Not today. No, I can't take that yet.

I've been standing on the sand for—I don't know how long. I see Logos near the water's edge, racing backward from the incoming shallow waves, following them as they recede, then backing away from them again.

I'm really in two places at once: that past, getting more vivid each time I reach into it; and this present. I begin to see that no easy transition is possible between them. At the end of each stint of writing, I'm in a mood that I can actually choose to stay in or break out of. If I stay in it, I seem not to be here on this island with this puppy. If I break out of it, I put distance between what I write and what I do in these Nantucket days. And with distance, I get a fresh purchase on that past when I go back to it each time. But what a rupture it is, breaking away. I feel loose flesh dangling for the rest of the day.

I call Logos to me and turn toward the long path through the dune grass that leads back to the streets. Maybe I should write during the afternoon; get the mail and a last walk on the beach before the sun sets. Or even if I write in the morning, go out for a long walk immediately afterward.

As we turn into our street, a little girl in a blue coat comes running toward us with a setter on a leash. Abruptly the dog sits, bringing the child to an unplanned halt. She stands in front of him and tugs and coaxes, but he doesn't move. Now we're very close to them, although Logos circles to the edge of the road, out of the setter's reach.

"Hi," I say. "What's wrong?"

"This dog does this all the time. He does it just to make me mad. He stops, he just stops, just like that, while we're running, and then I can't make him get up again. He gets up when he wants to. See?" The dog illustrates by starting to walk off, pulling her along with him. He sees Logos but doesn't consider him worth pursuing. Nevertheless, and for no apparent reason, he now allows the little girl to lead him back toward me. She wants to talk. She's pretty, with long blonde hair, perhaps ten years old. She examines Logos and asks his age. I tell her.

"Awwww." The sound women make when they look at babies.

She knows all the dogs in Siasconset. She calls it " 'Sconset." I ask her whether " 'Sconset" is a nickname for Siasconset, or whether "Siasconset" is pronounced as though the first two syllables don't exist. She looks at me and in the next instant understands what I want to know.

"There are two names." She pronounces both of them. " 'Sconset" has two syllables; "Siasconset" has four.

She's ready to show me what else she knows. I ask her about the dogs I've seen on our walks. If I know their names, I'll be able to send them on their way faster. "Who's the big black dog?"

"That's Midnight. He's a Labrador."

"And there's a little black-and-white dog. He always seems to want to fight. Anyway, he always makes Logos run between my legs."

She thinks a minute. "That's Fido."

Naturally. "And then there's a brown dog with one tooth hanging over the edge of his lip."

"That's a girl. That's Judy. She's a boxer."

I thank her for all her information and start to move toward my house. "I'll see you around," I call back.

"Oh, good!" She smiles so broadly that I stand surprised: she likes me. I walk into my driveway and turn to watch her before we enter the house. The dog has sat down again, and she is tugging at him without success.

Some days it's too much trouble to look for my journal on the shelf, lift it over to the desk, open it, and start writing. I should keep it open on the desk and write in it as I pass.

So today is Saturday. Saturday night, quiet and alone, and somehow I don't ache to be out at a party somewhere, or drinking with almost any acquaintance, to make the night go by. All day I didn't know that it was Saturday. It's the first Saturday I can remember that hasn't struck me as Saturday. Well, what's so Saturdayish that the way of spending it should matter so much? It's the morning of weekends, the recurring promise that more excitement will happen on this day than on any other day, the sense that all Cambridge is preparing for some party or other, the smell of the holiday morning in the Square. I was almost never a part of Saturdays, especially of Saturday nights.

Here I'm at my leisure all week long, not just for two weekend days. De Grazia's *Of Time, Work, and Leisure* taught me the sense of that word: the fullest use of my time in accordance with my own specifications. I'm beginning to know what it's like to do only what I want to do: it's feeling no constraints of any kind. From other people, from myself. Perhaps a day can be packed full, if it can be spent that way.

I watch Logos jump on his ball and roll his body on top of it. Clumsy, loose-limbed, utterly free, delighting me with every move. Tonight he'll be housebroken completely, I think, and then I don't have to keep such close watch on him.

8

Lying in the bright room, I try to figure out what day it is. Sunday. Not generally a good day. In fact, the worst day of the week. Everyone is at home. But where I live is never home: I'm always trying to leave it, and Sundays close off all places where I can go to avoid the boring, empty, aching sameness of my days. Getting up early on Sundays is a very poor idea: the whole miserable day stretches out endlessly.

Today doesn't feel like that. I lean my head on my propping elbow to consider. Because yesterday didn't feel like Saturday, either? No. I know. Because Saturdays back there held out a hope, but here I've deliberately cut off hope. Sundays can't contrast with Saturdays so sharply now. Sunday here is like Tuesday or Monday. Or Saturday. A day that may take me closer to what I want to know, if I think and write and try to shape the hours around whatever the contours of my self will turn out to be. I'm tearing out one more old habit.

All the newspapers in Logos' hallway are untouched: he's housebroken! His triumph and mine send us out the back door into the sunshine, and although I shiver waiting for him to come back to me, the world is too new this moment to close myself in any more than I have to.

I've begun to wonder whether I might be able to get down the whole of high school. Mimi and Joyce and Isabel are my only solid ties with those years.

Joyce. I haven't kept a single letter from her. For chunks of time during the twenty years since high school we didn't write. And yet, when we meet, she goes out of her way to make me understand that she cares about me.

Even before she set foot into that junior-year English class, the word had spread that the new girl's father was the manager of the Palace Theatre. I stayed away from her for just that reason, irritated to watch everyone jockeying for her favor. Then one day we happened to talk, and soon we were meeting between classes, eating lunch together, waiting for each other after school to walk home together, talking for hours on the street corner where our ways parted. "Through hell and high water," we told each other. Even our parents knew that to look for one of us was to find the other.

But not much more than a year later Joyce married a boy I couldn't stand, and I was off to Chicago and Goodman. Whenever our doings crossed thereafter, we'd pick up our friendship again. Then silence for years at a time.

Where does that take me? I shake my head.

Isabel, for all her redheaded disdain of the politics involved, became president of our senior class. My problems and hers were alike, at least in trying to convince our parents that we knew what we wanted. I may not have known what I wanted, but I thought I did, she writes in 1944, and maybe if they hadn't made me fight for it so much I might have been freer to see what I really did want. What Isabel wished for me was the opportunity to prove the truth to myself, or to my parents and everyone else. Well, I've proved something to my parents and everyone else, but that wasn't worth doing. I haven't proved any truth at all to myself yet, except this thing that I'm trying to do here.

Yet I can sit at this typewriter, off and on ever since midmorning, and not be touched, as I was yesterday, by remembering merry-go-round music. I seem to have turned this writing into something having to do with feats of memory. I go away from it easily. I have the feeling that it's not going anywhere. I've learned from it so far, though, that I can remember. Tomorrow I'm going to start with the men and work back.

July 1944, on the night shift at the rubber labs the year I worked to get money to get back to Goodman Theatre. I can remember what it felt like to go to bed at nine o'clock in the morning, and to awaken at three in the afternoon. The taste in my mouth was set for breakfast, but my mother was preparing dinner; "supper," we called it then. Even then it struck her as strange that I'd want something other than what anyone else wanted. When I'd come home in the morning, after smoking at work all night, she thought I should cook breakfast, because it was the time of day for the others in the house.

Buzz, leader of that swing shift. He was good-looking behind those glasses. He walked like an Indian: straight, lean, reserved. But he was cruel. The night I walked all the way to Highland Square so I could call him without my family overhearing, he let his landlady, who was his lover, listen on the extension. They were laughing by the time I understood, and then I was ashamed. I called Robert, the research chemist who had adopted me, the wild kid needing a friend. He came for me through snow and cold in his blue Hudson, and he let me cry myself out at his house before he delivered me home. He and his wife saw how shattered I was and didn't even ask me what had happened. I was crying again by the time I got to bed. I remember that Daddy either put me there or found me there when he came home from bowling, and he couldn't stop my crying. But I remember that he said, in the despair that he showed only to me: "Life is just one damn thing after another." That not very profoundly stated truth has remained in my memory for eighteen years, more as a signal of his misery than of some beacon I can use to steer my days by.

Here's a letter from Isabel's brother, dated April 1943, two years before he was killed in the war. Tibby: reckless, so young, with new money and only a life to throw away. We'll get a plane when this is all over, he said, and you and your love, and Issie and her love, and I, we'll fly the country. "P.S. Why do you study, you should enjoy life. How does it feel to be in love?" Dear Tibby: Maybe I've never known. Illiterate Tibby, but he had his hands on what mattered: when he was doing something, he knew whether he did or didn't want to do it. But if I didn't study then, I wouldn't have enjoyed life either, never having quite learned the trick. What I savored was the acclaim someone else could give me. What is it like to savor the thing I'm doing?

Sitting on a log washed high up on the beach, I watch Logos at the water's edge. A shallow wave comes in, slaps down, and sighs backward, and as its crest hits the sand, Logos leaps onto it to catch it, and then chases the receding water, reaching for the lost wave one more time. The reach after the chase always lands him paw-deep in the water, and although he concentrates closely on the new wave forming, when he unaccountably finds that the water is up to his elbows, he flies backward, above the point at which the new wave slaps, then sighs away from him. He utters a little cry at each failure. His leap becomes more focused, and his chase, faster. Then abruptly he turns away from the water, nose high, sniffing the air, and trots off to explore the possibilities of other games.

Yesterday I thought I knew what wanting is: being aware of myself as under no pressures from anyone, or for any reason. But what I really know is when I'm doing something I don't want to do. Sometimes, anyway. That can't take me very far. An animal, an infant, can learn to pull back from the fire. I have to find what will draw me toward something, not simply what will keep me away from it. I need Socrates' *daimon,* but turned inside out. His voice could tell him only what not to do, and then only after he was on point of embarking upon some action wrong for him. Mine will also have to tell me what I *want* to do. No doubt Socrates knew what he wanted to do without needing to be told.

I miss Logos. I stand and then see him, far down the beach, digging. I start to walk slowly in his direction.

Wanting. *What* have I wanted? No: What have I *wanted?* Not right yet: What have *I* wanted?

A dull hopelessness runs through me. I'll never be able to understand wanting. Can I say what, exactly, the idea is? I try, but I find only the tiredness in me. I catch up to Logos and start to turn toward one of the long stairways. He, guessing my direction, runs ahead of me to lead the way.

The warm, sharp, strangely sweet taste of the bourbon hits the center of my throat. The first swallow always shifts me into a new gear. Glass in hand, I go back to my desk to try again to write of the day, but I barely lift the pen before I put it down, shove the journal away, and sit watching the late-afternoon sun across the moor.

One week already. Seven days falling on the heels of one another, tumbling me along. Not bored, not lonely. Working by thinking. But the thinking is a kind of fighting. I'm defending, and laying siege, all at once. I'm even the prize. But I'm also the only one who'd want it.

Someone is breathing steadily beneath my bed. If I can figure out where I am, I'll know who that is. I lean over the edge of the mattress. The tip of a furry tail prompts my giggling. I call Logos' name in a low tone. The even breathing continues. My watchdog. I reach down to flick the visible fur. Sudden scrambling. But the bottom of the mattress is too close to the floor to let him stand up. He sticks his head out from under the iron railing of the bedstead and, clawing repeatedly to get a grip on the waxed floor, flattens his body to crawl out to freedom. I slide out of bed quickly to prevent his jumping up onto the covers. Our morning reunion is held on one of the needlepoint rugs, until I realize that this glorious excitement might crack his newly won control.

He follows me, nails clacking, down the waxed steep stairs and outside. The air is cold but not crisp, not the crispness of Cambridge winters, but harsh enough to keep me in the kitchen, watching Logos from the window. The clear sky invites me toward the sea. After coffee.

Logos' new bell-shaped tag clanks as he moves. The Commonwealth of Massachusetts, in the person of the Nantucket Town Clerk, granted me his license this noon on condition that I restrain him from killing, chasing, or harassing livestock or fowl. Logos lifts his head to make sure I haven't left my desk since he fell asleep. Another jangle or two, and he settles flat on the rug.

The same hour during which he slept has seen me unmoving in this chair. The page in the typewriter is empty, and nothing I try will let me inscribe even one word on its whiteness. My thoughts wander back over our morning walk, the dim office of official Nantucket, the insurance agent's cheerfulness. But no writing. Perhaps I need to take a day off from time to time. Do I dare? There's no time to waste any longer. The money goes down each day. True, the check for my final month's work came in the mail today. But I have to keep some money in the savings account to help me get to, and settle into, wherever I go when I leave here.

I forage among the possibilities of what to do with the new money, aware of my tense shoulders. I let them fall a hand's breadth to their natural position. A stupid habit. I still do it, even knowing why. It's how I used to hunch over my book, reading fast to get as much read as I could before my mother called me downstairs to wash dishes, or dust, or help with the laundry, or peel the potatoes. To do something in her house. Even when I lived there, I thought of it as her house, not our house. Her house, which she kept ready for the times her friends and relatives would visit her. In between, it was something we weren't supposed to tarnish too much, and I, the eldest daughter, was chosen to be her assistant.

I think of her as being always occupied cleaning her house. I hold a vivid image of her: she passes the kitchen clock, glances at it, then gasps. Even as a little girl, that gasp caught my curiosity. I'd watch her to try to understand what important event required her daily race with the clock. So far as I could see, nothing unusual ever happened. Yet each day she gasped when she looked at the clock. I remember figuring out what the gasp meant: "There won't be enough time!" She wouldn't have enough time to wash the dishes, so that she could make the beds, so that she could wash the walls upstairs, so that she could clean the mirrors, so that she could get the evening meal ready. And all of this took place on some interior schedule that she followed faithfully.

It wasn't until I lived away from her house, in apartments with other girls or by myself, that I understood one sudden day how little she had been doing, for being so busy. I knew how long it took to clean the place I lived in: fifteen minutes a day, some days; an hour a week to do the whole show. But I cleaned my place only to smooth the way for the other things I was doing. That was when I understood what she had been doing with her life: she cleaned her house. I understood then, too, why she was always so shocked by the passage of time: cleaning her house was her career, and no matter how well it had been done yesterday, she had to make new gains every day, or else be a failure.

I still hunch my shoulders, waiting for her to call me away from whatever I'm doing, hurrying against her deadline, a deadline that will arrive at some as yet unknown time, a deadline set by somebody else. But here there's no deadline. Except the one set by the amount of time it will take me to run out of money.

A real circle. Do I bank the check as savings, or do I use it to help me do what I've come here to do? I'll wait to decide. I tuck the check in an envelope and place it in the drawer.

I've written nothing of all this. It flew in too fast. Anyway, I knew it already. The writing didn't make it come to me, the way the writing of the last few days helped me make new connections. I push the typewriter aside and reach for the journal. But I rebel against writing down the details of grocery shopping in Nantucket, of the straightaway drive into the town, of being able to find my way around the streets, even of the walks along the sea. What will happen to my plan of keeping the journal of the day's outer doings, when what I do is already so familiar to me?

Four o'clock. A day lost.

It's a way to spend an evening, studying the muscular structure and skeleton of the dog. But where do I find out what to feed Logos? The Kennel Club books says: "Meal and water and fat." I don't know what meal is.

The SPCA booklet is in the kitchen. Leaning against the refrigerator, I learn that there are three basic forms of dog food: canned, kibble, and meal. Explanation of how kibble is made. Nothing about what meal is. I think of cornmeal, oatmeal. Hard to imagine either of those mixed with water: it would turn to paste. And fat: bacon fat?

I slam the booklet down on the sink. Why do people have to be so vague? What fats are there? Who manufactures meal? How much do I feed the pup? Logos eats so little. I've got to get him eating again. Puppies are supposed to eat more than grown dogs, but I don't seem able to find the food he likes.

Damn it, damn it, *damn* it. I make a hard fist with my right hand and punch the side of the refrigerator until the fleshy edge of my hand hurts. I make a pillow of my arms and lean up against the cold smoothness, burying my head. I can't do it. I can't think my way through thirty-seven years of not knowing what the hell I'm doing. What a fake, a fraud, a phony, an ignorant bitch I am. I sit here on an island with a typewriter and some paper, expecting the truth to unfold before my waiting eyes. I'm playing a part: another role for the big actress. Footlights up. Houselights down. Curtain. Scene: the hermit in her retreat.

A warm body pushes against my legs. Paws reach to my knees. I look down through my arms. What will we do, Logos, you and I? You're in my hands, and I'm such a dog person that I can't even feed you properly.

I sit on the floor near his water bowl, and he puts his chin on my belly, his face inches away from mine. I stroke the silky head; the golden eyes explore my face. Yes, we must try to figure each other out. Your job is probably easier than mine. Maybe you're ahead of me already. You, at least, don't get in your own way.

9

My fingers on the typewriter keys, I look at the same blank sheet that I inserted into the roller yesterday. No, not today, either. I shove back my chair, grab my coat and my keys, and head for the door almost before Logos can realize that the walk is first this morning.

At the end of the driveway, I know I've forgotten something. I stand still, feeling in my pockets for keys, paper handkerchiefs, gloves. What, then? I start to walk slowly. At the road a sudden gust of cold air hits my face in a more startling way than usual. I know: I have no lipstick on. I start to go back into the house, and then stop again, confused. It feels funny without lipstick, and my lips are drying so fast in the cold. Logos is halfway down the road, sniffing the tracks of those who have gone before. I watch him for a moment, thinking of unlocking the door, going upstairs, finding a lipstick, putting it on, putting it away, coming downstairs, and starting out all over again.

"Lipstick, for the love of God!" I say out loud. Logos turns toward me, puzzled. How could I not have noticed that lipstick is for them, for other people? And there are no people here. I walk swiftly to catch up with the puppy.

We swing onto the smooth wet sand edging the low tide and turn north toward the lighthouse. Then I stop. Habit, already? To fall so quickly into patterns, when I've vowed to break as many patterns as I can notice? I turn abruptly south. The new direction lays a certain force against my motion. Surprised and annoyed, I find myself working to overcome it with each of my initial steps.

The coastline starts to curve westward. I'm rounding the very tip of the island. No bluff, only low dunes on this coast. Gradually they spread out more broadly until I, near the water's edge, can almost not see the houses of the town. Logos moves so swiftly across the sand, nose down, that he seems to glide.

As I watch him, my peripheral vision is caught by a small moving object. I turn toward it. A solitary car is traveling the paved road at the distant edge of the dunes. Curious to see a car out here, close to the sand and shells and seaweed and debris washed up by each high tide. I stand waiting for it to pass along the stretch of road on my line of vision, even though it's a thousand feet away. Special event: a living person is driving that car, purposely heading in some direction toward some goal unknown to me. I feel an impulse to wave. Silly. The driver doesn't look toward me as he passes. Why should he? I'm not as untoward a part of the landscape to him as he is to me. I don't think he even saw me. Who would expect to see a woman and a puppy walking near the water on a cold November morning? I watch the car disappear down another road that probably leads toward the post office.

So: still acting. I wanted that man to see me, to wonder who the woman is, alone on the beach. Still starring in plays I invent as I go along.

I've tried so often to stop it. Withdrawing from dramatic school hasn't prevented me from acting on my own stage ever since. I left Goodman Theatre in the fall of 1946. Now it's the fall of 1962. Sixteen years of making people look at me. Look at me: I'm being passionate. Look at me: I'm being intellectual. I even underplay having my doctorate, to make eyes open more widely when I, oh so reluctantly, announce, oh so quietly, that I have my degree.

But I did try to stop, very hard, the summer before I finally began to write my dissertation. Why then? I still don't know. Just because Jim left for South America? It was only one more miserable ending to an affair. Why should that breakup have so galvanized me into trying to tear away the incessant acting? Yet I think of that time as taking me to some extremity that I had never before reached.

At eight in the morning I watched from my window while he took the few steps I could still see before he turned the corner, lost to me. Without sleep, empty and sick for having been deprived, one more time, of a man I wanted, I washed my face, changed my clothes, and went for a walk along the Charles. Eight o'clock in the morning, early June, Cambridge from the river: hushed, calm, fresh, clear, beautiful. I walked for two hours trying to register the fact, the unalterable unbearable fact, that Jim was gone.

I look far out at the slowly moving waves. Three years later, I still don't know why he mattered so much, why that day of his leaving started me down a new path, why that day I knew I had to try to make myself stop acting. Jim's going away was a fact I had had at hand for a whole year before it took the form of a trip to South America. He had gone away first by marrying someone else while I was in Europe. He had gone further away by writing to me in Germany that he would nonetheless like to meet me somewhere in the spring. And he had gone furthest away of all by welcoming my initiative that we pick up our affair when I returned. Then why did his leaving the country strike me as something so final for me? That day I couldn't know that he'd come back, and that after his divorce a year later, I'd be in his car one night listening to him talk and I'd think: How he bores me!

But that day it was final. And I had two hours in which to shift gears from a lost Jim to a lost dissertation topic. So I kept the 10:00 appointment with the pretentious faculty member, and I listened to him move quickly from critical remarks about the topic I had proposed for my dissertation to critical remarks about me.

"You don't belong in philosophy," he said.

I remember thinking that if he had said that the day before Jim left, or the day after, I might have been angry, or at least apprehensive about my future work. Instead, I heard his words from a vast distance. He thought that what he was saying mattered, and it didn't at all. Because Jim had left two hours earlier. Nothing else could match the impact of that fact.

Did I reply to those words of his, or did my face simply register my indifference? I remember that he embroidered his remark with what I understood to be the limit of his kindness: "A lot of bright people don't do well in philosophy. That isn't to say they couldn't do well in something else. Why don't you get out of it?"

From my far place, I saw him as trying to distract me from attending to my own thoughts, and so I stood and thanked him for his time and left. He was merely telling me that the ten years I had spent studying philosophy were wasted years, and that I had no talent for the field. What made him think that that would matter on any scale on which the unit of measurement was that Jim had left two hours before?

Home, but needing company. To Rick, finishing his senior year at Harvard while his wife worked, my buddy for long midnight walks and a beer. By noon, I persuaded him to spend the day with me in serious drinking, and by four o'clock I was following him around some market helping him check off his wife's grocery list. By dinnertime he was as drunk as I. "You have to eat with us tonight. Can't have you not eating." By nine, as summer darkness began, I staggered onto my bed, to sleep for the first time in almost two days.

Next morning I took the first of a series of steps that led me to Dr. Kant. But it was summer, and his vacation was about to begin, so that by the time I faced him over his desk in the fall, I had met, and also lost, Mike.

A rain of sand flashes into my face, and I cry out. I spin around, wiping the sand from my mouth. Logos looks up at me from the deepening hole he's been digging at my feet, and then returns to his work, first one paw, then the other, serving as his shovel. Now he shifts his position, downwind from me, and I consider the possibility that he may have aimed that batch of sand at me.

I look around and realize that I've been standing on one spot for a long time. I push back my sleeve to look at my watch: no watch. I check my pockets: not with me. Did I lose it on the way here by not fastening it carefully enough? Couldn't have: the sleeve at my wrist is too narrow.

I have a sudden image of the watch on my bureau. I forgot to put it on again after I washed my face this morning. I find myself smiling. Alone, how can it matter when I do what I do? I'll go home when I'm tired of walking.

When I'm tired. When I'm tired.

I play the phrase over and over. Why is it familiar? Oh, yes: I went back to sleep the second morning here, and I did it because I was tired.

I start to walk again very slowly. And then I stop. I see that by having left the watch at home, I've thrown out not just one more rule, but a whole collection of them. Not only does it not matter when I go home, but it doesn't matter when I eat or sleep or walk or read or do anything at all. Incredible piece of knowledge! Wait. To say it doesn't matter has to mean that it doesn't matter to *me*. Is that true? Yes, that's exactly what the gain was the morning I went back to sleep. I went back to sleep because I was tired.

It's coming very fast, and I'm trying to hang on to it.

Because I was tired. Not to avoid some problem, not because I had to get a certain number of hours of sleep in order to meet someone else's schedule. I went back to sleep for a good reason: because I was tired. So not wearing my watch can teach me the other good reasons for doing things. Going home because I'm tired of walking, or because I want to write, or because Logos needs water. Eating because I'm hungry. Reading because I want the refreshment of another mind.

I make some sound that is close to a laugh. Some quiet part of me has been working on my behalf today better than the alert and watchful part. Forgetting my lipstick and my watch is exactly what I set myself to do by coming here: to get rid of habits and beliefs and ways of thinking that aren't genuinely mine, that have been imposed on me from the outside, somehow.

Logos is not visible. I shout for him. His head appears over the edge of a dune a few feet to my left, and then vanishes.

"Hey, Logos, let's go home." I start to cut across the broad sweep of dunes toward the road where the car turned a little while ago. It will be a new route home, a new route down to the sea. The newness of it speaks to something long buried within me.

Logos isn't following me. I stand without moving, just as he looks up from his digging to realize that I'm no longer where he saw me last. He starts up the beach in our old direction, still not seeing me. He runs a few hesitant steps, swings around, and then stops to take his bearings. I raise one hand inches only, and the deviation from my stillness is all he needs. He races toward me, galloping, and over-reaches me. I rough the fur of his neck when he comes back my way, and then he bends all his attention to streets he hasn't been down before.

Why do I have the feeling, here by myself, that all I have to do is set myself to remembering, and then I can indeed remember almost anything at all? But when I've needed to remember—taking exams, lecturing, wanting to make a point in a philosophical discussion—those times I couldn't remember. Trying made me forget even more.

The difference has to lie between one kind of remembering being personal, one being professional. Where does that take me? Nowhere. It's not true, either. I still don't know why the carousel music harrows me, what it reaches for in my memory. The difference can't be between being here and being back there. Or between being alone and being with others. Is it being with certain others?

I ought to be able to write something about remembering and forgetting. It seems to be the focus around which I've been playing today.

Something makes me look out the front windows. A car is parked across the street from my house. Imagine seeing two cars in one day. I go to the kitchen window to get a closer look. The car is empty. By the time I throw on my coat, find some outdoor shoes, and close Logos safely in behind me, a small boy and a man carrying a gun are walking toward the car.

I call out to them: "Please go away. You're too close to my house.

I can't have hunters near where I live." I'm more angry than afraid, but I'm trying to be polite.

The man looks at me in silence. His contempt is so strong across the fifty feet separating us that it taunts me to pull out the stops.

"The police have told me to report the license number of any hunter who might be a nuisance. I'm standing here memorizing your license."

The man swears, but only loudly enough for me to know his displeasure. He does something to his gun, puts it into the back of the car, hustles the boy into the front seat, and still without having addressed a word to me, drives down the road, pushing the motor as hard as possible in each gear, until he is gone.

I curse him in turn, and head back into my driveway. The puppy's face peers through the kitchen window. And then suddenly my eye is caught by the NO TRESPASSING sign to the right of that window. And the one on the front door. And on the left side of the house. And on the garage doors. Just as such signs pepper the vacant houses along the bluff and throughout the village.

So the hunter didn't know that someone was living here. Well. I'm sorry to have come storming out at him. Still the signs do forbid trespassing. Maybe I struck him as banshee enough so that he'll warn away anyone else who might be thinking of hunting out here.

Logos leaps at me as I open the door. I pretend to chase him, and he flies around the house. I don't let him catch his breath before I mock-lunge at him again. This time he runs in an intricate pattern to evade my capture. We cut across the lawn, out to the road.

Almost before I realize that I'm awake, I begin to cry. I seem unable to stop the tears. They cover my face, but I'm not sure why they flow now, before the day has even begun. Then I know: it's about Thanksgiving Day. One more holiday disconnected from any human caring. Knowing, I feel my jaws press my teeth together, and the tears stop. June's letter yesterday, not quite saying that she couldn't invite me to spend the day, and yet saying it all the more loudly. I wouldn't have gone, would I? But I wanted to know that there's a place where I could have gone.

There's no place where I can go, where I belong, where I want to be.

The way I fling off the covers teaches me that I'm angry. I stomp down the stairway to let Logos out, not playing with him on the way. I close the door behind him. He knows what to do by now.

Small bits of fur on the floor catch my eye, and I stoop to examine them. I wail a loud curse. Logos has chewed away great patches of the lining of my fur boots. I've never even worn them, and they're wrecked. My anger bursts. I throw both boots across the room, and then lean against the wall, pounding until my fists ache.

The door sticks when I try to open it, and so I kick it hard. It opens. Logos is still off in the high grass, checking the morning news. I call him. I see from the face he turns to me that he hears the harsh note in my voice. Head lowered, he walks toward the door. I reach out to grab his collar and drag him in.

"Bad dog. Look what you did." I thrust his face into a boot. "And did you swallow the fur, too? You'll be sick and I'll have to spend money for a vet. Bad dog." Logos squirms loose and runs into the living room to escape me, then returns to the kitchen doorway. He seems so confused that I stop raging and sit at the kitchen table.

Quietly he comes to me and I stroke the top of his head lightly. It is the merest outline of a gesture noting his presence. But he sees it as a renewal of our perfect friendship, because instantly his paws are on my lap, and he licks my face, making his little cries. I catch my breath, and then let it go.

"Okay, I'll tell you what. Today we'll go all the way out to the lighthouse. On the sand. I'll even take some water for you in a jar, so you can run and run and run and not have to come home because you're thirsty."

The beautiful face looks up into mine as though he understands every word. We'll have a holiday in our own way.

Turning out the lights on my way to bed, I notice a tiny white object on the rug, reflecting the light of the floor lamp. I stoop to pick it up. There is a reddish patch in one shallow end, the other end is pointed. I'm slow to understand that it's a puppy tooth. Logos comes over to see what provokes my interest, and I roll him over onto the floor, pretending to play, then quickly open his jaw. Some new teeth are more than halfway through the gum: he's teething. I play with him a few minutes, and then I look for the dog book to read about teething. I learn that if he doesn't get a good bone to chew on, he'll chew on anything. I go back into the kitchen, put my boots into the hall closet, and try to anticipate what objects in the living room he might gnaw on. Nothing at floor level. I start up the stairs.

"Come on, Sweet Puppy." It has become his second name.

IO

We walk along the bluff until we reach my favorite wooden stairway. The bluff is at its steepest here, but the person who designed the stairway transposed that handicap into this victory. From the top of the bluff to the line of surf, the stairway combines with the dunes to form a series of restraints. The walk down the first third parallels the line of the water, but to look at the sea I must turn my head at a ninety-degree angle. The bench on the landing lets me sit, but to see the water only in the context of the immense length of the shore. The next third of the stairway repeats the feeling of the first. The final turn, leading straight to the sand, shows me how distant the shore still is. By the time I reach the water at last, the effect is one of great release.

I always do sit on the bench, however. The bench has virtues of its own. Sitting here, I'm cantilevered out from the bluff. Above me, the line of great old houses. Below me, the sand and dune grass. And the view outward encompasses the entire sweep of the shore: northward to the lighthouse, southward to the blunt eastern tip of the island. Suspended, neither on land nor sea, I sit and look and think.

Even Logos is pleased by the time we reach this platform. He flops down, breathing hard, reminding me that this resting-place is almost two miles from our house, and that he's only four months old. Then, too, he doubles my distance on any of our walks, simply by rushing ahead of me, turning to see that I haven't yet caught up, coming all the way back to urge me on, then impatiently rushing ahead again. So here he lies, almost asleep, his eyes opening from time to time to make sure I'm still with him.

My eye travels over every inch of the side of his body, watching until his breathing begins to steady itself and deepen. I have fallen in love with him, no question about it. Suddenly I realize that I didn't think beyond Nantucket when I bought him. Did I imagine that I'd use him for company here on Nantucket and then hand him over to someone when I pick up my life in a city somewhere, where dogs are an inconvenience? I didn't plan anything at all with him. I certainly didn't plan to love him.

My thoughts stumble across the knowledge that my life will be longer than his, but the thought emerges in the form that I want him with me always, and then his get, and then his get's get. So I have to register him with the American Kennel Club in order to mate him with a purebred female. The breeder said he'd charge me fifteen dollars more.

Fifteen dollars. My checkbook reads something over three hundred dollars. Three hundred dollars for four, perhaps six, months here. I sigh. Yes, I'll do it. I'll cut down on other things. Funny idea. The only other things there are are food, fuel, phone, and electricity.

Heavy overcast erases the line dividing the different grays of the sea and the sky. A southwest wind is blowing fog parallel to the land. The day becomes darker even as I contemplate going down to the sand. A light rain begins again, and instinctively I start up the steps toward the bluff and home. But the rain remains scanty and I turn back down the stairway, onto the sand, next to the water where gulls ride the waves near the shore. I look for the leader gull, as I learned to do at Malibu where the gulls lined up on the beach in the rain, standing for hours unmoving except when one of them would take a step or two beyond what must have been the limits tolerable to the leader, who would turn instantly, having somehow seen it all, and so, scowling and raising his wings just so much, he'd force the offender back into the quiet line again. Here, too, one gull sits ahead of the formation, facing northeasterly, waiting it out.

From time to time Logos shakes the accumulating wetness from his fur. My rainy walk in November might not be such a good idea for him. I begin a slow trot toward the short stairway that will get us to the back roads fast, then home.

I use three bath towels drying Logos. He's content to settle down with his back against the fireplace I never light, while I write to the man from whom I bought him, enclosing my check.

Noon and I'm hungry. Thanksgiving dinner will be a tuna casserole. Lunch will be an egg-salad sandwich. Why not?

The rain is coming down heavily now, and I stand at the window watching the trickles mark out their own paths. Why is this day different from any other day?

My father, asking the question of the youngest child during the Passover service. I see him, intent on the reading, serious as no one else at the table was serious. I see his essential sweetness, made even more obvious by his concern for the prayers, a concern that set him apart from the rest of us, giving him a distinction he didn't normally possess.

Now he lies in a hospital, treated as though he's no longer a human being, and I'm helpless to change any part of his life. Nothing can stop the brain deterioration. Nothing can stop my mother and brother from thinking of him as a recalcitrant child. Almost nothing I can do will avail him.

"Daddy," I said, placing the bound copy of my doctoral dissertation in his hands as he lay in bed in my mother's house, "this is my thesis. I did it for you. See, I dedicated it to you." And I opened it to the page where his name stood alone.

"I don't care about that," he said, running the words together, looking distantly across the room, pushing the book away from where it rested on his chest. "I don't care about that," pushing my hand away as I tried, gently, to make him look.

He doesn't mean it, I said to myself, standing, looking at the now thin face, hearing the familiar voice. He doesn't know what he's saying. And so I removed the book, and kissed him lightly. Lightly, because if I put my arms around him, I'd collapse onto him, puzzling and frightening him more.

Daddy. Dear Daddy. Why should loving be so hopeless and painful? Whatever gave me the idea that loving brings joy? Leaning against the window, my whole being contracts into my tears.

It's not working out. I've lost the patience to sit down and write while I think. The thoughts come too fast, or they come in their own time instead of when I'm ready to welcome them. Or they leap from problem to problem, not letting me pursue one single thread all the way to its end.

And yet it's only the writing that isn't working. The thinking goes on by the hour. It's hard to stop the thinking. Being with a psychiatrist for fifty minutes twice a week, even daily, doesn't take that into account. Why couldn't a psychiatrist spend a week, two weeks, a month, with one person? Not just talking together, but eating, walking, being out in the world together. Then the doctor wouldn't need to rely solely on the patient's report: the doctor would have his own standpoint on what had been said or done. If the therapeutic problem is to make the patient see how he distorts his version of reality, what better way than to call the patient's attention to it while it's happening, rather than days later when it has already filtered through all the layers of the patient's lies? Why couldn't a therapy be run all day every day for weeks, so that a psychiatrist could listen as a genuine friend, could teach me to trust him unconditionally?

Joke. It's because no psychiatrist could conceive such a plan that I'm here to do it myself. It's because no friend could be such a friend that I'm here alone. Being here alone, I don't have to put a face on at all. I don't have to isolate a therapeutic hour from the rest of the day, because here the hour has expanded out to encompass the day. Without neighbors, I don't have to pretend to be cheerful when I leave the house. Knowing no one on the island, I don't have to *seem* to be anything at all. When I start thinking my way through some remembered torment, the only thing that stops my thinking is my endurance, not somebody else's decision that we have no more time for it today.

Anyway, no one can tell me more about myself than I already know. No one can care how it all turns out more than I do. And that's why no one is here with me now.

If I fail, I could never make up for it by looking for some relationship with other people, because I'd know that I carried within me a permanent failure: it could neither be overcome nor forgotten.

I'm walking back and forth in the living room, sitting in one chair, then in another, then up again and into the kitchen, moving with no purpose except to keep moving so that what I'm thinking won't burst my body.

If I fail in this, I'll know that from now on, nothing I ever do will matter. Getting a job will be only a means for staying alive, rather than a reason for being alive: I'll never be able to pretend that I have a work that occupies my mind, some far-ranging series of studies that will make use of my knowledge and skill and interest. Because I won't know what my interests are, or my skills.

Holding a man will be only a response to a body hunger, like eating: I'll never be able to pretend that I love him or any other man, because I still won't know what loving is or what sex means to me, or what my own sexuality consists in.

So I can't fail. I haven't made much headway yet. Twelve days. But I still have time. I have to try to get back to the typewriter. I know that I need some record of what I think about here, so that I can see the pattern of it when I've written enough to look back on.

I return to the typewriter one more time. I try to force my thoughts onto one topic, just one, that will start me writing again. The image of my father comes before me with such clarity that I close my eyes to ward off the pain.

I stand at the window, looking out onto the sunny day. Logos is awake and stretching, ready for a run. I could make a sandwich to carry in my pocket down to the water. Sit on that log high on the beach and have lunch. I seize on the diversion gladly.

To think of Daddy is to enter a path ending in hopelessness and frustration. There at the dead end stand my mother and brother, having the lawful right to deal with Daddy as they will. Mother, who cares only to keep her friends from thinking that Daddy is insane, conceals his true condition and thereby makes people wonder all the more what the trouble is. She can also collect all that pity, being brave about her suffering. But she's absolutely incapable of trying to grasp what Daddy must be feeling, and so she's incapable of alleviating the horror for him in any way. The doctor she uses for Daddy gives her a special cheap fee, and so it escapes her that Daddy gets cheap medical attention for the bargain.

I've tried to circumvent them so often. The doctors I've talked to, the articles I've read, the medical appointments I've arranged, the social-service worker who tried to help me find a nursing home, the physical therapists at the rehabilitation center: all of these attempts end by having to confront my mother and her chief adviser, my brother. Both of them refuse to accept the diagnosis by the chief doctor in psychiatry and neurosurgery at Western Reserve Hospital.

"Get out of it," he said to me the day I went to his office to talk with him myself, not trusting my mother's version of what he had advised. "Let your mother take care of him. She has a lot of guilt to work off, and you haven't the time or money to take care of him. Go finish your doctorate, and try to forget the whole thing."

"But I love him. I have to try to help him." I sat, not understanding his words.

"There is nothing that you, or anyone else, can do. The brain damage is already extensive, and it's getting worse. It may go on two years, ten years, I don't know. But brain tissue does not regenerate. There is no way he can ever get better. So get out of it."

I never once doubted his medical analysis. It was his psychological advice that I couldn't follow. Maybe I could have "gotten out" if my family had accepted his diagnosis, and if they had treated Daddy accordingly. But I hate the way they treat him so much that I'm still trying to take him out of their hands. Three months ago he weighed barely one hundred pounds, and he was refusing to eat. How long can he live?

I try to envision learning that he has died, and I fight away the sick stomach and hot throat. I realize with shock and terror that I don't know what there is to do at death. My thoughts stop me in the middle of the road. Who will help me? I've run out of people.

Randall. As I say his name, I know how right he is. I think of him last August in Washington where I was looking for a job. Randall, with his two little girls in palest orange-and-white dresses, as we inched our way around the base of the Washington Monument, their first visit and mine. He, dressed with elegance, as always; his hair gray, short enough, very right for his lean face; the spare and agile body. That peculiar walking trot of his: he always looks as though he just catches himself from falling. The active face, the lively eyes, the dry, hard mind. Once we thought of marrying. I mean, we tried to think of marrying. We matched on every score, except that there was no warmth between us.

"What have you learned in ten years that's important, Randall?" I asked, in the cab on the way back to my hotel.

"I learned about loving," he said, turning to me from the front seat. He surprised me by not being embarrassed at saying the word.

"Loving isn't something I'd have predicted for you. I always thought of you as connected to people only from a distance. What happened to change you?"

"Mary. She just kept on loving me, until I could accept it. Then I could return it, and grow with her in it."

I look at him, and he at me, smiling deeply.

"I was very smart ten years ago," I said. "I chose you for what you could become. And look at you: you've become it. I'm glad you're happy. I couldn't have taught you what Mary did. I don't know what loving is, even now."

The cab stopped in front of my dismal hotel. "I have the feeling that we've been talking in these last few minutes as though we might never meet again."

He helped me out of the cab. "Don't let it be the last time. You must come and meet Mary." He kissed my cheek. "Good-bye, Timmie."

I waved to the children, and walked to my room. And lay staring at the ceiling, comparing my grim life with his, until it was time to catch the bus for New York.

Yes, Randall will help me. I can't wait to go back to the house to write him.

The mail brings a letter from the contract research company I visited in Stamford before coming here. They want me to consult for them. The man is sending, under separate cover, the report he will pay me to read and analyze. He still thinks that technological research requires some understanding of epistemology. People who aren't in philosophy persist in believing that that's about how we learn, rather than about the warrants for what we claim to know. What have I to do with people like this? They don't really want to know philosophy: they want to know psychology, but they don't know there's a difference.

I have an answer to why I should have anything to do with them: they're the only source of money I can see, and I can earn it while I'm here.

I curl up in one of the chairs near the fireplace, drinking the golden heat that will in time levitate me toward preparing the evening meal. Suddenly I'm very amused. Here I am, defending the purity of philosophy, trying to prevent its being dirtied by hands that don't know how to deal with it, yet I don't have the first idea whether philosophy means anything at all to me, whether I *want* to spend my life doing philosophy. I have to begin thinking about all of that. Soon.

The liquor warms me slowly, and I linger over it, waiting for the insurance agent to bring me the new 1963 registration for my car. It's nearly seven when I hear his car in the driveway. He hands me the plates, we exchange remarks about the weather, and he is gone. I had no intention of inviting him in, nor had he an idea of being invited. Yet as I hear his car back out, I find myself wondering whether I should start to look up the people on Nantucket whose names I collected in New York.

But there are no people who would talk about this thing with me. And I can't imagine bringing myself to talk about anything else, as I'd have to, with new people. So there can be no relief from this, except what I myself find.

Anyway, relief is the wrong kind of idea. Like dancing on the way to a grave. Finishing this will be relief enough to spare for the whole of my life. If I finish.

The room is dark when I awaken. Logos breathes peacefully beneath my bed. There is no other sound. I lie quietly trying to fall asleep again. Left side. Right side. On my back. Counting. Breathe deeply and hold my breath to raise the oxgyen level in my blood and become giddy. I remain fully awake.

I reach for my watch, but in the dark I can't read its face. Irritated, I return the watch to the night table and fall back on the bed. And then an unfamiliar idea comes to me: I can turn on the light. I fight against it even as I consider it. My hand hesitates all the way to the switch. My eyelids close reflexly at the light. When I can focus, I lie in the light-filled room as though I've entered another world, large and new. Why should this familiar room feel and look strange? Because it's light in the middle of the night. But the night is no darker at two-thirty than it was at ten-thirty when I went to bed. And the light was on then, throwing the same shadows, brightening the same portion of the floor, the bed, the table. The newness disorders my thoughts, and I'm unable to sort my way through them. I reach for my book, but I read only half a page before I know I'm going to be awake a long time. Something hot to drink could put me to sleep. But that's downstairs. I start to read again.

It strikes me that the idea of going down to the kitchen gives me the same feeling that the idea of turning on the light gave me moments ago. A restraint, almost as tangible as a hand, stops me now from getting out of bed. Just as it half stopped me from turning on the switch. I must understand. Immediately.

At the foot of my bed lies my robe. Under my bed lie my slippers. But to reach for either one warns me of a battle of unaccountable intensity with what? With whom? Working against that presence, I stretch out my hand for the robe, then wriggle into it. I throw back the covers, swing my legs over the side of the bed, find my slippers, and slide my feet into them. Then out of bed. I stand, feeling space opening out to me, astonished that nothing terrible has yet happened. The newness begins to be so exciting that I smile. Logos slithers out from under the bed, stretches, then falls again onto the rug, ready to move when I do, but not sooner.

Yes, something hot. Cocoa. Maybe even graham crackers. With butter. So many lovely ideas, all at once. And then the force of it hits me, and I sit back on the bed as though thrown. I'm breaking another rule: When you go to bed, you stay there until it's time to get up. If you wake up in the night, just go back to sleep. No lights.

My mouth falls open. Is it possible that I have lived thirty-seven years as though I were still the little girl my mother had to make go to sleep? Bed is a place where you stay, once you're put there, until daylight at least; preferably until everybody else is awake. I think swiftly back on the terrifying nights of sleeplessness throughout the last ten years. I've never turned on a light to read myself back to sleep, never gotten out of bed after the night began. I shake my head in wonder.

I sit on the floor to pet Logos. "Hey, Sweet Puppy," I whisper. That too? No talking at night.

"Hey, Logos," I shout. He's on his feet, alert instantly. We both clatter down the stairs, I turning lights on throughout the house. While the pot of cocoa is warming, I go back upstairs for my book. Each movement unravels something in me. Eating crackers and drinking the hot brew, with Logos asleep nearby, I read until I start to yawn. The sky is now a visible gray. I think I might be able to fall asleep; I really think so. I open the outside door for Logos, and by the time he comes back in, I almost feel the warmth of my bed.

My room is losing its shadows to the new day. I switch off the artificial light that has burned all these hours, and settle under the covers. I've done a tremendous thing tonight: I've found a way to fall asleep when tiredness isn't enough.

II

I trail longing thoughts for some indefinitely particularized male. Who would like it here? I stop on the sand, trying to imagine someone walking along the water's edge with me, talking with me on my cantilevered platform, throwing sticks for Logos to chase. Not Stan: he's night and city. Maybe Mike. So much taller than I that each time of being with him surprised me by the distance I had to tilt my head. I always lost the first few minutes of our time together by being astonished at his looks. Each feature all but perfect, yet there was a certain roughness, a force from inside him, that kept it all lighted and in motion. The curly dark hair. You just kept wanting to look at him.

Yes, imagine Mike here. I begin a long silent conversation with Mike. It takes me a good way out to the lighthouse. When I turn back, Mike is still not here. Nor is he likely to be. Nor is anyone likely to be.

I'm spoiled.

The chain of ideas comes so fast they almost pass me by. I have the feeling of reaching after them to pull them back to look at.

I'm spoiled because I always use my looks to get something I want when I'm not sure I can get it by ways that other people have to use. And then I wonder whether I deserve to have whatever I've gained. I think of myself as beautiful, and yet I'm always surprised to be told that I am.

How can I begin to untangle all this? It's like standing between two mirrors and watching the images reflect back and forth to one another. A mirror should be able to tell me what I look like. Yet it's when I look into a mirror that I'm stopped from thinking myself beautiful. Once every now and then if I look long enough, or if the light happens to be just so, I begin to get some faint hint of what people have been telling me for the last twenty-five years. But most of the time looking into a mirror is a repetition of the bewilderment I remember when I was thirteen.

A Sunday evening meeting of young people at the Temple Israel. I'm there under protest. The misery of putting myself on the line at dancing school, and then being ignored, was too fresh to have lost its bitterness: sitting on the chairs against the wall and waiting to be asked to dance; never being asked by the best dancer, or the best-looking boy, but rather by the shortest boy, or the ugliest; sometimes not being asked at all. The Sunday night meeting was my mother's idea. She wanted me to meet other Jewish boys and girls, since I seemed to show no preference for Jews over non-Jews in the children I knew at school. Did she tell me why I was there, or did I guess? No matter: I never trusted anything she told me anyway.

Some of the boys and girls were in my high-school class; most of them were new to me. I had no idea what the meeting was supposed to be about. I knew only that I was ill at ease, waiting to be the last one asked, if at all, to whatever there was to be asked to. But just before the meeting began, two boys changed seats to be sitting in front of me, so they could turn to talk with me. And when the meeting was over, I was the center of a ring of people, the girls having come over to share some of the glow. It was easy to laugh: I was excited in a way I hadn't known was possible.

Stuart, the best-looking and the most popular boy, asked to take me home. To drive me home: me, alone in a car with this boy! On my doorstep, he kissed me. For months afterward, I'd go out onto that doorstep when I was sure no one could see me, at night when the family was upstairs or gone, and I'd re-create that kiss. But this night, I was so stunned by the firstness of everything that when I finally turned the key and went into the house, I placed myself in front of the bathroom mirror, staring, wondering, dreaming, baffled.

I can still see that face. Maybe that's the only face I ever see, even now: that thirteen-year-old looking to see what there was in that face to get all that attention that evening, what there was in that face to prompt that kiss. The kiss was my initiation, not just to sexuality, but a new reality, to a whole new way of giving and receiving, of asking and taking. By kissing me, Stuart showed me that I was Alice: a person, not just a member of my family. He didn't *have* to kiss me because I was related to him. His reason was that he wanted to. And the basis for his wanting was my face, what I looked like. I didn't have to ask to be kissed; I didn't have to kiss someone first, in order to get a kiss in return; I just had to stand there, and look like whatever I looked like, and that received a kiss.

It was beyond my understanding. I needed the mirror that night to show me the girl who was receiving all that attention. She was no one familiar to me. I think she's never become familiar. I think that the face I see when I look into a mirror now is still the face of that thirteen-year-old before that evening. Why compliment, why kiss that face? And yet, people do.

I've walked too far for the puppy today. He's been falling behind, even stopping to rest from time to time. When we enter the house, he goes straight to the fireplace and settles into what I know will be a long sleep. I remove my coat and boots. I have today hit upon a knot of ideas that carries somewhere within it something to teach me. Mirrors and my face. My face and receiving attention. My face and loving.

I take my drink to my desk to look out the west window, where there would be a sunset if the day were not overcast. Where there would be light if there were not shadow.

Holding a cup of coffee, I lean one elbow on the top of my typewriter and wait for the news to reach my intellect that another day has begun. Hard to tell. Same overcast sky I looked out on late yesterday afternoon. In between, a sleep and a forgetting.

Wrong. No forgetting. I have to think about mirrors. Mirrors mirror: they reflect. As I must reflect on what mirrors mirror to me. On why it is that when I look at a mirror I see one face, whereas when other people look at me they see another.

The coffee is still too hot to get down in two good swallows. Sipping is not satisfying: the heat is too intense at my lips for the flavor to get into my mouth. Sitting, imperfectly alert, mindful of the coffee more than of my thoughts, I realize with astonishment that I'm now touching the edge of what is genuinely peculiar. Not that I see my face differently from the way other people see it, but that I've chosen to believe what they see rather than what I see!

Slowly I place the hot cup on a protected surface and, frozen, understand what I've been doing. I have turned other people into mirrors for me. I look at other people in order to see myself. If they think I'm beautiful, why, then, I am.

Where is the soft place? Where will it give? Where can I push it? Other people. The "they" I came here to get away from. The ones who make the rules that I follow even as I rebel against them, those rules I've been breaking in small steps for the past two weeks. So: it's not just my face that other people have given me.

But I'll start with my face. And my voice and my body. This whole organism that I've turned into my facade. Even up to last month when I saw it begin to come apart in Laurel's mirror in New York. A mirror, again.

Because I was beautiful, and had an interesting voice, I had to be an actress. No, not accurate. I started acting in the second grade, playing Old Nokomis in *Hiawatha,* sitting hidden in the wigwam through the entire performance. And after that in every play, taking every opportunity to appear before an audience throughout grade school and high school. I was acting because it didn't occur to me that I couldn't. Up to a certain point I wasn't doing it for the applause or the attention; otherwise, I, at thirteen, wouldn't have been so astonished at the attention given me at that meeting.

I see now: from that Sunday evening on, some part of my innocence about being on stage was rubbed away. Acting became a way of guaranteeing that kind of attention, but magnified and focused. That evening was the first diluting of the purity of my reasons for wanting to act; at the same time, it weakened the confidence I had had before. Whether I could act, which I had never questioned, became my preoccupation.

I corralled the director of the Goodman Theatre school. "Will I be a good actress?"

The moments until he answered told me what I was afraid to hear, and yet I waited while he inhaled a long pull on his cigarette and flicked the growing ash. "I don't think my job is to make predictions about great or good actors or actresses." He spoke, not looking at me, in that Russian-French-British–accented voice that I had heard range from a low pitch for sarcasm to something nearing a shriek when someone on stage did something to outrage him. "I can teach you, all of us here can teach you, the techniques of your craft. What you yourself have to contribute to that, once you've found your own way to put it to use in the theater, is something I would not be willing to talk about. You should not have come here to be made a great actress. It is not something that can be made."

"But I want to know . . ." I was slow to find my words.

"Yes?" He was not really encouraging me. He found the interview unpleasant and wanted it over. I thanked him and left. Incredible: I *thanked* him.

By the time I put my thoughts together, I could only interpret his restraint as his lack of interest in my talent, or rather, as his recognition that I lacked talent. Secretly I must have agreed with him. It struck a note in me, his dismissal of me.

David, on the other hand, gave me his enthusiasm. David: a teacher of acting, not an administrator at all; interested only in what he could make happen on a stage; Russian, like Dr. Gnesin, but less educated, his English carrying a barefaced accent that bespoke his impatience with whatever might distract him from the theater.

David was on my side from the day of the rehearsal in which I accidentally knocked my elbow hard against the bench. Yes, I was supposed to struggle with the girls who were carrying me; yes, I was supposed to be in pain; yes, I was supposed to speak lines while they tried to calm me. But when I smashed my elbow, I screamed because it hurt, and I was crying while I spoke my lines.

David rushed backstage when the scene was over. "Koller, you were magnificent! I felt your pain. When you screamed, you had me on the edge of my seat. You were really in it." His eyes glowed.

"But, David, I hurt myself. I banged my elbow and it hurt. I wasn't acting: I really screamed. It still hurts."

"But you made the scream be part of your character. You used it in the scene. You didn't stop the scene and say, 'I hurt my elbow.' Your instincts are perfect. You will be great. You have real talent."

"But, David, it wasn't acting. It was real."

"Koller, who knows better: you or me? Don't argue."

A year after I left Goodman, having decided I couldn't act, I saw him in some theater foyer. "Koller, you should have stayed. You had more talent than anyone there. You were an actress."

It would have been easy to believe him. Why didn't I believe

David's open admiration, which I won from him on terms he himself set up? Why did I believe Dr. Gnesin's equivocal remarks, which I construed as his being kind about my lack of talent?

Mirrors, again. I turned these men into mirrors. If they saw me as talented, I was; if not, then not.

I reach for the coffee cup: cold. On my way into the kitchen, I fumble among the threads of what I've just been thinking. That I made those men into my mirrors is only part of it. What I haven't touched at all is that they disagreed, and I chose one rather than the other. Why? Because I had started to believe that I couldn't really act, couldn't be the kind of actress I wanted to be. What kind was that? An actress who would be able to draw an audience, not just because of what I looked like or because of my voice or my manner, but because of my ability to project a character as someone real, as someone having her own life, way of walking, reasons for crying, taste in clothes. But to do that an actress has to *feel* the character, feel as the character would feel throughout the performance, night after night. Otherwise, it's not acting: it's merely giving the actress a chance to strut.

It wasn't something I could do. I could only feel *myself* playing the character. I couldn't help knowing, as soon as I'd hear certain lines, that I was supposed to be angry or happy; I prepared myself to be angry or happy; and when I became angry or happy I was fully aware of myself as playing a happy or angry character. I was never *not* aware of myself on stage. And that, according to the Goodman view of the matter, was wrong.

Now, twelve years later, I know I could have decided that if I couldn't act that way, I'd find some other way to act, a way more congenial to what I knew I *could* do. I knew even then that there was another way: Coquelin's way. But at Goodman no one talked about Coquelin, even though his ideas permeated the French theater. Only Stanislavsky deserved to be studied.

So I decided that I couldn't act Goodman's way, and then went on to decide that I couldn't act at all. I broke off the main line of my life the night I decided, and I've been outside and dangling ever since. Going back to college, going into philosophy, working for advanced degrees: none of it reached into me, tearing me up by the roots as that decision did. I had a sense of being at home in the theater. Nothing I've done since has reinstated that feeling.

And yet, perhaps it was my ignorance that let me be at ease on a stage. Because it was when I began to learn acting as an art that I began to be afraid and insecure: I couldn't ever feel what everyone told me I ought to be able to feel.

Leaning against the refrigerator, waiting for the coffee to reheat, I think of the night-long talk with my Chicago roommates, ending with me upright in the armchair, my back against its back, my eyes wide, totally amazed. "Well, then, I have to stop acting." And then the silence in the room as I heard the words out of my own mouth, and Pat watching me closely.

"Timmie, sleep on it," she said. "Maybe we've done you a disservice, trying to get you to look at things other than the theater. Wait a few days. Acting has been your whole life. A few more days won't matter."

"No." I remember staring at her, trying to hold down the room that was slowly going out of focus. "No, the reasons won't change. I have to stop."

That was only days after my twenty-first birthday, a year after Hiroshima, sixteen years ago. I'm still unattached: to anyone, to any work.

Logos wanders into the kitchen as I pour my cup of coffee. He sits and wiggles his tail, telling me that our walk is being too much delayed this day. A gain: it took me until noon to discover that today is Sunday.

Looking through my files, I come upon my copy of a security questionnaire listing all the jobs I've had and all the places I've lived. I count the jobs: thirty-five. I didn't bother mentioning a few. Like the very first one: selling toys at Christmas, working on Saturdays and two afternoons after school. For thirty-seven and a half cents an hour. The toys were so sleazy they fell apart lying on the shelves. And expensive. By the last few days before Christmas, I was persuading people not to buy them, especially people who shouldn't have been buying them. I remember those people: they had a look of too much longing, as though they were adding and subtracting pennies, giving up necessary things in order to put those junky toys under their Christmas trees. The toy department was always packed, in spite of me. The store dismissed me after the holiday rush. Not that they knew what I was doing.

Playground leader part of the next summer. Cashier in Joyce's father's movie theater until school started, at fifty cents an hour. How dirty money is. I had to wash my hands for a long time each day to get them clean when I left the cage.

The candy-department job in that specialty food store in Chicago. Pieces of candied fruit would fall on the floor whenever I'd weigh out what the customer wanted, so that by the end of the day, I had grown an inch taller from the debris that stuck to my shoes. I'd get back to the boardinghouse long after dinner was over, and I'd have to eat a meal in the kitchen, never hot, never enough.

All those nasty little jobs in Chicago. Selling blouses. Working in the school cafeteria for my lunch. Modeling at the Art Institute.

For the second year at Goodman I had to pay my own way completely, so it had to wait until I saved some money. I lived in Akron to cut expenses, hating it, and worked in the rubber-research laboratory. Before the year was out, I had to get away. Off to Texas to visit Christine.

Everyone was Old Whoever to her. I was Old Sarah.

"Why Sarah, Chris?"

"Well, Sarah Bernhardt, you clown."

"Listen, Chris, someday some girl like you is going to call some girl like me Old Alice." She hooted. But the name stuck. Even her parents, stopping by our tiny Chicago apartment, called me Sarah. I never understood her job at Navy Pier, but it netted her an officer, a pilot, and I was a bridesmaid at eighteen.

The visit to Corpus Christi lengthened. So a job at the Naval Air Station.

And on and on. Adds up to twenty years of supporting myself, with occasional minor assistance from the family.

Thirty-five jobs. And none of them meant anything to me except as a means of feeding myself and paying the rent. I was always working *toward* something, but I never, ever, got there. Even when I finally took my Ph.D., I didn't begin the work that I had been preparing for. I tucked the degree away until I could think about whether I wanted to use it. Whether I could use it to break down the distinction between a job and work: you work when you spend your time doing something you want to do and, almost in passing, you get paid for it. Everything else is a job. I think I've never worked. I think I've only had jobs. Because I was never doing something I wanted to do, not knowing what I wanted to do.

How small that circle is. I track around it as though I were riding one of the horsies on a merry-go-round. Is that why that music so horrifies me? Nailed to one spot while everything else goes around. Hobbled. The psychologist I talked with in Chicago a long time ago: "You are hobbled by something having to do with authority. You're as unable to move as though your legs were bound together by a board." She wanted me to begin therapy. A joke: I had only rent and food money. Two years after leaving Goodman, even with one year at the University of Chicago chalked up to me, the only way I had of earning money was as a typist. Therapy was out. Anyway, I despised the idea of it then.

I shovel all the papers back into their folder with impatient hands and toss the folder into the file box behind my chair. I go to the window on the moor side, clear away my books, and plop down on the window seat. Gray Sunday. I need a drink. "Need?" No, I don't know what I need. I'd better stop using words like that until I understand what they mean.

I wish there were someone to talk to. About funny things. To sit with in a dark bar. To tell stories to. To drink with until that giddiness arrives and stays and warms. To hold. Perhaps to hold.

I delay picking up the mail until just before the post office closes. The Stamford report arrives. I tuck the thick package under my arm and read my other letters on the way home.

The sun is down, but the sky is still red. How quickly the temperature falls. Crossing our lawn, I realize that I've noticed the relations of sun and earth, the movements of winds and water, the aspects of the sky, the way the air smells, as though I've never been outside in my whole life until I came here. Maybe the difference is that here I simply open my door and I'm outside: no obstructions, no hallways or stairways or elevators. No people to have to exchange conventional greetings with.

Logos stands before me, legs spread in that wide-apart position that tells me he wants to play. I start to chase him and then, caught up in the running itself, I drop my mail and follow after him, finding a burst of speed I don't remember using since I was a little girl. Logos looks back at me, surprised, and then moves ahead so swiftly that he rounds the house and comes up behind me, both of us reaching the scatter of my mail at the same time. My laughing is great gasps, and Logos finds the spectacle so unusual that he comes up very close to make sure that I'm that same old woman who always plods along behind him.

The report is worse than I expected. You don't find out until page eight what it's about, and even that statement is incomprehensible.

No. No, no. I won't read any more of it.

To break my annoyance, I get down on the floor to pet Logos. His eyes open briefly, and then he emits a long, low, delicious groan. The sleeping male.

"Hey, Logos," I whisper softly into his ear. The ear flicks at the passing air. I should let him alone, but I'm very restless, and it's only eight o'clock in the evening.

With Mike. Yes, I ran that fast with Mike the night we met. We drank and laughed and talked, because the closeness between us sprang up so fast. I told him of going backstage the year before to talk with Gerry, now a star. Better: a superb actress, saying all the right things about why she was acting. And then returned to my grim basement apartment, still in graduate school, still working for—what?

"Ah, Timmie," Mike said, leaning at one end of the bar in the apartment I later deeded to June. "Rich and famous? You don't want that, do you?" And I didn't know, until Mike came to my side of the bar and put his arms around me to hold me while I cried, that I was also jealous of her.

Being with Mike was being children together, both of us temporarily reprieved from duties we knew we had to face sometime, knowing we'd be helpless when the time came. Like me, Mike never stopped acting. The difference was that he had been a real professional for ten years, while I had been only a student. It was our common burden, and yet it provided us with a special kind of fun: we knew the same lines from the same plays. Something would remind one of us of a line, and the other would remember the rejoinder; and then we'd grin at each other. We even used Shakespeare the first time we decided that we should leave each other. I wrote a letter for the post office to deliver to him five blocks away:

> If we do meet again, why, we shall smile;
> If not, why then, this parting was well made.

And in the next mail came his reply:

> If we do meet again, we'll smile indeed;
> If not, 'tis true this parting was well made.

That first long night of talk could not end. We got the idea of walking along the Charles to watch the sunrise. At dawn we ambled out into the empty streets and, as we reached the end of my block, the excitement of all the good things that I thought were in store for me with him rose up in me, and I shouted, "Let's run!" He was ahead immediately, and then something surged in me that made me go faster than the fastest I could try. We stopped at the corner, I breathless from laughing, but Mike's face was clouded and serious.

"You wanted to win," he said.

I looked at him, shocked. He was accusing me of something, and it was false. "Mike, I was running because everything is so good. It felt good to run. So good that it made me want to run harder."

"Timmie, you wanted to beat me. Are you competing with me already?"

I should have heard what he was saying, but I heard it only just now. I said whatever I thought would keep him with me. It occurs to me now that nothing I said made him stay; he must have decided that he'd give me another chance anyway. Because that piece of glory between us lasted—oh, at least a month.

Mike came to me when I was vowing not to lie to anyone, even to a man, perhaps even to myself. It was one of the things that drew us together, because he was vowing it too. But I almost didn't know how to try, and he was hardly the person to teach me. Yet we knew the worst part of each other merely by knowing that we had been actors. Knowing that, we had almost nothing left to confess. Then we had only to make ourselves tell the truth. But before we could notice that we didn't have to practice deceptions on one another, Mike found that his only salvation lay in his not being a party to saving me too.

And even though I helped set up the scene for the farewell, I couldn't really believe that he had gone. I called, I wrote, I plotted ways to be in places where I thought he'd be when I thought he'd be there, and I was nearly always wrong. When I did encounter him, it threw me so completely off-balance that I'd stammer or drop something or trip, like a little girl with her first boy.

Why didn't I let him alone? He gave me the feeling that he had had to tear himself away from me; that he really wanted to be with me but that we couldn't possibly help one another, and that that was very sad; that by leaving me he was stopping himself from doing me the harm he knew he'd invariably attempt if he were to stay.

Jean, no longer roommate, now married, newly a mother; no longer a graduate student, now degreed. I'd tell her the story over and over, and she'd try to be nice. "Timmie, he's done this before. You are one of a long line of women whom he has left with exactly that feeling. George and I shouldn't have introduced you two. But we thought you'd see it coming, because you're both so much alike. Timmie, forget him." I told myself that she really didn't understand.

I have never, not once, accepted the end of any of these things. Yesterday (no, Saturday) I even considered what it would be like to have Mike here. As though the option were mine. As though he were very much alive in my life, there to be phoned or written to. But he's not.

I make myself say it out loud: "Mike is not available to me. Mike doesn't exist for me." I'm not sure what I've just said.

Logos has been asleep under my hand all this time, and I'm stiff from sitting on the floor. I rouse him, take him outside, go to bed, and lie wakefully a long time, wondering how I'll ever figure out what I'm doing here.

I bring morning coffee back to bed and prop myself up with one thin pillow through which I feel the widely spaced iron columns of the bedstead. I get out of bed again to raise the shades on the glorious morning. The moor spreads below. I try to remember what I thought a moor would look like before I saw one.

Another pillow from the other bed in the room lets me settle in more at my ease. A pity that the Stamford connection won't work out. To get the fifty dollars a day they're offering me, I'd have to spend my time reading garbage like that report, and that's not my idea of how to make my way through the hours of the day. Very sad.

Maybe I can simply put them off. I don't have to tell them how impossible the report is this very day. I can keep them in reserve as a source of income until I know where my next cash is coming from. That in itself is a new way of doing things: being provident.

Maybe it's not possible to tell the truth when a roof and bread are at issue. But if you can't say what you mean then, nothing's to stop you from making another exception, for your friends, say, and then another and another. And then you're lying if you tell yourself that you still know how to tell when you're not lying.

Or maybe the important distinction is the one between work and a job. You can lie to keep a job, but there should be no occasion for lying if you're working.

But think of all the ways there are to lie, and I'll have done every one of them. Pretending to like something because someone in authority does. Evading a question. Saying only part of what I believe.

Not saying anything at all. Shaping my words to fit what I know will be acceptable. Smiling when someone intends to be funny. Looking serious when my thoughts are elsewhere. Agreeing when I haven't even thought over the matter. Drawing someone out just because I know he wants to talk. Trying to amuse in order to avoid talking about something I'm not sure of.

Acting. For the dear love of God, how could I not have understood it before! Those are all pieces of acting. And I don't know where it ends. I have to try to think of one thing I've done that was for free.

I stop walking. Has everything I've done been payment for something? By pretending, by acting, by lying, what have I been buying? What? Oh, please, what has my acting bought for me?

The midday silence surrounds me. Logos digs in the wet sand near the line of the advancing tide, barking when the water sweeps over the hole. My mind goes blank, confronting some blackness whose extent is too wide for touching. I watch Logos for a little while, and then slowly cut across the dunes toward the paved road that is one of the long ways home.

I ought to be able to know what I've been getting in exchange for my evasions and my smiles. Does it have something to do with the way I've turned people into my mirrors, so that I believe them, rather than what I myself see?

The linkage retreats when I try to press it. Mirrors. For the dozenth time I remember the afternoon last summer in Ohio, while I watched Weck in front of her mirror, hurrying to be off to teach her class in jewelry design. God knows I wanted her to stay and talk to me, to tell me why I was always chasing some man who had left me, why I was still without a good job a year after my Ph.D., why I was about to go to California when I hadn't an idea that I could get a job there. Why I did what I did, when I was always so unhappy doing it.

She finished smoothing the makeup onto her face and reached for the black pencil to outline her eyes. Leaning close to her mirror, she said, "You know, you can't keep on blaming everything on your mother." She stretched her neck backward a little to see if she had done the eye properly. I watched, chin in hand. Eyes so black. Almost liquid, like her voice. She was a Mary Ann, her true name, yet everyone used the nickname that abbreviated her maiden name.

Weck leaned toward the mirror again. "Just because she didn't give you attention when you were a little girl, you can't hold her responsible for . . ."

I barely listened: I knew her reasoning. I found myself wondering why Weck sometimes used such stilted language. Twelve years of being friends, yet she seemed to feel she had to make up for not having gone to college when she spoke to me. She could have said simply that my mother didn't love me. Instead she said that my mother didn't give me "attention."

Suddenly I stopped breathing. I stood, feeling that my mind and my body were being sliced apart. I struggled under the ripping. I screamed at her: *What did you just say?*"

The shocked face turned to me, her marking pencil describing an arc in the air. "Alice." She may have been whispering. "Alice, what's the matter?"

I was crying. "For God's sake, what you said. You said she didn't give me *attention,* but what you meant was that she didn't give me *affection!*"

I fled out the door, screaming, crying without control, propelled up the stairs to the room I occupied in her house, and flung the door shut behind me, falling on the bed to let the tears pour out.

She ran up the stairs after me, knocked on the door, then entered, shaken but trying to soothe me. "Alice, what did I say to hurt you? I'm sorry, whatever it was. I didn't mean it, whatever it was. Please stop crying."

"Weck." I spoke between gasps. "I can't stop. You didn't hurt me. You made me see that I—oh, get me something. I want to tell you."

She brought me water to drink and held the glass for me because my hands were shaking and my teeth clicked against its edge. She removed the glass, watching me without speaking, then: "Tell me. Please tell me what's the matter."

I looked at her and opened my mouth to speak. But a great cry came out instead, and I curled into my tears all over again. Weck left and returned with another glass. "Don't say anything. Just drink one swallow." The liquor slapped my throat to spare her from slapping my face. I took another swallow. The crying began to subside.

"Weck, I want to tell you. I had the words *attention* and *affection* mixed up too, but I didn't know it. When you used one for the other just now, it was as though you punched a button that released the machinery that was holding the structure of me together. A long time ago, when I knew she couldn't love me, I must have decided I'd take the next best thing: I'd get her attention whatever way I could, even to have her yelling at me. All those years of fighting with her while I was growing up were my way of getting some, *any*, substitute for her affection. What I got was her attention: her needling, nagging, ignorant, unloving attention. And I didn't know that's what I've been doing until just now, when you said . . ." The cries whooped out of me again. "Weck." I could speak if I swallowed every few seconds. "Go on to your appointment. I can't stop crying yet, but I will soon. I'm not crying because she didn't love me. I've known that for too long. I'm crying from the shock of finding out what I've been doing to try to make up for it. The energy I've wasted, to try to get her to look at me." Weck touched me lightly on the shoulder and was gone.

I knew that day that I had grasped a piece of truth unlike any I had come upon in all my years of trying to understand what I was about. Today, a year later, the whole memory retains the same quality of being unimpeachably true.

Pieces of unimpeachable truth: no diet for a philosopher. Everything I know in philosophy forbids me to accept the truth of that afternoon in the terms on which I do nevertheless accept it. I know only that it carries a mark by which I recognize it: it belongs to me. In fact, I've done away with every other criterion for truth merely by being here alone, trying to tear away everybody else's standards to see whether anything remains that is mine. Particularly, specifically, uniquely mine. I didn't realize until just now that my whole intention is to work out my own truth, something that is true for me alone. I can't let it matter whether anyone else would find it true: true about me or true for themselves.

Logos strolls over to the corner cabinet as I start to turn off the lights for the night. He barks, looks at me impatiently, then barks again. I grin at his way of letting me know where his ball is. Then, even as I watch him, he comes straight toward me. Very gently he takes my hand in his mouth. I'm startled enough that I almost pull it back, but I want to see what he'll do next. He tugs, just a little, and I relax into the pull. My hand in his mouth, his teeth not even indenting my skin, he holds his head high, as though he carries a trophy, and prances with me across the room to the cabinet, where he drops my hand and stands looking at me expectantly: I am to get his ball for him. In wonder I kneel, reach under the cabinet, retrieve the ball, and hand it to him. Gravely he takes it, lies down facing me, and waits for our game to begin.

"Oh, brilliant Logos!" I hug him. His performance deserves a game. We play in the half-lighted room until I yawn.

In bed almost asleep, I realize that tonight is the first time I've thought of philosophy as having any bearing at all on what I'm doing here. I'm sobered to understand that what I learned during those brutal years at Harvard seems to exist in a different compartment from this hands-down battle against some unknown enemy for some imperfectly glimpsed goal. But I know that what I understood with Weck that day was true. For me.

12

I'm reaching for the towel to dry my hair when I hear knocking at the back door. The sound is so extraordinary that for a moment I think I may have misheard it. Can it be Logos' tail thumping on the floor? The storm door banging in the wind because I didn't close it tightly? I stand, water trickling down my body, the towel still in midair, when the knocks sound again. I wrap the towel around my head, throw on my robe and slippers, and go downstairs to look out the kitchen window. There stands a young man whom I do not know. I step back quietly before he can see me and try to decide whether to open the door. Who is he? What does he want in the middle of the day? I glance out the front window. No car. Then he must be someone who lives out here.

I open the back door just enough to stick my head out, the storm door still closed against him. "Yes, please?" I'm not encouraging.

He is surprised at my getup. "I left some of my things out here in the Elstons' garage last summer, and I've come to pick them up. I just wanted to let you know what I was doing in the garage. I needn't trouble you."

I feel helpless wearing nothing but a robe. I don't like the idea of his rummaging in the garage without my being there. "Would you mind waiting a few minutes? I've just stepped out of the tub, and I want to dress."

Logos has come to see the visitor too and somehow gets in the way of my closing the door. I pull him out of the way by his collar, and then fly into my clothes. I rub the surface water out of my hair, dismayed at having to go outside with this wet head. I comb my hair, which thereby fits my scalp as though sculptured to it. In the mirror I see what I always expect to see. The sole virtue of this face is that it's clean. I don't need to be pretty for this boy. I don't need makeup. I start down the stairs, and then hesitate. Well, some. Not lipstick, though. I go back to the mirror, swiftly brush color on my brows, and go outside to the boy.

As I unlock the garage door for him, we tell each other our names. Ralph is big, wears rough outdoor clothes, knows exactly what he wants to do about the frames stored in the back of the garage.

"You don't need to take them away just because the Elstons don't own the house anymore. They certainly won't bother me. My car doesn't use the whole garage."

"You didn't buy the house." He speaks his thoughts abruptly; his remark is more statement than question.

I grin: imagine owning a house. "The owners live in New York. I'm just renting it for a few months. How were you going to take the frames away with you, anyway?"

His car is parked in the road, beyond my driveway.

"Why don't you come in and have some coffee before you move them, then?" The invitation is out before I even consider it. As though confirming it, Logos circles Ralph, sniffs his boots, and then joyfully places both paws against Ralph's legs. Ralph reaches for the paws, stoops, and finds the place to scratch behind the puppy's ears. Logos collapses in a slow roll, and lies on his back, soliciting more.

"I had a dog for nineteen years. He came with me everywhere. Finally had to put him to sleep two years ago. I'll never have another dog."

Silently I watch him handle Logos. I try to say something, but I know he would repel my words. He stands up. "Yes, I'll come in. But I don't drink coffee. I'll stay a few minutes while you have some."

There is almost no room to move around the kitchen with two people in it. Ralph hangs his jacket on the doorknob without asking what to do with it, and sits at the tiny table. We talk rapidly about dogs, Nantucket, the postmaster, Siasconset. He is recovering from an accident. I look at him curiously. He seems in perfect health.

"What are you doing out here by yourself in the middle of winter?"

I go to the stove and fiddle with the coffeepot. I've been avoiding people on this island in order to avoid hearing just these words. Will it ever be possible for me to tell the truth when people ask me direct questions?

"I'm doing some thinking. And writing." Well, it's part of the truth.

He looks puzzled. "What do you think about?"

It didn't work. I decide to trot out my degree. It might help change the subject.

He looks at me coolly. "That's very impressive. The people whose house I take care of in Nantucket both have Ph.D.s. In psychology, I think. I've never been to college myself. I'll tell them about you. Maybe you could meet them."

The idea of talking to psychologists appalls me. I say that that might be interesting later on, then scramble around in my thoughts for something to talk about. "What do you think of the vet out here?"

"There's no vet on Nantucket."

"Of course there is. I've been taking Logos to the SPCA on Pleasant Street."

"Mr. Lema. He's not the vet. He's the dogcatcher. Or he was. Did you think he was a vet?" Ralph grins at my stupidity.

"He never told me he wasn't. And he's been giving Logos his shots. I'm damned. That explains the funny feeling I've had about him. He couldn't tell me what books to read to learn more about Logos."

"The vet comes here once a week, from Boston, I think. Find out from Lema. I have to go now." He takes his jacket and is out the door while Logos is still getting to his feet.

For half an hour afterward, I move through the house, unable to settle in one place. Echoes of a voice other than mine still sound. To have talked for the first time in almost three weeks. The mere fact of being able to talk shouldn't be such an event. What is there about talking, about having to talk, that gives me this peculiar sense of opening out, of letting someone in. I have the feeling that I must gather myself in again. I'm not ready to be with people yet.

I fluff my hair. Dry enough. I find my fake-fur hat, coat, boots, and we're on our way. I race Logos to the ocean. He wins: I give up in two blocks. Once on the sand, I find my log, thinking of nothing except the salt smell of the air that bathes me.

Everything about Randall's letter is gratifying. He offers me his services as a lawyer and a friend, whenever I shall need him. The cream-colored paper is the heaviest bond, suitable for the enduring words of the law. He encloses an offprint of something he's just written, a review of a book about the Supreme Court.

Stupid girl: I'm thinking of him, too, as one of a set of present alternatives among whom I need only choose, thereby solving one of my major problems. As I thought of Mike yesterday. As I think of George. Or Stan.

Stan. For ten years men seemed to me to be walking around with signs reading I AM NOT STAN. So that no matter how long any of them lasted, my final judgment on them, one by one, was, "You're not Stan."

I think of an April afternoon in our newness together, walking in the Yard, laughing, tossing each other ideas, so aware of each other's presence that not even our fingertips needed to touch. Ahead of us on the diagonal path leading to the library a man approaching us stopped for a long moment, then slowly resumed his steps. Stan and I both waved. He was a classmate.

"You took my breath away, both of you," he said, nearing us. "It was like seeing Sex Itself coming toward me." He kept on going, smiling and shaking his head in wonder.

"Well." Stan grinned at me. "I can see how he'd say that about you."

"Me with you, Stan."

Perhaps we touched then.

No, it wasn't his looks. Short, fat, and bald.

Marilyn, giggling: "Alice, why do you call him that? He's not short." Marilyn, whose friend he was first, during our early months at Harvard.

"Well, he's not tall."

"Or fat." The chest whose outline my fingers can still trace, the lean belly.

"Okay, he's not fat."

"Or bald. Well, maybe balding."

"He combs that yellow hair over a pretty visible patch of scalp."

It was not his looks that made him seem to be the other half of me.

But I have to notice that Stan is not here. Nor Mike, nor George. None of them, except now Randall, knows where I am. None of them would even try to find me. And the reason is: none of them cares. In any important sense of the word, none of them cares.

Why, then, do I continue to think of them as possibilities for some future relationship? I seem to believe that once I decide which of them I really want, all I have to do is plunk myself down in front of him, and we shall be happy ever after.

They are *not* possibilities. Aloud: "They are not possibilities."

Logos looks up, stretches, rolls onto his back, and falls asleep again, his forepaws in the bunny position, his rear legs spread wide for balance. Soon he'll start to fall slightly to one side, and then gradually, like an accordion, piece by piece, legs and paws will follow and he'll be back on his side again. There.

Since they're not possibilities, why have I been thinking of them? I pour the last shot from the bottle of bourbon and take the drink back to the window seat. The reddened clouds are turning purple. They darken further, swiftly, until only the palest light remains in the sky. If I could stop the world now, cutting off what preceded and what is to follow, this sky could be indistinguishably dawn or twilight.

I've let myself be misled. I was supposed to be thinking of these men only to try to understand what I do when I deal with men. Why it always ends with one or the other of us not wanted but not believing it. But I haven't been able to understand any part of it. I've been doing nothing more than reminiscing. What it all comes down to is that I have no idea what I do with men, and so I can't yet ask why I do what I do.

There must be some way of getting outside the story. To hear it from a standpoint that some detached observer would take. Cool but friendly. The storyteller and one of the main characters at the same time. Too tough.

Storyteller. I smile at the old nickname, and finish my drink. The room is as dark as the outside is.

But I could tell the story about *her* instead of thinking of it as being about *me*. By changing the pronouns I can get some distance. I, the storyteller, can be the observer of Alice, this ignorant female. Yes, I'll try it. Tomorrow.

I've forgotten where Logos lies asleep. I call his name. Near the couch a stirring. Near me I find the desk and turn on the light. Now the dark is only outside. And in me.

Logos is not on the doorstep when I go to let him in before breakfast. I call him, expecting him to come to me out of the tall grass. I run outside to the front lawn and shout his name, loudly, then again, and stand, shivering, looking toward the water tower. Emptiness and silence. My heart pounds abruptly, and I am immediately turned inside out. I rush into the house for my coat, then run to the road to call him again. Which way, which way did he go? The moor? I cut across the lawn again and make my eyes divide the rows of purpling scrub. Not here. Back to the road, turning left, running but looking backward every few steps until I come to the intersection. Which way, ocean or golf course? My ignorance makes me wilder. Did he run away? Did he go out to the main road and get hit by a car?

Car. I run back to the driveway, fling open the garage doors, get into the car, and swear: the keys are in the house. Out of the car, into the kitchen. Where did I leave them? Out the door again, my peripheral vision makes my head snap to the right. Trotting across the lawn from the direction of the water tower, all ease and puppy grace: Logos.

I'm still trembling. I know I must keep my hands in my pockets or else I'll hit him. He comes straight to me, skipping the last few steps, delighted to see such an old friend first thing in the morning. I stoop to hold him with both arms. He endures it for five seconds, then squirms free.

"You clown! Where did you go?" I'm actually waiting for an answer. Logos prudently goes to the door to be let in, and I accede, watching him with new eyes. He's growing up, growing away from me.

Idly I follow the pattern of the sunlight on the ecru rug, trying to remember what bright idea I elicited from my glass of bourbon last evening. It eludes me. Something about a new method. I need something new. Time is going by and I'm still walking in swamps.

Wait. I packed Polya's *How to Solve It* in the carton of books I brought with me. Here it is. The philosophical part of me is almost wholly skeptical. I know there are no "methods of discovery," in any strict sense of the word *method*. Yet Polya speaks of "heuristic" as "the study of the methods and rules of discovery," as though there were a set of steps which, if pursued in order, would lead to a discovery.

The other part of me that never amalgamated with the philosophical is desperate for clues. I flip through the early pages to refresh my memory, and I realize how much more modest Polya is in his text than his publishers are on the jacket. He knows that at best he can outline a series of what are only hints, suggestive steps that might usefully be followed if you're willing to take a chance and have the time. And if your problem is more or less technical, preferably geometrical. Unlike mine.

I find myself reading more closely than I had planned. Perhaps he has something for me. I go to the typewriter and copy out portions of his two-page schematization of his whole book, and then sit back in my chair, staring helplessly at the page. No, I'm giving in too soon. He's trying very hard to make clear something that is impossibly difficult, and I have to try to see what he means.

First I must understand the problem: he underlines it. God knows we agree. He even tries to analyze what that understanding might consist in: the problem is made up of an unknown, of data, and of a condition. I have to ask, "What is the unknown?" The solution to the problem consists essentially in linking the unknown to the data.

The data: this mass of memories I've been digging up and adding to daily. The unknown: what is the unknown? I shudder. I still can say it only in the terms that Dr. Kant gave me: I won't be able to understand why I live as I do until I understand what, exactly, I do. So to discover the unknown is itself a piece of heuristics. I have to find some way to set forth the data so that I'll be able to see the pattern of my behavior emerge. I have to find some way of telling myself what I do, before I can understand why. So the unknown is what it's always been: a problem in description. Rendering apparent what is now obscured to me. Making clear what wasn't clear before.

Maybe it's a piece of philosophical work after all.

The insight takes no edge off my despair. I'm back to where I always start: my nose close down on the details of what lies smack in front of me, with no way of rising upward from it to gain perspective.

I begin to see that the whole idea of a method for discovering things is *ex post facto*. You succeed in doing something, or you do something so well that you yourself want to know how you did it. So you go back, trying to re-create the steps that led you, not quite by accident, not quite by design, to where you wanted to be. You call that re-creation your "method." But what guarantees that you picked up all the significant steps, like loops dropped from a knitting needle, or that you put them together again in the order in which they originally occurred?

Like Leonardo's "method" for teaching his pupils how to sketch the faces they saw on the street. He categorized all foreheads, all eyebrows, all shapes of eyes, every conceivable aspect of the human face, then numbered them, and gave the list to his pupils. Instead of sketching faces when he saw them on the street, the pupil took a description of the face in terms of items on the list: Eyebrow 22, Nose 64. The pupil was supposed to sketch the face later from the list of aspects checked off. And Leonardo was perplexed when his pupils couldn't make their sketches resemble the faces they had seen, because his sketches looked like the faces he saw and he had given his pupils his foolproof method.

But it wasn't a method at all. He had no method: he just knew how to draw. But he believed that what he did could be said. His list was his attempt, so sincere, so useless, to articulate the steps of what he did.

But there is saying, and there is doing, and almost always people do something better than they can talk about it, as though the minded body defeats every attempt to select out only the mind part as deserving sole responsibility for the success.

I push back my chair and jump up with great excitement. How did I come upon all this? I've based my whole life on something utterly opposite: if I didn't know a method for doing something, I couldn't do the thing at all.

Acting, for one thing. I stopped acting because I couldn't act according to the method that Goodman taught. But what I'm saying now is: there's acting, and then there's trying to say what you do when you act—your method. But the method is at best a shadow cast by the actor who is trying to *say* what he does. So Stanislavsky says: I *feel* myself being jealous when I play Othello. And Coquelin says: I am aware of myself as the actor who knows where the audience is, where the exits are, how my costume fits, whether the other actors are tired or in a good mood. Coquelin, aware of all these factors in his craft, *guides* his Othello-costumed body in and out of tenderness, jealousy, doubt, rage, and sorrow, all the while speaking Othello's lines.

The problem for the craft of acting is: Which of Stanislavsky or Coquelin is reading his interior experience more truly? Grant they were both great actors. Which of them was better able to say what he was doing? For that matter, which third person might say it better than either of these? Or which fifth or fifteenth?

I'm almost skipping around the living room. I never understood the problem in these terms before. I might still be acting if I had thought that the method I was being taught was merely one version of how acting can be spoken about.

Abruptly I stop moving. I construed that method as a standard I had to meet in order to count as a really good actress; and when I found I couldn't meet it, I let it disqualify me. A standard, a rule: this is how we do things. Someone else's rules. Again.

I feel like crying, but I shake my head to rid myself of the tears. The movement seems to release connections that up to now have lain knotted and unyielding.

If I had understood that that method was only one man's way of talking about what he himself did while he was acting, I might have been able to see whether it matched what *I* did while *I* was acting. I might have found that it matched in some places but not in others, and in time I might have found my own way of talking about acting: my own method.

But that would have required my knowing, my being sure, that I could act. And until I went to Goodman, I *was* sure. Rather, it didn't occur to me to question whether I could. What made the difference? The standard. Before Goodman, I had no standard to gauge the quality of my acting. I got the applause at the end of the play, people told me I was good, and that was that. But at Goodman, people didn't tell me too often that I was good. That's when I began to question whether I was. The only available way I had for answering my doubts was to ask whether I could meet that standard.

Shocking, nauseating. Mirrors, again. Am I beautiful? I let other people tell me. Can I act? I let other people tell me. How have I *let* other people have such power over me? It's as though I don't believe I know . . . what? What should I know that I don't know?

I think back to the day I finally saw my face telling me my age. But if I don't really think I'm beautiful, why should it matter that my face will now have lines and shadows marking it? I know: it's that I'll stop being treated as a beautiful woman.

But I should welcome what's true. If it's true that I'm not beautiful, then I should be glad when people stop treating me as though I were. What I've known all along will be even more obvious to everyone else now. I should welcome getting older because it diminishes the distance between what I've known and what other people tell me.

If thoughts have sizes, this one is miniature. But, oh, it hurts, this tiny idea. It exposes a surface that I've kept guarded. Well, look at it. This is what I came here to do: to see what's true.

So I do know something: I know what I look like. Now and always, no matter what anyone might tell me.

But this piece of knowledge is not the thing I should have known about acting. I try to pick my way back to the path I spent the morning carving out. Surprised, I come upon my own tiredness.

Logos is as offended as he is bewildered to be standing in the bathtub having his fur soaped and soaked. I work swiftly on the rear parts even as I know him to be preparing a third time to jump over the side. The rug almost floats on the water he carried out with him the other two times; I myself am wet enough to have been in the tub with him. The rubber hose keeps detaching itself from the tub faucet, and my hands race against Logos' predictable last try. The most important thing is to rinse him thoroughly, said the book; the dried soap could act as an irritant on his skin, leading to all sorts of what I'm sure would be expensive complications. The hose breaks away from the faucet just as I finish washing his tail. I grab for the long-handled pan that I luckily anticipated needing. I fill it from the streaming faucet and, sweet-talking Logos, I pour it over him, then fill and pour until my arms ache from sustaining the contrasting pressures of holding him with one hand and rinsing him with the other. When I release him, he leaps out onto the floor and heads for the door, but I've outguessed him: the door is closed. I sit back on my haunches to catch my breath for the next round of toweling him dry.

He looks unexpectedly scrawny, standing there with water flowing off him so steadily that he himself might be its source. He holds his head down, and I am instantly touched: he looks as though he's just been beaten. I start to reach for the pile of towels. Suddenly it's raining in the second-floor bathroom. Instinctively I duck my head. Logos shakes his fur again, but most of the excess is already on me. The third time he lowers his head, I leap for him and encircle his belly and back with a towel, then rub. In seconds the drenched towel hangs heavily in my hands; another towel and another; I use six before I'm willing to consider him dry enough to leave the room. Outside the door, he gives one last shake, just to show that he's in charge of his own body. His fur stands out thickly all over; he looks well nourished and well shaped and well cleaned.

My sigh propels me into cleaning up the bathroom, and in the middle of the process I take a fast bath too. Logos is in for the night. No whiff of cool air may touch him.

Settling into bed, I look at the twin bed on the other side of the night table. I could let him sleep there. He'd be out of drafts, and he's certainly clean. I consider what precedent I'm setting. By never letting him on top of the furniture, I've kept him from knowing that there are surfaces up here to be lain upon. If I let him sleep on the bed, he'll have some new and dangerous knowledge.

I'm fighting the rule-ness of it. But it's my own rule: I can break it tonight, if I choose, and reinstate it tomorrow, if I choose.

"Logos." I pat the cover of the other bed, inviting him up. He looks back and forth at me and at the bed, hesitating long enough for me to doubt the wisdom of my waiver. "It's okay. Come on." In one jump he's on the bed, turning in a tight circle to find the spot to curl into, and then lies quietly down. I think I see some look resembling triumph, but it quickly turns into a peaceful gleam.

Here we lie, my friend and I, on opposite sides of a night table. I haven't had anyone at eye level on a bed for a long time. For a moment, I expect Logos to talk, to contribute his share of the entertainment. But he falls asleep so fast, and lies in such contentment, that he pleases me in his own way, by being so much at home. And gives me the same peculiar feeling.

I fall asleep in my robe with the light on. It awakens me some time later. I turn it off and climb under the covers for some legitimate rest.

Logos' eyes are less than a yard away when I open mine in the morning. The feeling of having a roommate flashes over me and I laugh. He starts to gauge the distance from his bed to mine, but I stop his leap by throwing off my covers and lifting him down to the floor. "No, sir. That was all the bed you're going to have until the next time you need a bath." I run my hands through his fur. It feels so soft and smells so fresh. He is quite thoroughly dry.

This morning I wait for him when he goes out. He seems to linger deliberately, but I'm determined to have my way. When we go back upstairs, I find some bits of what look like rice on the cover of the other bed. While I dress, I try to remember what that's a sign of.

I find the dog book on my desk and run through the index until the right word triggers my memory: *tapeworm*. The description of the symptoms include poor appetite.

I head for the phone to call the vet, but then I notice that the sun is at its lowest point in the eastern sky. My watch is somewhere here. Ten minutes before seven. Hell! Three hours before I can call. I shove the typewriter to one side, and place the watch at the center of the desk. It's the first morning I've wanted to know what time it is since . . . I can't think back to when.

Then how do the doers learn? Stanislavsky was taught a method, Coquelin was taught a method, both when they were as young in the theater as I was. That each of them described his own method at all means that what they were taught didn't suit them. It means there was a gap between what they were taught and what they knew. What they found themselves doing on stage. What they observed of what other actors did. What they thought would work in a certain scene, even though no one had suggested it to them, even though no one had ever tried it before. The way to eliminate the gap was to try to say what they knew, to articulate their method.

I'm on the trail of some connection here, but I don't seem able to catch hold of it. It has to do with the fact that I gave up at exactly the point at which these actors dug in. I said to myself: What I'm being taught doesn't match what it feels like to be on stage, therefore I'm not competent to be on stage. They said to themselves: What I'm being taught doesn't match what it feels like to be on stage, therefore what I'm being taught isn't the whole truth about acting, so I must help it along as best I can.

I left; they reshaped the craft of acting. They knew something that kept them in the theater; if I had known it, I might have stayed. What did I *not* know?

They wanted to act.

It comes to me so purely, in such simplicity, that it cuts through all the knots and windings of the past two days.

And I didn't want to act.

Involuntarily I shake my head. No, that's not quite it.

I didn't *know* whether I wanted to act.

Wanted to. My whole focus was wrong. While I was rushing from person to person to find out whether I *could* act, I should have been looking into myself to find out whether I *wanted* to.

But I took for granted that I wanted to. Why did I do all those plays before getting to Goodman if I didn't want to act?

I hold my stomach to stop being pummelled. I was acting because everyone kept telling me I was good. Mirrors. Even here.

I walk: desk to couch, couch to table, table to fireside chair, chair to stove, stove to refrigerator, and there I lean, crying. The endlessness of reflecting myself in other people's eyes. Turn a pair of eyes on me and instantly I begin looking into them for myself. I seem to believe there is no Me except in other eyes. I am what I see in your eyes, whoever you are.

I choke on a laugh: to be is to be perceived; the monad mirrors other monads. But then I hold my breath: I must have done this in philosophy, too.

Why can't I see? What's wrong with my own eyes? If I knew how to look at what I see, then what? Then I wouldn't need other people's eyes.

How do I learn to look? Oh, no: I'm asking for a method again.

Wait, wait. Something is trying to be understood. The doers, the ones who do something really well, are taught a method. The method serves them, up to a point. But then some sureness about what they're trying to do lets them cast off that method, or start to. Something they know impels them to bridge the chasm that lies between the safe inadequacy of what they've been taught and the fulfillment that they uncertainly sense will exist on the other side. And the only way to get to what can't really be guaranteed but can only be hoped for is to make a leap. Once on the other side, they look back and then throw down a footbridge, their method, for their followers to use.

I now know that their daring consists in their knowing what they want to do. If I could learn how to see with my own eyes, I'd be able to make a comparable leap, leaving behind everybody else's rules.

My own truth, again. I'm beginning to understand how badly I need it. Now I even see that there's an outright conflict between what other people see and what I have to learn to see. I shouldn't regret that other people might not find my truth to be the truth they'd see about me. I should consider it an achievement.

When I call the SPCA, Mr. Lema tells me I missed the vet yesterday, that he comes to the island on Thursdays. If the planes are flying. I briefly debate telling Mr. Lema about finding the rice, but I'm so irritated at myself for having thought he was the vet that I say nothing.

"Thank you. I'll call him next Thursday."

I hang up, suddenly aware of new disadvantages of isolation.

But why have I *needed* other people's eyes? I must not have trusted what I could see, and so I turned to what they could see. And yet, not every "they." I chose which ones I'd believe. I must have had some reason for choosing Dr. Gnesin's opinion over David's, for instance. Or for believing the people who told me I was beautiful, even though I suspected them to be wrong. Of course, being beautiful isn't something you get an opposing opinion about. People don't walk up to you and say, "You're not beautiful."

Let's try the easy way first. Say that I believed people who told me I was beautiful because I *wanted* to believe them. But then I'd have to conclude that I *wanted* to believe I wasn't a good actress, because that's what Dr. Gnesin was telling me, instead of wanting to believe that I was good, as David told me. How do I make sense out of that?

Or being smart. Now there's something I *knew,* from the time I was the littlest girl until the catastrophe of those exams at Harvard. But I did, finally, question even that, didn't I?

Very odd. There's some sort of pattern starting to come through. It's that the source outside me starts to dry up, and that sets me to doubting myself. Lines appear on my face; I realize the familiar compliments aren't coming to me as often as they used to; I fish for them; and then I end by doubting whether I ever was beautiful. I didn't get overwhelming praise for my work at Goodman; I sought it from what I decided was an authoritative source; he disappointed me; I concluded that I couldn't act. Years of getting the best grades, winning scholarships, knowing that I could learn anything simply by setting myself to do it; then unbelievably failing the Harvard exams; and in all the years since, wondering whether I was really smart after all.

In the next instant I hear my own words. I said, "the source." The source of what? Of rewards! How could I have missed it? Compliments, applause, praise, admiration: they're all rewards. That's why I stopped doing the things I tried: the reward started to slack off.

It's not possible to calm my heart, although I press my hands against my chest to try.

That's why it took me until yesterday to discover that I never knew whether I *wanted* to act. I wasn't acting because I wanted to act: I was acting for the applause. Even studying philosophy was all part of the same thing: I just transferred the action from the theater proper to a university. I've never known whether I *wanted* to do philosophy, either.

I'm sitting quietly now, watching the connections take place as though they were outside of me with a life of their own.

I know now what I bought with my pretenses and my lies: the applause.

Is it possible to cry? My second year in graduate school: working as a secretary to one professor three afternoons a week, and typing the lectures of another from a tape recorder in the evenings in someone's office in Emerson Hall. And trying to study for the exams again. And being totally without Stan, by his choice. And feeling cut off from all the students who had been friends the year before, when I still showed promise of being among the bright ones; they had now passed exams that I had failed. And so at just past midnight, I packed away the tape recorder, walked down the empty stairway of the building that had become my prison, out into the streets of Cambridge, and went home. I took a deep breath, which I couldn't catch, and instantly went into hysterics. Was Jean at home, and did she try to comfort me? I dimly remember that I was trying to explain it all to someone as I lay across my bed, pounding the mattress, screaming.

And the purpose of going through that was the applause? Find the applause in that. The applause that I knew would come when I finally had my degree: the admiration would reach beyond my face. I seem always to have been aiming for something extraordinary, something out of the usual range. The early days at Goodman, when David asked each of us in his acting class to say what we wanted to do in the theater. I said: "I want to be the greatest actress of my generation." Not many people who heard me let me forget that I said that. It may have been what each of the others wanted, but they said things like: to play Cleopatra, to help found a repertory theater. While I: greatest actress.

What a ferocious appetite I have for attention. To be the greatest, the best, the most unusual, the very different. And in pursuit of that, I withstood years of living on pennies, of lowering my head to buck harder at the wall that had already laid my scalp open. Forcing myself to stay in philosophy, for instance, yet not willing to admit it until near the end, when the investment had become so great that I *had* to stay and finish the degree.

"I'll show them!" Pacing the room where Stan and I were studying between exams in May of our first year. "I won't take their damned degree!"

"No." Stan, as tired and tense as I; Stan, who had grasped the point and was trying to teach me that being in graduate school was being at war. "*Taking* the degree is showing them."

He passed with the highest grades. Even before the exams, everyone knew he was the best student; afterward, there was no honor Harvard withheld from him. I didn't pass, and so I fell into the background. Not passing meant not being appointed teaching fellow for my second year; it meant not being involved in new things, but rather going back over the same work. Because the department let me try again, having made a special concession to my novel way of failing. Passing completely needed four B minuses; passing conditionally needed three B minuses; I had two. And two C pluses. The department actually voted to pass me at one point in their deliberations: they thought I was smart. But then they found that someone else had the identical grades, a person they didn't think was smart. They couldn't fail him and pass me. ("Why not?" I asked Henry when he told me afterward.) So they passed us both, conditionally. One more B minus, and I'd have had to repeat only one exam; as it was, I had to repeat all four.

I still groan over the arithmetic, as I used to every night, turning over in bed as if I could turn away from it. And the difference between a B minus and a C plus is of course very vast; it so clearly marks off the deserving from the undeserving; it's a line so sharp that absolutely anyone can tell where the B-minus mind ends and where the C-plus mind begins. It would have to be, to justify the torment accruing to me for being on the wrong side of that line. But I've taught since then, and graded, and I know how it's done. So they couldn't have thought I was smart, after all.

Yet last summer in Berkeley, Stan said: "You don't think you finally passed the exams because you got smarter, do you?"

"People don't get smarter."

Stan, his eyes on the freeway signs to be sure of taking the correct turn: "That's my point."

I remember almost snapping my head toward him in my astonishment. He thought I was smart enough to have passed the first time. He even implied that the department thought so too.

"I suppose you're giving me the excuse that my operation during our first year kept me out of classes half a semester." From the passenger seat, I watched his face closely.

"I don't have to give you the excuse. It was perfectly legitimate. You're the only one who seemed to think you didn't need extra time to catch up. Let's say it was legitimate the first time you didn't pass. After that . . . well." His shoulders raised slightly, and then he was silent.

After that . . . well. After that, I became terrified. The second time, three of the four exams won the highest grades. Faculty congratulated me on the streets, stopping me to shake hands. But the fourth grade was a D. And the third time, a C. By then I had shrunk into myself and was slinking around back streets. The fourth time old friends held a special review class and let me talk my answers to their probing questions as we walked along the Charles for hours. And so the fourth time I passed. And took my degree a year before

Stan did. Now, sitting next to me in the car, he was telling me that no part of that nightmare was attributable to any flaw in my intellect. And that he wasn't the only one who thought so.

He thought. They thought. The department thought. I've *got* to stop using other people's eyes. I must find some way to know what *I* think.

But I can't bear this anymore today. How do I stop thinking about it? No one to talk to. No radio to bring another sound. I have to move, fast. Go somewhere fast. Can't walk: I'd think again.

"Oh, Logos, why can't you help me?" And he does. He comes into the kitchen and sits here, looking up at me. He cocks his head to one side, trying to understand. My smile encourages him to ask for a walk. He barks twice, tentatively.

"We'll take the car."

My tires furrow the pebble surface as I back out of the driveway.

13

I must talk to someone I know, somehow, at some time before the day is out. Who? Can I even consider catching the ferry and going to Cambridge for the weekend? But who's in Cambridge, to *talk* to? June. No. She has what's almost a commitment not to be close to anyone. Unfair. She's put me up and fed me and listened already. Who am I to insist that her listening be done with concern? But, oh, how I want someone to listen caringly.

Who else in Cambridge? There's no one. That's why I'm here: because there's no one to talk to. In Cambridge, or anywhere else in driving distance.

The knock on the door startles me. As I cross the living room, I think of the apartment with Marilyn our third year in graduate school, and how, no matter what room we were in, a knock would cause each of us to take a sharp breath. We'd converge, quietly so as not to be heard, and stare at each other. Who could it be? We'd take turns answering, only after we had assessed the likelihood that someone she or I wanted to avoid was not on the other side of the door. The gasp following the knock became almost pure reflex by the end of the year, so that we'd do it, and then laugh, but silently, pushing each other to answer the door.

"Ralph!"

"Have you tasted the Nantucket scallops?" His look is intense.

"You're sure you're not bringing me news of fire. Where's your car?"

"I walked."

"Six miles?"

"It took only an hour or two. You told me you walk a couple of miles every day."

"Usually. What's so special about Nantucket scallops?"

"Very tender, particularly when they're just an hour out of the water. If you're not busy right now, let's drive into Nantucket and I'll buy you some and cook them for you. You have to cook them in just a little butter for just the right amount of time."

I look at him silently. Drive him into Nantucket and back, and then make lunch here? I wanted to see someone I knew, and, like the fairy tale of the fisherman and his three wishes, I forgot to specify how well I knew the someone. No, I said someone to listen, caring. But that's impossible. So someone I scarcely know, someone to whom I won't talk in that way, will have to do.

Logos rides in the front seat, Ralph in the back.

"Why does Logos sit up there with you?"

"He hates the car, so I keep petting him and talking to him while we're moving. He used to tremble a lot and whimper, but now he's quiet. He rests his head on my leg sometimes; he's learned to keep out of the way of the gearshift."

Ralph says nothing for a mile or two. Then: "There's really no connection between you and that dog."

I look into the rearview mirror immediately, expecting to see the teasing on his face. He catches my eye and returns the look. He isn't smiling.

"You must be joking. Logos and I are together all the time. You haven't spent time with us. You don't see him fall asleep near my desk while I'm working, or sit near me while I'm eating. I can't take two steps away from a position I've been in without his following me. I sometimes have to tell him to stay where he is when I'm getting up for only a minute. Even when he's asleep, if I move from my chair, he awakens instantly and is ready to go where I go. Isn't that being connected?"

Ralph shrugs in the rearview mirror and turns to look out the window. I continue to detail the extent of Logos' belonging to me. I am unwillingly aware of being defensive. Ralph says nothing for the two miles preceding the right turn that takes us into the town.

"How long have you had Logos?"

I think back. "November eighth. Today's December first. Three weeks. Why?"

"Well, it takes time for a person and a dog to be close. Puppies follow people anywhere. If you gave him to me, he'd follow me in half a day. You feed him. You play with him. You shelter him from wet and cold. He doesn't want to let the source of all that out of his sight. He doesn't know yet that anyone else would do the same things, and he's not old enough to know that he can do a lot of it himself. He's using you. For all I know, you're using him."

I cover my rage with an attempt at civility. "Using him? What for?"

"Oh, you live alone out there. He's company for you."

He's right, but, "Why is that using him?"

"Listen, I don't really know about things like that. Turn right when you get to that corner. Now go up that alley. Fine. I think the man just brought in his catch."

He's out the door, closing it, and gone. For a moment, I consider leaving him here and going back to Siasconset. I'm angry about half a dozen things, and I can't sort them out if I have to make small talk over lunch. I stroke Logos' forehead, cupping my hand as I reach his ears, smoothing them back against his head. The silky warmth of him is under my fingers. "Using him." A living being to touch. A consolation for not having a male of my own species. The shock runs along my back, and I take my hand away. "Don't I love you, Sweet Puppy?"

Why did I think he'd be exempt from the stupid way I foul up relationships with people? I realize in that moment that I've relied on my loving Logos as some sort of point of stability. Now even this has to be examined. I want to run somewhere.

Why am I sitting in this alley waiting for a boy I hardly know? He made me see something I might not have seen, or not have seen for a long time. That's my answer. I should be grateful to him, even though he's undone me. But I don't have to tell him what I'm thinking. I can be pleasant. He didn't mean to jab at me. He simply said what he thought.

Driving home I pretend we haven't talked about Logos. I get Ralph to tell me about places on the island, and people. He's awkward with frying pans and the stove, but he convinces me he wants to cook the scallops his own way. Lunch is meager. I haven't kept food on hand for anyone else.

Ralph realizes that I want him to leave. He starts to remove the dishes from the table, but I take them from him. He looks at me silently, uncertainly. Then: "I dreamed about you last night."

I'm at the sink on the other side of the cabinet that divides the kitchen. Fortunately so. This boy has more surprising things to say than anyone I can remember talking to. "Oh? What was your dream?" I almost guess what he'll say.

"You were out here alone at night, and some men broke into the house. And I heard it somehow in Nantucket and came out here and saved you just as they were about to attack you. It scared me, and woke me up."

I succeed in not smiling. So my face has lured someone else. Even without makeup.

"That's really why I came out here today. The dream was so real, I had to check to be sure you were all right."

"Oh." Having him dream about me makes me triumph over what he said about Logos and me. But abruptly I shake away my revenge. This child wants to protect me. And I can't begin to explain to him that the only thing I have to be protected from is my own blindness.

"I've got to get back to Nantucket." He's at the door.

I offer to drive him, but feebly.

"No, I'll walk. In case I want to call you, do you have a phone?"

I start to give him the number, but he's out the door with a wide wave of his arm. I know he'll find it himself.

Fog close to the shore obliterates the horizon and substitutes in its place an expanse of hovered-over water. I can see only fifty feet out. Even the line of the shore is cut down. I realize that the limitlessness of the horizon is one of the reasons that I keep coming here, but it's gone today. The fog softens the air, a compensation, perhaps, for what my eyes can't see. But walking here is unsatisfying: the edges of me remain rough. I sit for a time on my log, giving Logos a chance to dig himself a good hole. Watching him, I remember that I have to think about him too. The depth of my sigh is sufficient to raise me to my feet, and I lead the way home.

By evening the frustration of not talking to someone who can hear me leads me to the telephone. I'll call Marilyn. Take a chance on a station-to-station call to Illinois. Not likely she'd be out, even on a Saturday night, with her third baby due.

An unfamiliar high-pitched voice answers the phone. A baby-sitter. Hell!

"Do you expect them back soon?"

The woman can't hear me. I hold my mouth close to the phone and slowly repeat my question. They will not be back until after midnight. Midnight in Illinois is one in Siasconset.

I leave my name and number for Marilyn to call tomorrow.

"Where did you say that is in Massachusetts?"

Shall I laugh or cry? "Nantucket."

"Wait. I'll write that down. Nanfucket."

I start to giggle, and then hang up and laugh until I remember how long this Saturday night will be.

The sun hasn't been high long enough to begin burning the mist from the moor. The sky is unclouded, brilliant.

I have to try to explore the affinities of a dozen threads in my thoughts. I even have the feeling that I'm close to being able to tie them together. But this morning something is stopping me. Maybe if I take Logos for a walk now, I'll be replenished again, able to tolerate what I know ends by exhausting me.

No, the alternative isn't a walk. The alternative is having to continue living in terror and disgust and failure. Unless I do what I came here to do. Now.

Where am I, then?

I've never done things because I wanted to do them, but because I'd get applause for doing them. That I made it central means that I've turned things wrong-end-to. Now I am here, wanting to have my own eyes, wanting no one else's rules for doing anything or for being anything. How do I get from there to here?

I tilt my chair onto its rear legs, and put my own legs up over the top of the desk. Balancing, I let my thoughts wander back over the murk, hoping to pick up a clue to start pursuing.

Actors do want applause, though, don't they? I can't believe that an actor would go before an audience to perform and not want the applause at the end. The difference is that I seem to have wanted it throughout the performance. Maybe there's such a thing as an appropriate amount of applause. Appropriate, say, to the size of the job done, or to the quality of the job. If there is, then I've gone astray in my inordinate need for it. A need that's completely unrelated to the appropriateness of it. What is there about applause that has given me such an appetite for it?

How am I going to get a piece of truth out of all this fraud? A piece that carries its own mark, like what I understood when Weck spoke that day in front of her mirror.

Incredible that I knew so long ago not just that my mother didn't, but that she *couldn't,* love me. And that that long ago I gave up trying to get her to love me and was willing to settle only for getting her to look at me, to give me some attention. So I provoked attention from her, in the form of screaming quarrels. I used every occasion to show her my contempt, and she gave it back in kind. She made me fight her at every step to get permission to do anything major, and when she gave it, it was with her muttered threats that I'd come to no good. If I went to Daddy instead, she'd snipe at his way of talking with me in a pleasant voice as we exchanged reasons—she called it "spoiling me." She couldn't even acknowledge other people's praise of me. Upstairs in my room during her bridge parties, I'd hear her friends: "Sarah, aren't you proud to have such a pretty daughter?" And she'd say, "I don't believe in giving her compliments. It will make her conceited."

But I understood all this at Weck's last year. Why am I trembling now, thinking of it again?

Suddenly the two lines of ideas crash together inside my head. The applause I played for everywhere and the attention I made my mother give me were exactly the same thing: substitutes for her love. I tried to make the whole rest of the world give me what she couldn't give me. If I were the greatest actress, maybe she'd look at me. If I were a brilliant philosopher, maybe she'd look at me. And if she looked at me, I'd have her attention, her real attention, which was her affection: I'd have her love. So of course I could never get enough attention from other people, because they were always giving me the wrong thing: they weren't giving me her love. I've never believed that I'm beautiful because she never told me that I was.

I lay my forehead hard against my desk, and my arms encircle my head. I have to realize that my thirty-year trail away from being a little girl has been nothing more than standing on the same spot, moving my legs up and down. I've never stopped being that five-year-old, old enough to know that I was missing something, but not old enough to know that it surely ought to have come to me without my having to pay for it. And I've been trying to buy it, lying and pretending ever since.

So, all the years are wasted. I've been doing things for a reason ir-relevant to the doing of them. How could I have known what I want? I've trod only the surface of things, hoping to extract from them something they couldn't possibly contain.

But I don't want anything from her now. I've hated her too long: nothing resembling love is left in me. I don't even want her love now, not from that woman for whom I have no shred of respect. She's al-most the perfect model for what a human being shouldn't be. Grow-ing up I used to think: I want to be what she isn't. She's incapable of telling the truth. She is pure willfulness. She's never done a com-pletely generous thing in her life, never undertaken a disinterested action simply because it was right to do the thing; she wouldn't even know what I'm talking about. Her only concern is what people will say. I never knew what a home was until I had the apartment in Chicago with Pat and Laurel. She made her house be a showroom for furniture, not a place where people could be at their ease. I never knew what food could taste like until I left her house. She could at least have been a good cook. As a woman she is without charm or grace of any kind. I still don't know what being a woman is, because I had no slightest clue from her. She's been an obstacle to be gotten around in everything I do, everything I've ever done.

In fact, in fact:

"I'm *like* her!"

I cry out the words and throw myself onto the couch to turn my face into its back. It doesn't keep out the sight. I'm like her: the only truth I've ever told is the kind that would get me my applause. My only concern has been what people will say. I've even known it: it was the thing I came here to get away from. And I am as unwomanly as she: not fat and awkward as she is, but inside. My way of re-sponding to a man is without grace. So she won. She set the whole course of my life as though I had never raised an eyebrow to stop her, and then in the bargain she determined my choice of weapons.

I'm not anything extraordinary, then. I'm not anything except a copy of her. And now I have to live, knowing that. I can never fool myself again. I can never again pretend that I've undertaken to ac-complish important useful things: I've been only a little girl asking to be held in my mother's arms.

"Logos." He raises his head from sleep. "Logos." I start to tell him that we're going to the beach, but I don't seem able to get past his name. He continues to look at me. I watch his body twist slowly from his sleeping sprawl to an alert horizontal. He's waiting for me to say something to him. "Logos." He sits. If I could tell him what I want to tell him, he'd jump and run and be very glad.

And then I start to cry.

14

For two days I use all the different paths down to the water. I go home only when hunger and darkness drive me there. Logos can now fall asleep even on the sand. Whenever I stop, his small body drops quickly down beside me. I know he longs for a quiet bed at the house, but I can't leave him there, and I certainly can't stay there myself.

The fog wanders, rolling just above the sand, muffling the incoming waves. I kick the sand every few steps, then turn to see the pattern I've made. But the fog cloaks everything beyond half a dozen footprints. I continue in my original direction. Or stop, watching the waves break.

I'm aware of the randomness of my actions during these two days. Lines that bound me have been cut. All to the good. But bound, I was also anchored. Now I'm cast loose. Free. Aimless. Literally: without an aim.

Acting. Philosophy. Politics. Teaching. Writing. They all present impenetrable surfaces to me now. What is the theater like? What would it be like to be *in* the theater? Or *in* philosophy? At thirty-seven I can't go back into each of them to find out. And yet, how else will I know what I want to do?

How do I begin to *think* about what I want to do? Is it something I can simply think about, sitting on an island, away from any contact with the people or situations I'd be dealing with?

I tumbled into acting: I didn't choose to do it. But I did choose philosophy, although my route was roundabout. I didn't know what philosophy was when I went back to school to study it. I thought it was the history of ideas. I wanted to know what goals people had found valuable, what beliefs they had found worth preserving. I didn't know what philosophy was until I began writing my doctoral dissertation. By then I wasn't thinking about wanting to do it, but only about getting the thing done.

Yet I was very excited to go to graduate school. I remember thinking that now I'd be able to study philosophy all day long. Too bad the graduate student council didn't publish their unofficial guide to graduate life until my second year. "Remember," they told me, too late, "that you are not here to get an education. You are supposed to be educated already. You are here to get a degree."

I stop walking, my hands deep in my coat pockets. What is it like to want to do anything at all? I think I don't know. I don't know what wanting is.

If I stand still on this spot, maybe the whirling will stop. Not know what wanting is? Ridiculous. Wantings move the day along. Wantings pave the path for a life. Or so I've been told. But then, my days don't move along: they lead me against obstacles. And the path of my life has been one giant merry-go-round, circling the same trajectory endlessly. What I've thought were my wants were merely well-disguised attempts to get her to love me. All my wants were collapsed into that one. That one has kept on reproducing itself, thickening a shell around me, throwing up layer upon layer against intrusions from any other want until that one could be fulfilled. But now I've torn it out, slitting the crust that kept me preserved as an infant. An infant: not innocent, but ignorant. And it's as an infant that I now have to turn my eyes toward the world.

My eyes. Good God! That's why I had to use other people's eyes: because mine were closed off beneath the layers that mummified me. My eyes could see only one thing, could use only one criterion for what was valuable: Will it make her look at me? But now I can see what there is to be seen, because I don't have to try to transpose it into something that it's not.

I swing around, almost dancing, and bump into the puppy, who has been sitting hopelessly by my side. He backs away, startled.

"Logos! Maybe I can *see* now!" He cocks his head. From a standing start, I race him up the beach. He wins. Panting, laughing, I follow him across the dunes that lead toward the wooden stairway up to my platform.

I can go back to the house now. I can sit still again.

Today's fuel delivery adds twenty-eight dollars to the November bill of thirty-five dollars still on my desk. Funny: it's not really cold here, and yet I'm spending as much money to pay fuel bills as to buy food. But heating a house is the last thing in the world I know anything about.

One of the last things, anyway. I don't even know what wanting is.

Oh, come now. I know the traditional philosophical views. I should be able to bring some of them to bear. Every introductory ethics text repeats that desire is motion toward an object or person, and that aversion is motion away. Motion toward: Some little engine in me propels me toward something, and that's wanting? Or is it that I know that I want the thing because I find myself moving toward it?

Something there is too slippery for me to get hold of. Since Sunday, I have to be suspicious of what I move toward, or at least, of what I've moved toward in the past. I still have to peel off the disguises in which my mother appears to me.

Where else can I find a clue? Perhaps in what C. I. Lewis called "felt satisfaction." Strange about those words. I'd try to compel them to yield their meaning when he lectured or wrote using them. I had the feeling that they were foreign, part of a newly acquired vocabulary, because I had to keep telling myself what they meant as I heard or read them. I never used them myself. Hardly strange: I never understood them. I simply assumed that I understood them, that the effort I put forth whenever I encountered them *was* my grasping of their meaning. Because Lewis also said that everyone knows that quality of experience to which the words refer, but that if someone didn't, we couldn't possibly explain it to him.

From now on I must stop being shocked by how much authority I have acceded to, in the unknown hope that the authority before me would magically turn into my mother, who would then open her arms to me. I have to stop being shocked, and instead become aware of the pervasiveness of it. I now have to examine every opinion I've ever held, in order to see whether I'd still hold it once the authoritative voice who spoke it to me is removed.

As now. I have to see that I don't know what "felt satisfaction" means. Or rather, what sort of thing it purports to be about. It's that word *felt* that hinders me. It must mean: the then-and-there sense or awareness of something. So that "felt satisfaction" refers to the sense or awareness, right then, of being satisfied, or of being in a process that throughout is satisfying.

I lean my head into my hands, tired already. I have to pick my way through ideas that other human beings have understood since childhood. I'm only beginning to see how long a road this infant will have to travel.

I'm looking for a certain quality that's good in the having, a satisfaction felt then and there. "Satisfaction" is stopping me now. I'll try my own net. A sense of excitement, an immediacy worth perpetuating, a quality of fullness. All right. That's what "wanting" will mean for me.

Now I have to try to think what things will give me this quality.

For a few minutes I cast about among some general categories: work, men, friends, some leisure occupation. No, I can't break through. I'm dealing at too abstract a level. Maybe I can look for examples of the feeling in what I've already done. I can't discredit my entire past perception of persons and situations. I have to try to unearth from that massive deception I practiced on myself the things that were true. Real. What do I use as a criterion to sort them out?

Yesterday I discovered that I could see. That I could if I tried. Now I have to learn what there is to see, and the only way to do that is by looking. Looking without prejudice as to what I'll find. Lewis again: We shall find what we shall find regardless of what we wish to find.

I start to pace the room. Logos gets up quickly, brings me his ball, and stands half crouching, waiting for the game to begin. I stoop and rub his ears. Slowly his body sinks to the floor, and he pushes his head toward me so that I may center more securely on that spot below his ear. I hear his low moan intercepted by a sudden grunt, then silence, then the moan again. I grin. That's it: that's the quality I have to remember. I place the puppy's head gently on the rug and lie down on the couch, my hands crossed beneath my head.

Suppose I circumscribe some arbitrary time. Say, the past year. What things can I remember doing during the past year that carried this sense of fullness? Clear cases only. If I hesitate, then I haven't happened upon a good example.

I think of three, then four. To my surprise. I sit up abruptly. I should get these things written down. I go to the typewriter for the first time in weeks and start the list:

Driving down to Princeton with the top down at night, slightly drunk, reading directions by my dashboard lights, to see Stan.

In four hours, I fill one page, double-spaced. Thirty items. Thirty times in twelve months I've done things that I've found good in the doing. There's a ratio worth pondering. Thirty times in fifty-two weeks I was doing something I wanted to do. Once every twelve days, a couple of hours were worth living through.

What in God's name was I doing all the rest of the time? I don't even know how to begin answering.

Look at the list now. These things that were exciting in the doing: Are some of them alike? Do they fall into groups in any way?

I take the sheet out of the typewriter and examine it closely. For a little while, my thoughts seem fastened to these very specific written sketches. I force myself to hover at a slightly higher level.

Even as I try to uncover common features from the thirty items, I keep being drawn back to the first item on the list. Very odd. I didn't say "being *with* Stan" but rather "driving *to* him." Being with him was a feast only for the first hours; his three-year-old divorce opened nothing of him to me. But the drive down to him remains in my memory as something good. Very odd, yes, since I've spent ten years in loving Stan.

I run my eyes over the list, put it down, pick it up, and then go over it again. Driving *to* Princeton. The words punch a key that sorts out only things that conform to a certain shape and rejects all others. Half a dozen items on the list light their way to my eyes. Being out of doors; walking in the sun or rain or snow; driving with the top down, night or sunshine; walking on the beaches in California. Being outside, alone. As I am here.

I've *liked* being here!

Being alone here, able to get to the ocean every day, able to step out of my door and immediately be outside. All of this has been my natural setting. How incredible: I find myself doing something I want to do. No, that's not exact. I can be exact now, because the outcome no longer has a price attached to it. I find myself doing something I like. That's a stage along the way of trying to discover what I want to do.

A stage, but perhaps also a criterion. What I'll want to do will have to have this same quality of . . . what? Fitting me. I've been able to stay here so long without anyone to talk to because all this time I've been trying to pry myself loose from other people, from needing them as I've needed food. They had what I used to look for: they could give me their attention. And their attention was my life.

The pieces rush to cluster together. People are in cities, and that's where I've gone to find them, when all along if I hadn't been pursuing that little girl's goal I'd have looked for quietness and fresh air and watching the day begin or end in the sky.

Is that really true? I don't know. Yet part of it must be.

I'm getting very tired. I think I have to stop soon. But the list draws my eyes to study it. What else can it teach me?

See the way I've remembered the men of this past year. With one, maybe two exceptions, the occasions I've listed are occasions of communication: of warmth, of good talk, of connection as human beings rather than as man and woman. Very curious, too, because that's not what I think of myself as wanting from a man.

The interlacing ideas move me out of my chair. I still have to think about men. Why I lose so often. Why Stan dominates my life. Or is it George?

How can I help laughing?

Putting on my coat and boots, I grapple with the furry mass of yelping puppy who insists on getting out ahead of me. I think I haven't written anything as important as that single sheet of paper now lying on my desk. Ever.

The spectacular sunshine invites me to take our longest walk. My thoughts idle. I watch Logos prowl and sniff. Tomorrow the vet arrives. He's got to tell me what to feed the puppy to make him eat. We reach the barrier marking the dead end of the road, and I stop to look at the flatness of the land back of me, ahead of me, on either side. The utter stillness of the air carries no sound to my ears. Only Logos crackling the high grass in his explorations. The silence almost demands that I imitate it, and I hold my breath before I realize what I'm doing.

We cross the grassy area bordering the fairway and start up the low rise leading to the outermost putting green. Standing at its edge, I'm surprised to find the green still perfectly mowed. I step onto it and bounce lightly on the balls of my feet. The grass feels as if it could spring me three feet into the air. I hustle Logos away from the green and onto the fairway that leads straight to the clubhouse an easy half-mile away. Strange to remember the look and feel of a golf course, how it's to be responded to.

That's it. That's what I don't know. I don't know how to respond to things. I shake my head impatiently. No, that's not it. I don't know how *I* respond to things. I don't know how to find out what's going on inside me.

I stop walking, involuntarily placing my hand over my mouth. What have I said? But yes: that's why I don't know what I want, or want to do. I don't know how to use my own evidence. I don't even know what counts as evidence.

Look at the way I had to go about finding what I like. That's how a detective tries to reconstruct a crime from a few clues. I'm supposed to be able to *know* whether I'm angry or unhappy or irritated or cheerful or fond or loving. Know it with the same kind of certainty that I know that this is my own hand. Know it without going through a series of intermediate steps, back-end-to, as I did yesterday.

What is that "supposed to" I just said? Another rule that someone else made for purposes that may not be mine? Or does it say something about what human beings are like in their very bones?

The old circle. I never could feel on stage what everyone told me I ought to be able to feel: the character in her own individuality. All I felt was myself playing the character. Ten years later, choosing a dissertation topic, I picked my way back to the same problem. I decided that what I didn't understand was: What sort of thing are emotions? If they aren't the sort of thing you can *set* yourself to feel, then the kind of acting I had been taught wasn't possible for anyone to do, talented or no.

But that's not what I didn't understand. It's not even a question of understanding. I just don't know what my own feelings are. I don't now, and I didn't then. Offstage or on. Someone teased me about my choice of topic: "It sounds as though you want to know what feeling feels like." Even the tone of the comment implied that I couldn't be so foolish as not to know what feelings range around within me. I remember replying sarcastically. But now I see that that's a rather close description of what I don't know. Because I am that foolish: I don't know what to look for inside me. I don't know how to identify *that* I'm feeling something, let alone to give a name to it. I think I've been anesthetized, deadened.

Think of how many people have accused me of being theatrical, of exaggerating. I'm just beginning to understand that I behaved that way not for the effect it would have, but because that was my interpretation of what being angry, or being loving, or being fearful was. I learned it from reading plays, watching plays, working in plays, talking about plays. Of course it was theatrical: it had to be big enough to get across the footlights; it had to get to the last row of the balcony. And because I've never gotten off the stage, I've never noticed that I didn't feel the things I was trying to make other people believe I felt.

So. The basic puzzlement that catapulted me out of the theater was at the absolute core of my being. And I must have recognized that it was central during all the years of graduate school. Because when the time came to write my dissertation, I chose it as my topic. That was probably one of the few genuine choices I've ever made, in philosophy or out. And I didn't know it until just now. It even feels peculiar to talk about choices. It's rather that I stumbled into that topic head-down. On the other hand, I couldn't have avoided it, once I gave myself even a little rein.

I call Logos back to me. It doesn't matter where we settle on the fairway: no one is playing today. I sit on the cold ground, my knees to my chin, my arms clasping my legs. How have I remained alive, not knowing such a thing? Alive. No, it would be hard to say that I've been alive, particularly as an adult human being. It's rather that this adult's body has contained a nonmaturing seedling. Now I'm opening windows everywhere and exposing it to the light. I don't even know whether it can still grow, or yet what the most favorable conditions are.

I have to learn this thing, somehow. Yet I can't guess how even to begin. Do I open some interior eye to discover that I'm apprehensive at the undertaking? Sad for the time I've lost? Excited that there can be something new in my life? No, knowing what I feel can't be figuring it out from among plausible alternatives.

I rise to my feet. The wind is from the east, biting and strong. At least I know that: that I'm cold, that the air slices my face. The question is: Is that relevant at all?

15

A morning rain stops, then starts again as drizzle. The fog cuts off my view of the moor beyond the outer edge of the back garden. At ten I'm on the phone to make my appointment with the vet.

"The vet didn't come today. Planes are grounded." Mr. Lema has said so several times already this morning. "Call him next Thursday."

"But my dog has been sick for more than a week. What can I do?"

"You could go to Boston to see him there. Try the boat." He's ready to hang up. I let him.

The Nantucket Steamship Authority voice is bored: "No boat today." He hangs up.

I look at the phone in my hand, listening to the dead line. I dial the number again. "Listen, I just called you. Will there be a boat tomorrow?"

"Lady, I don't know. There hasn't been a boat all week. Every hunter who came here Sunday has been stranded. They call me every day, and believe me, if I knew how high the waves would be tomorrow, I'd tell you and I'd tell them. All I can tell you is to call tomorrow." The phone is dead again.

Hunters. I remember: deer season began Monday.

What do I do about Logos? I get the book about dog care and reread the section on tapeworm. Logos lies near my chair, looking up at me, waiting for something. "No, I can't play with you now."

Why am I pushing the puppy away? I know: he's making me go back to Boston. And there isn't a damned way of getting him to a vet at Angell Memorial unless we stay overnight on the mainland. The boat doesn't reach Woods Hole until evening. Two hours to Boston. See the vet the following morning. Hell and hell again. I have to spend *two* nights away. The only boat to Nantucket leaves Woods Hole at ten in the morning.

Can I go? I'd stay with June, I suppose. Maybe I don't have to tell her what I've come upon. I always *had* to talk about things very close to me. Did I believe they weren't real until I talked about them? Men. My plans. My pure misery. But maybe I can keep this mine by not talking about it. To June, to other people. I don't have to avoid seeing them, but I can avoid talking about this.

I'm backing away. Confronted with the possibility of talking seriously to people again, of talking on more than the level of courtesy where I deal with the postmaster or clerks in stores here, I think of ways of avoiding it.

I think I don't want to go.

No, that's not it. I do want to see some familiar faces. To laugh. To hear stories. But I'm not finished here yet, even though I don't know what I still have to do. I know only that I'm not at the end, and so I fight going back to the very place that was the center of my horror for so long.

I think I'm afraid I'll start to do things the way I did them then, as though none of these weeks here had taken place. I'll act. I'll exaggerate. I'll pretend something is funny just so the person telling the story won't be hurt that it didn't come out right. I'll pretend to be interested in what someone says to me just because he's interested in saying it. I'll dress for the stares. I'll wear makeup.

How can I stop doing all that again? The four weeks I've spent finding out what I do seem puny, now that I have to try to weigh them against the way I behaved for all the thirty-seven years that preceded them.

But I do have to have Logos taken care of. So I have to decide whether to go back to the old way. It would be for such a short time.

What sort of choice am I giving myself? I have no "old way" to go back to. It's gone: I've torn it away. Not all. Not yet. But what's gone can't simply be retrieved from the dustbin, like an old costume. And why do I still want to fool anyone, anyway? I have no "decision" to make about how I'll behave in Cambridge.

Will I ever stop? The theater is the only framework I know how to use. I still think of the world in terms of costumes and scenery. I leave here, even for two days, and I'm on stage again: How shall I act? what shall I look like? what shall I wear? But that's what can *not* exist any longer, here or anywhere else. I've done away with protections. I can't let anything cushion or come between me and my juxtaposition to my surroundings. What is that even like? I've surely never known.

No boat two days in a row. I'd better take the first boat that runs. The weather may break tomorrow and then close in again Sunday.

Before the boat office closes for the day, I call again. "I know you don't like to say anything definite about the weather, but do you have any idea how it looks for tomorrow?"

"Wind has gone down. Even if it rains and the wind stays down, we may go. But call in the morning to be sure."

"Oh, I know, I know."

When the night long-distance rates go into effect, I call June. I tell her about Logos, and that my plans hinge on the weather.

"Come here, of course. You can have the couch in the living room. How long can you stay?"

"Dear June. It's very good of you to make it sound as though it's no imposition at all."

"Silly. We'll love to have you. If you can stay Monday night, Joan's brother is having a marvelous party. Tennessee Williams will be there."

"June! Why?"

"Well, his new play is opening that night, and Joan's brother knows people in the cast. I don't really know whether Tennessee will be there, but maybe he'll come along just because it's a party. So bring a party dress. Stay if you can. Go back Tuesday instead."

"Maybe I will. I'll let you know when I get there. Look for me tomorrow night around ten. Buy us some bourbon. I'll split the cost of the bottle."

When I hang up, I'm alone again with my puppy in a second-floor bedroom of a house belonging to someone else. The lamp beside my bed is on. Otherwise there is darkness and silence. I've just been in touch with someone who is part of a community where there are parties that famous people may attend. The distance between here and there is so vast. How do I traverse it?

I know: I take what I've been doing with me.

The hunters seem unready to drive their cars aboard the ferry. They crowd the deck in groups whose outlines change a handful of times even as I watch, sitting in my car with Logos. The red caps and jackets, and the broad patch of red buckled across some backs and shoulders, testify to the use they make of their time. Other witnesses lie strapped, immobile and bloody, across the roofs of the station wagons.

When the loudspeaker announces that the car decks are open for boarding, I maneuver my car toward the ramp. I am not quick enough. A dead deer lies slung across the roof of the car directly ahead of me. I lower my head to concentrate my attention on the car's brake lights. They flare on, then off, as the line of cars moves slowly toward the great hole in the side of the ferry. Groups of hunters still stand on the dock, in no apparent hurry to leave. Now and then one breaks away, shuffling toward his car.

My car is stopped between two rows of red-faced men who stand so close to my car that one of them stoops to rest his hands on the top of my open window. "Please," I say, trying to sound unfriendly.

"Hey, look!" The man starts to put his head through my window. He stares across me at Logos. "Is that a real deer?"

"No." Suddenly I can grin. "He is a very dear."

The car ahead of me disappears down the ramp, and I'm free to roll toward the first leg of the journey back.

I skimp on courtesy to the men who come, in pairs or threes, to the curving corner seat I stake out for Logos and me. They trickle away, perhaps to pass the word that I'm hard to get along with, and I am left gratifyingly alone for most of the trip. Half an hour out of Woods Hole, yet another hunter makes a try.

"Your puppy is beautiful. Male?"

I look up from my book. "Yes. Five months old." To take care of the next question.

The man, middle fifties, surprisingly makes no move to pet Logos. "Is he in good health? Does he eat well?"

It's a novel tack. "No, as a matter of fact; he eats almost nothing. I think he has tapeworm. I'm on my way to a vet now."

"It's not serious. There are pills for it. When he's free of it, he'll eat again."

Mentally I take a deep breath. "Won't you sit down?"

The man settles himself comfortably. We talk of dogs. A month ago, when this same boat first took me to Nantucket, people stopped to talk with me of dogs. Has nothing happened in between? I listen to the amiable nameless man talk.

"One afternoon I had Pete hunting with me. He was behind me on this particular path, and then I saw I could send him on ahead. I whistled very quietly, a special whistle that he knew meant he should track ahead of me. Nothing happened. I looked back, and there he was, trotting along, his tail wagging when he saw me look at him. I called his name and he just kept wagging his tail. I said his name again, and then all of a sudden I knew what was wrong. He had gone deaf. I just sat down on a log and cried. I took other dogs hunting after that, but none of them could do what Pete could. When he'd see me get my gear ready, he'd beg to come with me. My wife would have to close him into a room, and she wouldn't let him out until I had gone. I don't know which of us hated it more."

I don't want to ask whether he still has the dog. He changes the subject for me. "Does your puppy sleep on your pillow?"

"No. I never let him up on furniture. He has a couple of different beds in warm places. Most of the time he crawls under my bed and stays there for the night."

The man grins. "He'll sleep on your pillow."

"No, I don't think so."

"You'll see."

I'm irritated to be told what will happen when I know otherwise, and so I become silent, wondering how best to disengage myself.

"You don't like hunters, I think."

"No." I remember his dog and try to soften my reply, but nothing kind comes to my tongue.

"I understand how you feel. I haven't hunted in five years."

His cap is red. So is his jacket.

"Oh, I take the gun, but it's not loaded. I take the dogs, but there's never anything for them to retrieve. It's just good to be in the woods, with the silence and the smell. I sit still and keep the dogs still, to let other animals go about their business at a distance. Pick up the signs of where deer lay the night before. It lets me go back to work fresh." He smiles at me, and I, surprised to find myself responding, smile back.

I reach down to scratch Logos' ears. "I think I'll give the puppy a chance to stretch his legs. We should be landing soon, shouldn't we?" I stand and reach my hand out to him. "I'm glad you stopped by." We shake hands. He rounds the corner slowly and is gone.

Logos is up and away, and I trail him, thinking of the two-hour drive that lies before me. And of what waits for me once I'm there.

16

Without unpacking, I follow Logos out the door and down the road, letting him set the course for his first free walk in four days. An enormous red sunset is being prepared, a reminder, as if I needed it, of the unobstructed beauty that has been here during my absence. For several minutes I welcome the familiar silence, even though I'm still riding the crest of the excitement of the Cambridge stay, and then I open the letters that have collected since Saturday. I look up from time to time to record the progress of the coloring sky, reading the letters swiftly for news, then stick them into my pocket to savor later.

Right now I want to repay Logos for the too short walks, morning and night, along the banks of the Charles; for having to be on a leash everywhere else; for the visit to the vet and its aftermath; for being left with June's son while she and I went off to the glittering party.

I throw a stick down the road and Logos flies to get it. He is just picking it up when I reach for a stone near me and fling it in the other direction. The streak that moves past me is brownish gold and gray, and I dance to see him run. I keep him speeding so fast that he seems to touch ground only as he turns his body into the direction opposite to the one from which he has just come. It takes a while for him to have enough. He stands breathing heavily, then slowly lowers himself to the ground.

While he rests I turn a slow circle to take in the whole of the low landscape. The top of the sun has yet to sink below the horizon. When Logos gets to his feet, we go quietly home.

I am out of bourbon and almost out of food. I contemplate my land-lady's bottle of gin, which I've been ignoring since I first came here. Gin makes me sick. I lift the bottle out to the light: one shot left, no more. Add some orange juice and I might not know the difference. Mixed, the gin loses its pungency. One long swallow, one deep sigh, and I wander to my desk to begin my reply to Etel.

I have an image of her as she wrote last Sunday noon, her chin-length black straight hair falling over her right eye and she only sometimes tossing her head to fling the veil out of her way. She with her bottle of Cointreau beside her in California, and I with my dollop of gin a continent away. She with her health dangling by a thread in a mysterious illness she never names; I deliberately trying to crack my own mind apart. She hired to educate the female young at a Dominican college, opening her girls to the questions she, a renegade Catholic herself, knows they carry within them; I having abdicated the responsibility laid on me by my doctorate. We know how to read; sometimes we even want to: we are the educated women of the twentieth century. Not that our education was handed to us, but that we tore it from the hands of men who professed to be able to offer it to us. No, not "offered": they dared us to take it. Both of us understood that our sanity was at stake at Harvard: we each knew that about the other the first time we talked, sitting next to each other by chance at a Spinoza lecture. I stayed and lost mine; she left, but she's no better off. The marks are there on both of us.

I want to reach out to her. There's a connection between us, and I want to consolidate it, so that it won't be broken. I can tell her what I've been trying to do here. Perhaps trying to write it out to someone who will listen closely may put it into perspective for me. And that may take the place of my not being able to sit down to the typewriter to write it for myself.

I get a long paragraph down, letting her know how I've imagined her just now, setting the background for what I want to tell her. One month of thinking, ready to go onto paper. I take up the gin again. It has already begun to reach me; warmth is spreading in my belly. I put down the glass and try to write again, but my fingers stay unmoving on the keys.

I don't want to write it: I want to talk to her. To write it, I have to find a beginning, a middle, and an end. But there's no end yet, and I don't know whether I'm in the middle or whether I've just begun. I can't simply plunge her in where I started. We know most about one another's work, far less about our history; for the rest, we've spent our time together trading our remarkably matching versions of the morass, what it has been and what is yet to come. It would take pages merely to get her to my starting place. Pages and hours.

No. I'm exhausted contemplating it. I can't write to her about this. Nor then about anything else.

I push the typewriter away and pick up the glass again. My silence will continue. If I were nearer the end, I'd probably have the whole matter sewed into a very tight ball. I'd be able to say: This was the problem, and this was the solution, and these were the steps that got me from there to here. Trying to write to Etel now, with my doubtful gains, is one more attempt to share out the burden with someone else. I took it on for my own purposes, and there's no reason to believe that anyone else cares that I did it, or why, or even whether the whole thing comes to an end. Or how.

Too bad there was only enough gin for one drink. Tomorrow I'll get bourbon. Tonight I would have liked . . . what? One wish, Alice. What would you have chosen with one wish?

That's easy: more light, faster.

I look again at the other letters that were waiting for me yesterday. The Radcliffe envelope carries a routine inquiry for news of me. In the same envelope is a letter from a Canadian college describing a job to begin next September: resident in a women's dormitory, plus half-time teaching; residency to be dropped in three years if desired, and full-time teaching to replace it; room, board, and pay. And then:

> While the College has no religious tests of any kind whatsoever, it is only natural that we would want someone who would feel some measure of real sympathy for the aims and ideals of an Anglican College.

We have no religious tests of any kind except this one tiny little religious test. How would they deal with someone like me, who knows all the refutations for all the arguments for the existence of God? I could have real sympathy for an Anglican if we found ourselves together at a tea party. But in my classroom my sympathy is confined to positions that can be defended.

How do I explain all this to that nice lady sitting in the protection of her respectable office at Radcliffe? This, and what I'm doing here, and the erratic path of the last twelve months. It's not possible. I'd be talking a language other than any she knows. No one could have been so alien to that school as I. Except Etel. And Marilyn.

Well. I'll write Radcliffe that I don't want to go to Canada, but thanks for thinking of me.

I start for my desk, then turn sharply and pace the full width of the living room. Damn it! I'll never break the pattern of what I've been doing. I tell myself that I'm going to examine everything I do, and yet this very minute I'm making it all into another play and waiting for the curtain to go up. This living room is not a stage, and I'm not playing a role. There is only a letter to be answered. I can answer it in the old way: lying, no matter how graciously, but lying. Or else I can answer it in some totally unknown new way, in which my only clue is to try to say what I mean.

At my desk I pull the typewriter toward me to begin drafting what I know will be a long reply. I close my eyes at the thought of having to write some of the things I now know I must write, and suddenly there comes an image of the little mermaid walking on the knives that were her legs.

I spend the morning composing my letter. Retyping it, something burdensome seems to go out of me onto the paper. But once in its envelope the letter makes me uneasy. It carries weapons for destroying an old and giant lie: that I've been in charge of my life. What can she reply? I am bewildered by the new path I've set my feet upon. But I *am* there. I do have to say these things. Now it's up to her.

The old woman who runs the liquor store cannot be made to smile. She has obviously seen every ploy that a serious drinker would try in order to get booze from her on credit. She makes me feel that I have to prove to her that I'm not drunk when I walk into her store, that my order for a fifth of bourbon is not filled daily, and that I can easily do without it. I give her my money; she gives me her bottle; I walk out carrying the brown package.

When I let Logos out in the morning, I lean against the door and burst into tears. Why am I crying? For an instant I become two people: one weeping, the other watching and wondering why. Noticing the division brings the tears abruptly to an end. My cheeks are wet, but nothing else remains of the outburst.

I pull the lone wooden chair out from the table and sit down. The party in Boston undid me, I think. People treated me as though I were attractive and intelligent and interesting, and I started to believe it. I even carried the idea back to Nantucket with me. It let me think, for a day or two, that I belonged in that world of persons with purposes and successes and human connections. But all along the secret accompaniment whispers: If you belong there, then why are you here?

Why am I here? There's no place else to be. What am I doing here? I don't really know. What am I trying to do here? To find some way to live. And how have I made out so far?

My thumb and my forefinger rub my forehead trying to press out some distillation of my month here. This: that I've probably never done a single thing I've wanted to do, for the simple reason that I've never understood what it is to want to do something. And this: that to know what wanting is requires that I be able to recognize what I feel, but that I don't know how to do that, and I don't even know how to begin learning how.

I open the door to Logos. He comes in wiggling his rear, trying to jump up to lick my face. He doesn't care that I'm the merest outline of a human being. Can a person love a person that way, Logos' way? Is that what loving is: caring, no matter what?

I wonder what I mean.

I turn my chair to face the window and prop my legs against the edge of the bookcase. A thinking position if there ever was one. If I try to write while I'm thinking, I freeze. That worked only for a couple of days, until I saw that reading the letters wasn't fruitful. Now I have to let the thinking come out, untouched by my attempts to transpose it into English sentences. All I can hope to do is to find some idea that stalls my thoughts, the way the idea of mirrors did, like a needle in a broken record. The thoughts kept grinding around that one spot until I noticed it and lifted the needle.

Logos comes over to my desk and settles himself to sleep near my chair. I've long since learned to look out for where he might be before I move from any stationary position: he could be underfoot anywhere. He still follows my every step.

"She says I follow you like a puppy dog." George, quoting the girl who was fighting to keep him even after he met me. I *fell* in love with George. I had to lean on the table in that packed convention room where we met to keep myself from falling deeper into his dark eyes. Like Alice tumbling down the well, floating, drifting, down, down. My only hope for climbing out was to keep him talking. If the talk were left to me, I'd fall silent and fall farther.

"No, I'm not here to get a job. I'm a mere graduate student, along for the ride. The fellow who was driving me back to Cambridge couldn't pass up the philosophical meetings."

I noted his accent without at once identifying it, then someone tapped my shoulder to talk for a moment, and when I turned around again, George was gone. I pushed my way past barriers of human beings, my stomach suddenly hollowed out and waiting to receive my failing heart. I prowled the room without finding him, and finally I interrupted people to ask whether they had seen him. Then he himself stood next to me, and everyone else instantly stopped existing. We talked again, and again the crowd separated us, and then the room thinned out, and I, one of the last to leave, was without him.

Who was he? Where did he live? How would I ever find him again? The girl I asked told me he was married, but she seemed unsure of her information, and anyway how could it be true? At the core of me was one large loneliness, gift of four New York months of trying to start the life to which my new doctorate entitled me. But that evening in New Haven the center started to burn, pointing me toward Cambridge, somehow, anyhow, to see George again.

I think of the morning I got up before the sky lightened, so that I could catch the train to Boston to see Dr. Kant. Through all the gray hours of that trip, I planned how I'd find George, call him, see him. But when I left Dr. Kant's office, I decided I couldn't call him because he really must be married, and then I decided that I could call him because I didn't really know. One call to Harvard netted me his phone number, but then I hesitated, leaning against the phone booth, my interior having become one immense drum. If he was married, I'd think of something to say and then hang up. I dialed the number. A man's voice answered: not George, but not a woman, either. The man called George to the phone, and then he himself was on the other end of the line.

"George. This is—"

He didn't let me finish. He recognized my voice. He could meet me where I stood in half an hour.

I pushed the clock through the minutes. Can I remember now what it was like to see him walk into that drugstore almost two years ago? He was very tall, and yet he seemed almost fragile to me: slender, awkward, and so much younger than I that I must have blushed when I looked into his face this second time. We walked almost a mile before we noticed how cold it was and that it was night and time to eat. We found a restaurant, small, brightly lighted, and kept on talking.

That night, and always, there was everything to talk about. Not just philosophy. He was interested in looms: how did a weaver's loom work? Or, much later, we puzzled over the cylindrical bits of chocolate, jimmies, that Brigham's dunked ice-cream cones into: How were they made? Not molded, not dropped; then how? We never quite got around to calling the chocolate factories to ask them whether we could watch the process, or to finding a weaver to show us how the weft and warp worked together. The fun was to figure out the principle in advance. And anyway, he had work to do, filling file folders with notes toward his dissertation. Two, three years lay between him and his degree, and I, having mine already, had to understand. From time to time, I did.

But that first evening we talked and ate, and talked and walked. We found ourselves in Copley Square, and searched out a bar he knew and talked again. The bar was red: red costumes on the waitresses, red chairs to sit on, soft red lights whose flattering qualities I knew very well. We sat at a tiny table, looking rather than speaking.

I bring my feet from the edge of the bookcase down to the floor. I must know something about what I feel. Because I do remember the *quality* of being in that bar with George. I was ready to break apart from the excitement within me, and yet I sat quietly. And waited. I may even have been aware that I was following Dr. Kant's lead. Not that he had told me how to behave in the particular circumstance of having a drink with a man nine years younger than I. He didn't give me a list: do this when that happens; do that when this happens. And yet, sitting in his chair, being kind, listening to me as myself, not to me-as-a-case, or me-as-a-type, he was trying to open my mind to the idea that there are feminine ways to behave and that I didn't behave in those ways. That assumes I knew what it was, what it is, to be feminine, and that I chose to behave otherwise. But I didn't know, I still don't know, so I couldn't have chosen.

Until my menstrual cycle began I never once thought that girls should do different things than boys do or that girls should do things differently from the way boys do them. When I understood that the physiological differences between males and females enabled sexual coupling, all that was simply a new set of facts about the world. Particularly compelling facts, to be sure, but no more capable of changing my basic assessment that men and women are alike than could, say, my understanding that a prism refracts white light into the colors of the visible spectrum.

Maybe more men than women can hoist heavy weights or pour molten steel, but there are no muscles in the human brain. A woman can undertake any career, any profession a man can. Men possess no moral characteristics that women don't also have; there are no goals that only men can pursue. Women can endure physical dangers, can stand up for their moral beliefs, can hold their consciences above their private gain, can be kind, thoughtful, and generous, can gauge the far-reaching consequences of their actions. They can also, of course, dissemble. To dissemble: to lie, to disguise, to deceive, to cheat, to pretend, to exaggerate, to underplay, to wait.

To wait. That was what I hated most to do. To wait for the phone to ring, to wait to be asked to go out, to wait to be kissed. Every man who tried to educate me began with waiting. "Timmie, wait for me to open the door for you." "Timmie, let me pick up your glove." "Timmie, let me light your cigarette." Did they think I couldn't do any of those things for myself when I was alone? And the same men who were teaching me to be feminine that way were exactly the men who raged about the women who had made them miserable in the past. They didn't see (*I* didn't see until just now) that they were trying to make me into the very sort of woman who would then be equipped to hurt them.

But that can't be what being a woman is: a creature who sits passively, waiting to have things done for her; an unthinking doll; someone who has no opinions except those that some man hands her, ready-made, not to be examined. How can a man value a compliment from a creature who has only the criteria and knowledge that he himself puts there? And anyway, there are things that men need that such a woman can't give them. I think of the men I've held in the night, talking courage into them for a following day's unendurable encounter. Or helping them think their way through problems before which they believed themselves without hope of solution.

Then why do men bother to invent that other kind of female? I know: because she'll give them no trouble. Except when she lies. But she won't give them those other things, either. For those things men come to women like me, even while they try to shape me to be like her. They talk to me, but they marry her. What a mucked-up world: not one man who'd let me be honest with him and who'd also want to marry me.

"Honest." My own word mocks me. I don't know what it is to be honest with myself, let alone with a man. Yet I've insisted on being honest with them. What did I even think I was doing? And how can something that was once so clear confound me now?

I started with George and the excitement of our beginning, but I ended up fighting the old battle about what it is to be a woman. What was the bridge between?

Yes. The red bar, and George looking at me, close, silent, while I waited for him to speak. He said, in time, "I wish I could tell you what's in my mind about you."

I felt a generation away. No experienced man, intent on seduction, would have taken a chance on so unsophisticated a remark. I smiled. "Why don't you try?"

He shook his head, and I saw again what a boy he was. "If I could tell you, I wouldn't have to wish I could. It's in here, in me, but I don't have the words to get it out to you."

I remember the bridge now: he made me feel that I had to sit quietly, on pain of frightening him away. His ingenuousness made me aware of how familiar I was with all the tactics men use for getting a woman to bed. His remark prevented me from calling on my repertoire of responses for countering any of the standard passes. By being so young, he disarmed me of my advantage and put me in the position of waiting for him to make the moves. With George, I fell naturally into the frame of mind that other men had tried to push me into artificially.

And I did that . . . why? Because Dr. Kant had taught me how to be a woman. But look at it: it's the same old idea of waiting. I sat and held my tongue, waiting for George to speak. And then when his words were different from what I expected, I knew I'd have to wait for other things, too. And for all of two months, sitting in New York, I did wait. But then I discarded everything foreign, including the restraint Dr. Kant had taught me, and moved back to Cambridge to be with George.

But that night in the bar, I knew, in some sense of "know," what the waiting was about. It wasn't just waiting to have men do for me the things I could do for myself. It was being the sort of creature I could be *only* in the presence of a man. It wasn't just putting my sophistication under wraps so that George couldn't see it. It was giving over the initiative to him.

Before George, I tried to do that once or twice. But with George, I didn't have to try, even though I sensed the awkwardness of the hands into which I was placing myself. With other men, it was exactly the sureness of the hands that drew me. Or what looked like their sureness: the transaction into which we were about to enter required that they be in charge. But with George, that exchange would be only one of the many exchanges that were in store for us. We had something intricately rich to share. That's what I knew, and that's why it didn't matter, not essentially, that my sexual experience was probably more extensive than his. Yes, I did feel like the older woman seducing the young boy the first time or two we were together. But after that our ages leveled off. Together we played like children. Better than childhood: the playing didn't have to end at dark.

I shove back my chair. I can't let myself be sad. I have to remember the wretchedness with George too, or else I'll be playing the same old game with myself one more time.

I watch Logos explore the field that extends from the south side of our house all the way to the corner opposite the water tower. He leaps over bushes, digs where the ground looks inviting, smells something carefully at almost every step, and races the tumbleweed blown by the wind. I examine the dead garden at the far end of the lawn. I can identify the rosebushes, but the other brown stalks are indistinguishable. The gardener will come at a time dictated by the calendar and under my landlady's charge. Beyond the garden is the moor.

Why can't I walk on the moor? The high bushes at the far edge of the garden restrain me. They might as well be a barbed-wire fence. I walk toward them, cross the line they mark, and keep going. The scrub underfoot makes walking difficult; I have to look down at my feet at each step. So not every new thing is worth doing.

A peculiar sound, almost a cough, arrests me.

"Logos!" Silence. I run back through the garden, onto the lawn. "Logos, where are you?"

He stands at the edge of the field. His head is low, his tail is lost between his legs, his whole body bends over the ground, and his back moves up and down, slowly, irregularly.

"Logos!" I race toward him, but he turns away when he sees me coming. His turning is a lurch, and I stop before I get too close. All at once he's unfamiliar to me: I see him as an animal behaving in an unknown way. I watch him from my distance. He heads toward the large tree bordering the field. His path is erratic. The movements of his back seem to propel him forward, and then abruptly he's digging at the roots of the tree. One paw digs with a long slow movement, then the other, and then, as though he couldn't do so until the hole was dug, he starts to vomit. His whole body seems to be pushing something out of him.

"Logos, what are you doing?" I watch, not knowing what to do. And then tears are pouring down my face and I am on my knees on the ground. "Stop him! Someone please make him stop!" I pound the ground until my hand hurts, and then I see him digging the hole deeper.

He lies down at the base of the tree, his paws over the edge of the hole, his head moving rhythmically. Logos and the hole in the ground call up an unendurable image that, in an instant, includes my father. I bend my head to my knees to shut out the picture.

When I raise my face, Logos is sitting up. His ears lie back, a ring of foam surrounds his mouth, and he looks at me, trying to read from my face whether he's done something wrong.

"Sweet Puppy, what can I do for you?" I stay where I am, afraid to frighten him if I move, not sure what he'll do if he starts toward me.

But he looks up at me with glassy eyes, concentrating on something inside him, and then trots off with a stiff-legged gait. Every few steps the heaving of his stomach stops him.

I know, somehow, that he wants me to stay away. I go slowly toward the house, hoping he'll follow. At the stone stoop, I turn to see him coming up behind me. He wants to be with me, but not near me, and so I let him go first into the house to find whatever place he chooses for lying down. He heads for the fireplace and, after turning a circle, flops down, rests his chin on one paw, and lets his eyes close. In moments, he straightens his back against the bricks, extends his legs, heaves a long sigh, and is asleep.

I stand in the doorway, my coat still unbuttoned, my hands red from the cold, my body shaken. I get on the phone to the SPCA and describe what I've just seen.

Mr. Lema is unaccountably unmoved. "What did he throw up?"

"I don't understand."

"Well, he probably got into something and then found it indigestible and threw it up. Why don't you go look?"

"Look?" My disgust apparently travels through the phone wires.

"Yes, look. I can't tell you what to do unless you can tell me what he threw up. If it's one kind of thing, it's not too important, and I can tell you what to do over the phone. If it's another kind of thing, you'll have to get him here as fast as you can. Call me back." He hangs up.

I go downstairs and look at the puppy in his exhausted sleep. The only way I can help him waits outside.

Chunks of carcass. Bones of a bird. Where did he find it? Did he kill it, or was it dead when he found it?

Mr. Lema tells me I should be glad. It could have been poison, or something sharp. Logos probably expelled it all. He'll lie around quietly for a few hours, but after that, he'll be fine again. Don't feed him until tomorrow, except some ice cream.

"Ice cream?"

"It would soothe his stomach. What do you have out there? Ice? Let him lick on a bowl of ice cubes. Call me tomorrow if he's not better."

I thank him and hang up.

Downstairs, Logos' breathing is quiet and steady. I lower myself carefully to the floor. I keep my hands to myself, although I long to touch him. Before this afternoon he was my beautiful puppy: funny, playing, outguessing me, too smart for his own good. But separate from me. Like a toy that had the unusual ability to breathe and move. But now he's mine in a way he hasn't been before. I make him mine by caring.

So loving is caring-for? Taking-care-of turns into caring-for, being-concerned-about? As Dewey said. I saw it with my own eyes this very day.

17

The brilliant day leads me out of the house after breakfast. The puppy trots importantly ahead of me. Does he remember how sick he was yesterday?

There must be people living in these houses. I do see a person or two once a week in the post office or in the grocery store. But no one is visible on the beach, and the streets might just as well belong to me.

George would love it here. All the times we walked: during the night, or at dawn, or in the late afternoon. And the places: along the Charles; from the Square to his house a mile away; the mile and more from his house to mine; from the Square to anywhere that took our fancy. I think that even if we had had cars, we still would have walked. It let us be together longer, it kept us out of doors, it left us open to whatever incident we might come upon, it let our talk range as widely as our steps, it let us skip or run or even sit wherever we happened to find ourselves when we got tired. And after months of covering Cambridge with our footsteps, each doorway, corner, street spoke to me of him. I couldn't have stayed in Cambridge after he left, with all those echoes springing out at me, and so I left before he did.

But he let me go. "Do you think you might come to Colorado?" was the most he could bring himself to say.

"Do you want me there, George?" It was the hundredth time I tried to make him include me in his life, and he saw it coming. I looked up at his face. His brows lifted in mock surprise, and he began to bounce his body forward on the balls of his feet, exaggerating his ordinary walk as I had once done to make him laugh.

"Why should what I want have any effect on what you choose to do? I want this: that if you want to come to Colorado, you'll come, whether I'll be there or not."

"You're infuriating! Why else would I be there except to be with you?"

"Yes, people do tell me that I'm infuriating, and now you've joined the majority."

"George, that's not fair."

"Look. Don't come there to be with me. Come there because your own independent wishes take you there."

Where the gravel road reaches the paved road, I stop Logos, make him stay, and cross the road myself. I look in both directions while he trembles with excitement on the other side. When I call him he flies across the road to me, and then runs to the nearest stairway down to the sand.

What was it Dr. Kant said when I repeated such conversation to him? Yes: "Alice, George is not committable. He is not ready, or not able, to commit himself to you or any other woman now. I don't know why, because, of course, I don't know him. I know him only through what you tell me. But it looks to me that you're hurting yourself if you keep believing that you can change him."

"That's telling me to break it off."

Dr. Kant sat silently, looking at me.

"You're telling me to let him go to Colorado, just like that. But then I'd never see him again. Because he won't ask me to go with him."

"Alice, can't you really hear what you're saying?"

Because his face was so kind, and because he was trying so hard to help me understand, my tears fell. I could only shake my head.

"You're saying that you're the one keeping this relationship going. That if you don't hang on to it every minute, fighting all the way, it will end. And yet you still don't let it go."

"But he's so close to me. We have so much to say to each other. He's more a part of me than Stan ever was. I can't believe that we shouldn't be together."

I waited for Dr. Kant to agree with me. He said: "And what of the other girl?"

"Well. He feels sorry for her."

"Alice." Gently reproachful.

"That's what he says. He says that I'm beautiful and witty and clever, so that anyone would be glad to take me anywhere. But that she's none of those things, and so he has to pay some attention to her to make up for it."

"And how did he get appointed to that role?"

It took me a while to reply. "I suppose he took it on himself."

"Exactly."

"What do you mean by that?"

"If you had your choice of spending time with a handsome, brilliant, entertaining man, or with a man who is dull, unattractive, but nice, which would you choose?"

"You're oversimplifying the whole thing. I know people, including George, who act some of the time in accordance with their beliefs about how human beings ought to behave toward one another. Not just in accordance with what they might happen to want at a particular moment."

"Alice, Alice."

I'm walking near the edge of the water. Logos chases the waves out and then backs up hastily as they advance.

I saw her once, but I didn't know it until later. No, I think I must have guessed that it was she. I just didn't want to believe it.

George and I left Jan's party, taking our host with us, to get more liquor before the stores closed. We joined hands, one man on either side of me, and fell into a running skip. They were both so much taller than I that I had to take two steps to their one to keep up with them without breaking the rhythm. It was fun, laughing-out-loud fun, and we moved into the street because the sidewalks weren't wide enough for the three of us abreast. We skipped through the driveway of the high school, chanting in time with our motion's rhythm, one or the other of us laughing or shouting that we were out of breath.

Suddenly someone was walking toward us, and George stopped to talk with her, unlinking his arm from mine. I would have gone on, except that Jan looked back, and then he turned around and said some friendly words to the girl. No one introduced me. I just stood there, a few steps away from George and Jan. The girl's face struck me as that of someone old before her time. There were wrinkles and puckers at unexpected places, and I remember thinking that she looked as though she were a piece of shattered glass. George talked with her only a minute or two, and then we all linked arms again and skipped the rest of the way without interruption. I didn't even ask who she was. I simply forgot her the moment we left her. On the way home, we set a slower pace and talked about philosophy, so that by the time we got the liquor to the party and Jan unwrapped the package, I was startled to hear him tell his wife that we had bumped into Elizabeth on the way.

I looked at Anne. "Was that Elizabeth? I didn't know."

"You've never met her?"

"Anne, try to imagine my meeting her."

Anne giggled in embarrassment, and then George entered the room.

My stomach contracts, my eyes close, my throat refuses to swallow, even now. The time George must have spent with her. Not just the times I knew about—things people would accidentally tell me, or seeing them at a distance walking hand in hand—but all those other times I couldn't know about, since they lived across the street from one another. The hurt is still there. I can't shake it off.

I kick the sand angrily. Logos sees the movement as the beginning of some new game and plants himself foursquare in front of me, his bright face ready for anything. I stoop to pet him, then find a stone in the sand and toss it as far beyond him as I can to let him run.

All I'm doing now is playing it back. It's no clearer to me now than it was then, why George behaved as he did, why he wouldn't stop seeing that girl, even though he and I had something that he had never had with anyone else. Why he could never tell me that he loved me. Why he couldn't ask me to marry him, or even to be with him, when he knew he'd be in Colorado teaching for three years.

I used to talk about him to Tony, into whose Hungarian refugee family I had adopted myself.

"Tony, how do I answer him when he says he does things that are his duty, but not things that he wants to do?"

"Alice, really. That's the sort of thing a child would say."

"You can't just call him names. You have to be able to answer him with a reason. Help me think of an argument against his. If I can persuade him that he's wrong, he'll admit it and he'll change."

"My God, do you really believe that? Then you're as foolish as he is. Go on, keep chasing him. You're a perfect pair."

God damn it, how is it that everybody except me understood what George was doing? None of them knew him. *I* knew him. But he baffled me. When I repeated some of the things George said, other people got the hang of him in a way that I never could. I was *saying* the things they understood, but I couldn't hear my own words.

Not being able to hear. Like not being able to see. I almost turn off my sensory equipment when it's a question of hearing what people say. And I can't sort out the things *I* see from the things that I've been looking at through other people's eyes.

I have the feeling that bunches of ideas are stuck together here. Where to split them apart? Slowly, now.

I hear the postmaster when he tells me what time the mail goes out, but I don't hear George when he says it isn't right to do things just because he wants to do them. What is it I don't hear? No, that's not the question. It's not the thing said, and it's not simply the person saying it. It's what special people say. People special to me. But by that reasoning, I'd have to be unable to hear what I say to them, too. Come, now.

But that's right! Maggie said that a dozen times while she nursed me through the aftermath of Mike. And Dr. Kant, and Tony, and Weck. It's all part of the same thing. I don't know what I do, and I don't know what I say. Somehow I don't have the right tools for describing things to myself. I can sit someone down and tell him the story of George, and when I finish, that person will understand who is doing what and why, but I will still be in the dark.

What happens when a person starts to become important to me? Not just a person: a man. Not just George, either. Mike. Stan. The only men I understood were the ones I didn't particularly care about. But then, there was nothing with them that had to be understood.

Aaaagh. I am like a cat entangled in a ball of wool.

A hundred feet to my left is my favorite stairway. The bench on the landing invites me.

The owner of the bookstore looks up from her desk when I walk in, greets me, then lets me alone. The shop could be in Harvard Square: good new books well arranged, no intrusion on your wish to browse. The bell on the door jingles, and another woman enters. She and the owner know one another, not just as seller and customer, but as social equals. They've been to the same Thursday party, they buy at the same shops, they seek out the same places in Boston.

I move toward the front of the shop where art books are displayed, and through the shop's large windows, I see Logos getting ready to jump from the open window of my car. I race outside in time to shove him back, open the door, snap on his leash, and bring him out for a short walk. I inform him very sharply that he has done a bad thing.

When I return to the bookshop, the women smile at me. We talk about dogs. The customer plays golf and has a springer spaniel who covers the course with her but who will not set foot on a green. We talk of other things. We introduce ourselves.

The owner thinks she has seen me before. "Do you live in Nantucket?"

"No, in 'Sconset."

"Good heavens." The golfer is astonished. "What are you doing out there?"

The predictable question, right on cue. "Well, I'm doing a little writing. It's very beautiful out there. I have the beach all to myself."

The owner laughs. "I bet you do. And does your husband work at the navy station?"

"I'm not married."

Both women stare at me. Courtesy prevents their mouths from saying what their faces ask.

The owner recovers first. "But you should come into town more often. Do you like the theater? There's a play being done tomorrow evening. At the Straight Wharf Theatre. I have tickets, or you can buy them before the performance."

I buy a paperback on aesthetics. We say good-bye all around. They hope to see me at the play. I tell them how nice it was to talk with them.

Driving home, I realize why I went into the shop. To talk to anyone who might be connected in any way to some of the things that are familiar to me: books, bookstores, the whole life of Cambridge before it became so dire for me.

But I can't enter the Nantucket of those two women. The only thing common to us is a certain surface, enough to occupy ten minutes of conversation. Each day I understand more fully how closed to me are the possibilities of human relationships. Not just the important ones: men, friends. But even the casual ones such as these.

Come to think of it, I didn't accept every opinion. I singled out the opinions of persons in authority, yes, but it was the authority of excellence.

Now there's a piece of subtlety for you. If I had been toadying to ordinary authority, I might have noticed long ago that I was creating surrogates for my mother. In fact, when anyone tries to *make* me do anything, I fight back, no matter what the cost. Think of my battle with the dean, than whom no one at Radcliffe was more powerful.

I don't trust my own judgment because I have nothing of my own in terms of which I *can* judge. Nor will I have, unless I find some way to know what I feel. To know whether I feel at all, or whether I'm a monster whose interior is stuffed only with the lines I've read in plays.

That has to be related to what I'm trying to understand now.

And it is!

I sit up on the couch and bring my legs to the floor so quickly that I almost stomp Logos, who lies with his back partly wedged under the couch. He groans awake, gives me a dirty look, then lowers his head to sleep again.

It is. What I can't see are things about myself: my looks, my talent, my brains. What I can't hear are things about men: their purposes in relation to me.

Their purposes? I didn't understand my own until last week. But *that's* the connection. If I didn't know what I was doing, how could I begin to understand what someone I was in love with was doing? If loving is what it was.

Christ! It's a set of Chinese mirrors, and nowhere is there a real object to be reflected.

The covers form a cocoon for my body all the way up to my nose. Their weight is enough to keep me motionless when I awaken. I must have collected, oh, eight blankets the night I stripped the other beds in the house. Under me, from my shoulders to my toes, are the two pillows I placed end to end to fill in the trough that is the center of the mattress. If I lie here without moving, Logos will remain asleep beneath the bed.

Purposes. What is a purpose? Something to be achieved, to be worked for, a future goal toward which a series of steps beginning in the present must be planned. But purposes aren't like blackberries, waiting to be found: they're brought into existence by human choices. So they depend upon a previous wanting, which shapes the path toward their fulfillment. I'm back at my old unknown beginning: not knowing what wanting is.

The only way to know what I want, supposedly, is through having a certain feeling. So either I don't have that feeling, or else I don't know how to recognize it if I *do* have it. Whichever it is, a lack or a blindness, it's a deformity. It has prevented me from seeing what I've been doing with my life. It has kept me from understanding my own purposes, and that, in turn, has kept me from understanding the purposes of other people, too.

I heave my body onto my left side impatiently. Instantly Logos starts to claw his way out from under the bed on the slippery floor.

"Easy, Sweet Puppy. Just stay there. Not yet."

I grin. Did he learn that long sigh from me?

I'm not thinking about the physical impossibility of feeling someone else's feelings. Because even if people could feel the feelings of others, I'd have the same problem with the feelings of others that I have with my own: I couldn't recognize them, either.

But that can't be how people understand purposes. Tony never laid eyes on George, yet he understood what George was up to. The only things Tony knew about George were what I told him. So if Tony had access to George's wants, I had to be the one who provided the bridge for him. Something about the very things I selected to tell Tony holds a key of some sort.

This is where I started: I don't know how to listen to my own words.

I throw off the covers, and this time Logos wriggles out onto the rug and catches up one of my slippers in his mouth. The new game he invented requires that I follow him to get back my slipper. The chase ends up at the outside door, and I let him out, as I do first thing each morning anyway.

Logos, prepared for his morning race across the yard, stops paw-deep in snow on the stone stoop, then retreats into the kitchen next to me. I kneel to reassure him. "Logos, that's snow!" I hold the door open for him to try again. He dips one paw into the cold whiteness, immediately lifts it out again, and holds it in the air for me to do something about.

"Okay, I'll show you what snow is for."

I fly upstairs, pursued by the puzzled puppy, and put on my clothes so fast that legs and pants, arms and sleeves, boots and feet seem utterly mismatched for one another. Buttons and buttonholes on my coat fare no better. The unfamiliar speed keeps Logos intent on my every gesture, so that, when I reach down to make the first snowball of the year, his nose follows my hand into the snow. I shape the ball, talking; I show him the arc my throw will take; I polish the ball to smoothness. A cry gurgles in his throat. Every inch of him is ready.

"Shall I throw it?"

Two high-pitched yelps reply.

I sling the ball the width of the yard, and Logos runs so fast that he catches it at the exact spot where it lands. He eats the thing that dissolves before his jaws move twice. He turns to me, astonished. I laugh out loud to watch him move his lips and tongue, and know how cool his interior has become, how incredulous he is of the whole experience. All at once he takes up a mouthful of snow and eats it with abandon. He thrusts his nose down and keeps it in the snow. He's on to something lying deep in that very spot. Or is it there, there, or there? His nose vacuums the entire front lawn, and the rear of him follows ridiculously along, his tail sweeping widely back and forth in joy.

In the next moment he falls onto his back and rolls his body in the snow from side to side in solitary ecstasy. Up again, as close to crowing as a dog can be. A second flying tour of the yard, nose down at intervals, stopping short, legs braced, he smells the new cool world. I throw another snowball, but he chases it only to have an excuse for taking another mouthful of snow. On his back again he skids, propelling himself in any direction that suits his captivated fancy. I am extraneous.

In the kitchen making coffee, I watch him from the window. What was the last thing I did that filled me with that kind of delight? I think and think, but somehow I'm unable to remember.

I'm not even sure what it would be like to form a purpose. Deliberately to form one, and then carry it out. I suppose writing my thesis can be counted as fulfilling a purpose. Even though it was part of a plan that was itself a sham. Because my real purpose in getting the degree had nothing to do with being in the philosophy department at Harvard. It was like going west to get to the east. Worse, because in the world I *can* get to the east by going west, but I can't get my mother to love me by getting the world to applaud me. And now I don't want either one. I just want to find out whether there's anything in me that's genuinely mine: my making, my doing, my choice.

And what does George have to do with that? Maybe he's simply the most recent man, and that's why he hurts the most, why I remember things about him most easily. Or maybe I'm using him as a convenient case study, so that if I can understand how things got so fouled up with him, I'll be able to understand how it happened with any other man I might think of in my long life.

No. I can't think of him as one more man. I even want to see him again. How *can* I want that? He was unbearable the last time I saw him. Then why can't I *stop* considering him as someone still alive in my life? I seem able to remember only the fun we had. Or the excitement of working with all the ideas that we brought out in each other.

Or the tenderness. The time I felt so miserably sick the evening before the X rays checking on my old operation. George, lying on the couch, reading to me. *The Little Prince,* was it? I sat in a chair, scarcely able to concentrate, but glad to have him with me. Once he looked up and saw me with my head in my hands. "Come over here," he said, and although changing my position seemed like arduous work, something in his voice touched me, and I went. "Lie down. Come on." And he held out his left arm to show me where to fit, and then he started to read again. I lay for a few minutes in the crook of his arm, and then turned onto my other side, and then onto my back, and turned again to face him. "I can't get comfortable." I heard the petulance in my voice, but I was beyond courtesy.

George examined my face for a long minute. Then: "Get on top of me." I lifted my heavily weighted body the few inches that put me in touch with him through the whole length of me. My head rested on his chest between the book and his chin, and almost instantly I was breathing in time with his breathing, my body moving up and down with his. He started to read again. I heard his voice and his heart at the same time, and the warmth of his body penetrated his clothes and mine. Gradually I became aware that I was falling asleep, but that it was in my power not to. And so I lay, deliberately suspending myself between sleep and waking, in order to savor the contentment that enveloped me.

I didn't write that on my list. Why not? Oh, yes: because it happened more than a year ago. I was happy that evening. I remember telling Dr. Kant that I was. I recognized that whole complex of feelings and called it by that name. And I was aware of it then. I didn't paste the label on later, after I had thought about it.

And yet it wasn't something I expected to be happy doing. I looked terrible, even worse up close under the light George was reading by. I felt terrible. I was frightened, knowing the pain of the X-ray examination the following day. Doubly frightened that the X rays might show new lesions. Meaning new surgery. I couldn't have endured that operation. All of this shaped my mood into fretfulness, and I behaved like a sick child. George gave me his body as a solace against my discomfort and as a shield against my fears.

That's loving, isn't it? Why don't I *know?*

Why, indeed? Two weeks later he told me that he had never stopped seeing Elizabeth. I hung up the phone and cried through the night. At dawn I dressed and waited until I was due at my office, my $1.50-per-hour typing job that was letting me be in Cambridge with George.

I remember that day. I said nothing to anyone; I sat in my little corner, rebuffing all conversation, typing cards of some sort until lunch, walking to the river for an hour, then returning to type again. Even refusing to take dictation because I would have had to smile and be polite when I felt only unmoving and dead inside. At five I had to face going home to Maggie, having to talk about it. Worse: having to think of where to go next, since there was no longer any reason to stay in Cambridge.

But George was standing at the steps of my office, waiting for me. When I finally spoke to him, my face felt like stone. "What can you possibly want?"

"To talk with you. Come and have coffee with me."

I remember being aware of a triumph, sitting at the table, watching him bring our coffee on a tray. I let him talk. That time, he was the one making the case to me.

A case? A joke. He had tried, he said, really tried, to break off with the girl, but she had begged him not to, and he really couldn't hurt her. "And anyway, she pleases me."

I pushed back my chair and started to get up, but he touched my arm. "It's not like what it is with you and me." He meant his smile to win.

"Why is it you can see how much you *might* hurt her, and not see how much you're *in fact* hurting me?" I gathered my coat and put it on, trembling.

"I can't hurt you as much as I'd hurt her if I left her. She has no one but me. You can have any man you want. You can go anywhere and be the center of attention. You're educated, and clever besides. She's not. She's just a nice girl, and being with me makes her happy."

I got up, skirted the other tables, and started up the steps. He scrambled after me. "Wait. I'll walk with you."

I waited. Why did I wait? Because I wanted that Eden, by then lost. We talked for two more hours, and the upshot of it was that he had his way. He had her, and he also had me. So that as the time closed in toward his departure for Colorado, I was clutching and grabbing in order to keep him with me, and he was fleeing like a cornered animal.

Dr. Kant said that if he wanted both of us, he couldn't really have wanted either of us. And that I was the one who let myself in for all the unhappiness that followed. More of what he called my "masochism."

I shove my chair back from the desk and get up to prowl the living room. It still irritates me to remember the rare times Dr. Kant dealt with me as though I were an exemplification of a theory. Most of the time he simply kept reminding me that I didn't know what I did. But he didn't tell me what I did. Perhaps he was trying to make me find my own way to see. Perhaps what I'm doing here is something I absorbed from his whole orientation of dealing with me in the very specific terms in which my life itself moves. The difference is that I don't have him to guide me.

I rest my head in my arms against the mantel, remembering him. I can't have him back.

And then I pound the mantel with my fist. But I've *got* to find a way to describe my own behavior to myself. To describe it as carefully as I can, in terms of who did what, when, where, and how. Or to describe it in any other terms that will let me see what I do, let me hear what other people say to me. That's turning out to be very hard. Not because I'm "unconsciously" concealing the truth from myself, but because I'm without working knowledge of a group of ideas that most human beings use without ever being puzzled by them. Like: what a feeling is, how to recognize a feeling of any sort, what it is to choose something, how I can have purposes that are my own.

For that, the term *masochistic* is no help to me. I wasn't aiming for pain: I was avoiding it. When I kept on seeing George after he told me he wasn't going to stop seeing Elizabeth, I was avoiding the pain of being absolutely without him. When I turned down the publishing offer in New York so that I could be in Cambridge with George, I was avoiding the horror of living alone in New York, of having only a few friends to see at carefully spaced intervals, of having neither intellectual nor personal excitement of any kind.

So it wasn't that I looked for pain and succeeded in finding it, as the notion of masochism implies. It was that I was avoiding pain but failed. Because it turned out that I couldn't endure knowing that Elizabeth was with him when I wasn't. And it turned out that I was bored to stupefaction being a typist in Cambridge. I just didn't foresee these things as lying in wait for me. So until I know *what* I'm doing, I can't know that a certain consequence is to be expected.

Maybe I didn't think of those situations as painful while I was undergoing them. Maybe I couldn't call what was happening to me "painful" because I didn't know how to call what I was doing by its name.

Like John in Chicago, who told me he had never been taught the names of the colors. It wasn't that he was color-blind, that he saw things only in shades of gray: it was that he didn't know how to put the label "blue" on blue objects, or "brown" on brown objects. I discovered it only by accident when he came to our apartment one day wearing brown socks with a blue suit. I teased him about his bad taste, and he looked so puzzled that I wanted to bite my tongue. "John, I'm sorry. You must be color-blind."

"Well, that's the reason the state won't give me a driver's license. When they held up the cards to find out whether I could tell a green light from a red light, it took me so long to remember what other people call the color I was looking at that the examiner decided I was color-blind. Green and red look different to me. They probably look to me just as they look to you. But it's like having to speak a foreign language that I don't know too well, when I have to tell you what color something is. So you tell me that I'm wearing brown socks with a blue suit, and that they don't go together. Okay. But nobody ever told me that before. If I can remember what things are brown in my drawer, and what things are blue, next time I won't wear them together."

"John, you are kidding me."

"Tim, I wouldn't kid you."

But that's what I'm like. I never learned that what was going on inside me was called "jealousy." Like John with colors, I didn't know that jealousy and pain go together. No, that's not quite it. I've read in books, I've heard people say, that jealousy is painful. But I don't know how to put the two ideas together and apply them to myself. And I can't put them together because I can't recognize them separately.

Then how do I know, how do I know even *now* that I was jealous *then?*

My head feels ready to burst. My hands try to contain my pounding thoughts. Logos is immediately next to me, sniffing out the possibility of my need. I stroke his head.

I have to understand this. Something happened to me a year and a half ago, and I'm now calling it "jealousy." What do I know now that I didn't know then? Because I called it by name just now without batting an eye. I think I've just realized that it *hurt* seeing George with her, it hurt guessing that they were together. And I know, at least I've been told, that those are some of the reasons for being jealous.

I see, I see. I've used a syllogism to discover something that I'm supposed to know without reasoning:

1. I hurt when I saw George with that girl;
2. Seeing them together is a reason for being jealous;
Therefore, my hurt was jealousy.

Shall I laugh? Could anything be more comical? I'm an idiot without qualification, and I prove it by not being able to stop crying.

18

My thoughts are so scattered, so unconnected. I need some path through them to let me see their pattern. Maybe this is what there is to know: that I have no way out.

I slam the pen down on the desk and storm to the closet for my coat. Boots, gloves, keys, Logos, hat down as close to my eyes as my brows. I move across the lawn almost running. Someone help me. Where can I go for help? Not to any person.

I'm halfway to the corner before I miss Logos. When I look back I see him sitting at the edge of the field, bending over something. "Logos!" He looks up quickly but doesn't come. Instead he lowers his head, then turns away from me toward the scrub. I run toward him, and then I see a dead bird hanging from his mouth.

"God damn it, Logos, drop that!" I make a grab for him but he slips out of reach. "You dumb dog! You were sick from doing that before." My voice is very loud.

He stands watching me, ready to turn in whatever direction he must.

"Drop it." I'm threatening him with my voice. He doesn't take his eyes off me; his mouth still holds the garbage.

"Drop it, you bastard! Hurry up!" I'm shouting now.

He starts to move backward slowly. My left hand swoops toward his collar and catches hold of it. My right hand comes down full on his rear. I hit him, and then I hit him again, and I keep on hitting him.

"Bad dog!" The palm of my hand stings. I rub it against my coat, and then still holding Logos' collar I straddle his body with my legs and press them against him to keep him from escaping. I open his jaws, forcing him to let go of the carcass, and toss it far out into the field. Then I let him go with a movement that thrusts him away from me. My hands are trembling. My throat is raw from shouting. My whole body throbs as though a motor were running full blast inside me.

I scream: *"Bad dog! I don't want you! Go away!"*

I spin around and run back to the house, across the lawn to the stoop, fumbling for my keys. Logos is next to me. "Go away!"

He gets out of the way of my sharp gesture, but he's through the door first when I open it. I throw my coat onto the kitchen table and lean my head against the cool window before I can bring myself to strike a match to reheat the coffee. Long minutes go by before I stop shaking. I pour myself some coffee and take it into the living room.

Scraping sounds, heavy breathing, from behind the couch. He's smart: he'll keep out of my way. I settle onto the couch and sip the hot coffee. In minutes the only sound I hear is the progressive steadying of my heartbeat.

When Logos squirms out from behind the couch, I pay no attention to him. He sits at my feet, looking up at me, but I turn my head away. And then, in a small and very quiet movement, he brings his body to face the same direction I'm facing, so that the two of us sit side by side watching some invisible scene taking place across the room.

I look down at him. I see the top of the small head, ears straight up and straining backward to pick up any smallest hint of a word from me. He leans against my calf, his forepaws on the toes of my boots.

Where can he go, this puppy? There is no other place but here. There is no other person but me. Just like me: there's only here and him.

I touch the silky head lightly. He turns his face toward me, unsure but ready. I put my cup on the table, and then shove the table aside and slide to the floor next to him. "Oh, Logos, I'm sorry."

He licks my face before I bury it in the fur of his neck.

"I'm sorry, I'm sorry." The smell of him is sweet and familiar. For a little while, he lets me hold him, and then he wriggles away, looks for his ball, and brings it for me to throw.

"No, just stay and keep me company." I want to be very quiet. I want to know what happened outside just now.

The day turns so cold that we walk only to the post office, pick up the mail, and come straight home. I haven't done anything today. It's too early for a drink, and too late to sit down at my desk. Too early, too late: Whose schedule am I on? "Too late" means I have no energy to start thinking now. "Too early" means nothing at all. I'll have a drink whenever the thought crosses my mind. I carry my glass back into the living room.

How is it that I recognized the fullness of my contentment the evening George read to me, and yet I can't remember feeling jealous? If I felt it then, I certainly didn't recognize it then. Maybe I couldn't recognize it because I was preoccupied with finding ways to get George away from her. Or because I was full of those imitation feelings that I, the actress, thought I should be feeling. God knows I cried enough, and there was nothing imitation about those tears.

Ah, Alice, but what were the tears for? Why, to have George again. Not George-cruel, but George-gentle.

The sun sets and the room turns dark before I realize that an hour's wandering thought hasn't roused up even one more occasion to set alongside that evening of permeating peace with George. I sigh. How can I get a clue from just one time? I need at least one more, so that I can see what the two have in common. Then I might have a starting point for understanding.

My laugh mocks me. No wonder I have the idea that I can't recognize my own feelings: the good ones are so rare that I forget ever having them.

Being three steps away from my first look at the water each day is as exciting as though I were about to meet a man. The difference is that here I'm never disappointed. The sea is always there and glorious, no matter what the wind or sun or lack of either does to it. It always catches me up into itself. From this point on the bluff, where my eye takes in the line of the shore with the expanse of water toward the horizon, the very familiarity of the view enlarges my sense of its beauty. My walk begins with this smile.

But the men weren't always there, not always kind, soon closed me in on myself, and, with familiarity, were gone. I shut my eyes against the sudden procession of the men. Too many, considering the number of times that I've been satisfied. I can count the times on one hand, but I don't even want to think of counting the men.

I keep going around a circle that gets larger without becoming clearer: men, loving, sex. When I was eighteen, all three were inseparable. Now I can think of them by twos as well: men and loving, men and sex, loving and sex. Something would burn in me, and couldn't be put out until he, whoever he was, touched me, held me, was lying next to me, on me, in me. But the fire was almost never put out, even then. And yet I always let him think so.

I was acting, and I knew it. Come to think of it, those were the only times I *knew* I was acting. There was a point at which I'd recognize that this time there'd be no orgasm either, and so I'd focus on making it happen to him. I'd use all the ways I knew to please him, sounds and movements both.

I got something from it: compliments on my skill; the sense of being alive all over my body. There was an ache that couldn't be eased, yes, but in time it went away. Even when I was in love, the satisfaction of an orgasm was rare. So that, thinking about it later, I'd remember the satisfaction as something very diffuse, ranging over all these other things.

How many men did I fool? Maybe all of them. The only man I didn't try to fool was Mike, and he was the only man who thought I was trying to fool him. But, oh, Mike, I spent a night with you that I'll remember to the end of my life. I can play back those hours, almost minute by minute, now, three years later.

The intensity of the memory stops me on the sand. I feel my face reddening. I stand still, longing with every part of me for a man who doesn't belong to me, who can't belong to anyone, perhaps not even to himself. That he is so much like me merely shows that both of us carry the same curse.

Abruptly I change my direction in order to throw off the images that inhabit me. This isn't what I want to be doing. This is no way to understand anything at all. With Mike, for the first time in my life I was trying not to be an actress. But what do actors know how to do, what do they know how to say, when they haven't got anybody else's lines but their own to rely on?

I know why I remember that night: Mike talked to me during the whole time. He was *with* me. We weren't two islands, touching only at localized points. We were two human beings who knew that words, as well as bodies, touch, and his words led me to where we both wanted to be.

I stare out at the water. Why did he leave me? What did I do to make him leave me? I shake my head. I don't see or hear him, either. Or George. Or Stan. Or myself. Or my damned-to-hell self.

Before I settle into bed to read, I call New York to make a hotel reservation for the Philosophical Association meetings on December 27. Will I really go? Looking for a teaching job now is only taking insurance against the day next fall that I might wake up, wanting to teach. I haven't decided whether I want to, and yet the only reason for going to the meetings is to try to get a teaching job. Think of seeing all the people I used to know. Think of having to answer the question of what I'm doing these days. I shudder in my silent room and pull the covers up around my ears.

Beneath the bed Logos breathes the long sigh that is the prelude to his night. I'll call June tomorrow evening to see whether she wants me there Saturday or Sunday. And check my clothes. I need a scarf to wear with the blue sweater. I'll look for one in Harvard Square. I fall asleep going in and out of all the shops I can't afford.

I take a last swallow of coffee and then force discipline upon the disordered stream of my thinking.

I can't see: I don't know how to describe the situations in which I find myself, in which I place myself. I can't hear: I don't know how to understand the purposes of people, of special people, of men, in relation to me. I can't feel: I don't know how to recognize what goes on inside me, what wanting is, what my own purposes are, or even whether I have any that are my own.

If I could only have *heard* what George, or Mike, or any man, was saying when he spoke, I might have understood what he wanted from me.

My eyes flew open. It occurs to me for the first time that what George wanted from me may not have been the same as what I wanted from him. I always thought it was; I never bothered to think that it wasn't. Being together was fun and exciting and close, and I wanted more of it, as much of it as I could get: I wanted to marry him.

I strike my forehead with the palm of my hand. How can I be so dumb? He didn't want to marry me. He said so a dozen times. And he obviously didn't want to be with me as much as I wanted to be with him. Then how could I ever have believed he wanted what I wanted?

I know. I never thought of him and me in terms of purposes, let alone purposes that might not be the same.

Oh, stupid, stupid female. To work so hard to bring forth this ordinary idea. What is more familiar than that human beings have purposes, and that their purposes more often than not conflict? And yet I've never taken up the idea of purposes into my thinking, just as the idea of choosing isn't part of my thinking, either.

I suddenly see how indissolubly connected they are. To form a purpose requires that there be things worth pursuing. You choose the thing you pursue from among other things worth pursuing. But you also choose the steps that will lead you to that thing and you choose them from among other possible steps. You're choosing both before and after you form your purpose. You're choosing throughout the whole course of your day. The existentialists have been saying so since Kierkegaard.

But I never made the idea mine. Then do it now. I'll have to fit it to me, to see where its ribs and joints are.

If George's and my purposes were different, what *did* he want from me? No, it's hopeless to try to retrieve that. But I know what I wanted from him: I wanted to marry him.

My stomach curls. I wanted to marry Mike, too. And Stan, certainly Stan. Don't turn away: look at it. I run my eye down the years of men and wince at each name. As far back as I can remember, I've wanted to marry the men I've been involved with.

To think of them all at the same time is like a nightmare from which I cannot wake. But I have to. Something here is trying to get through to me.

I've wanted to get married. And each time the affair came to an end, I'd try to get the man back. But then, in time, I'd meet someone else, and fall in love with him, and be glad I hadn't married the last man because *this* man was so right for me.

Except with Stan. I would have dropped any current man in the past ten years if Stan had asked me to marry him. Even George? I hesitate. Yes. No. I don't know.

I know Stan better than I know any other human being. I've studied him, as I would a text whose every line I had to annotate. I set myself to understand him in order to discover what he wanted from a woman, so that I could give it to him. I did learn; I still know. I told him that I knew, just before he got married. I was the only person who wasn't surprised by the news of his divorce six years later.

Strange, more than strange. I've given him the kind of thought that I haven't been able to give myself: I could find out what he wanted. Why did I do it? Because I love him. I loved him. I think I loved him.

Not the others? Maybe not the others. Why him? What *is* he to me? How can he have meant so much to me for so long without my meaning anything at all to him?

It began . . . I close my eyes, shivering. It began on the heels of another ending. Don't shudder, but don't forget it, either. I'm thinking about Stan now only because I said I loved him: best, most, only.

And so I have to find something about him that will let me distinguish the misery I went through with him from the misery I went through with any other man.

I was amused by the way Stan kept trying to get my attention our first semester at Harvard. I'd have coffee with him, but only because he was there. I even let him put me on the train to New York when I went there to forget the most recent man. When I returned to Cambridge, I called him the same day. We sat having coffee in a small glaring-white restaurant, and I suddenly looked at him and saw him. I touched his sleeve. "Stan, I went to New York to try to find something relevant, and it was here waiting for me all along."

Over the next couple of weeks I let myself fall in love with him. It's laughing-funny: I *let* myself do it. He had shown me that I was important to him, he had gone to some trouble on my behalf, there was a special warmth on his face whenever he looked at me, he so clearly wanted me to stay whenever I left him. I remember thinking that I'd fall in love with him so that, for a change, I'd be loving someone who loved me.

I kick the wrinkles out of the rug on my way to the kitchen. Reheating the coffee, I shake my head. I, the brilliant, beautiful, Sophisticated Lady, was going to do the favor of falling in love with the pleasant, not exceptionally attractive, rather smart, small-town boy. But he turned out to be the one who was brilliant. I had walked rings around the men I knew, but he had me racing to catch up with him. And how can anyone match what he, as a man, does to me? He has a net that he tosses over me to reel me toward him, so that I can't even look at anyone else who stands near. I'm almost physically connected to him, as to a part of his body, or as he to mine.

Am? What is this "am" I use? There is no present tense with Stan. Why can't I make myself believe it?

And I was the small-town kid, not he. He had a Genevieve, just as George had an Elizabeth. The only difference was that Genevieve was a continent away while I held him; I didn't know she existed until he was ready to break it off between us. I hated her the minute I saw her the following September; I probably hated her even before I saw her. Just as I hated Marcia when I learned he was going to marry her. He should have been with me. I was so convinced of it that I was willing to wait out that marriage. His divorce *couldn't* have surprised me.

The reheated coffee tastes so bitter that I dump it out and start all over again. He didn't get the divorce because of me. I wasn't even in touch with him for those six years. I was simply waiting for him to be unmarried again.

The day I turned my thesis in, I stood outside Emerson Hall, wondering how to celebrate. My green book bag hung over my shoulder: it felt so light, it was so empty. Except for the oral examination six weeks away, all the years of clawing my way through to my degree were over, and the empty book bag was the most real evidence of it. But I was empty, too: I no longer had something to do. I was freed by my own hand of the burden I had freely imposed upon myself. Who would know better than Stan what I had just done? I walked home very fast and poured a drink and called him in California.

I said my whole name clearly and right at the start. After six years, I couldn't expect him to recognize my voice, and he might know other Alices. His replying voice immediately connected to that part of me that no one else had gotten near in six years, and we talked for ten minutes as though we were at liberty to arrange to meet in the Square that evening.

A year later, when I heard that he was returning to Cambridge with his own dissertation, I wrote to tell him where he could find me. And where, Alice, was that? Why, in the $1.50-an-hour office where I was typing so I could be near George.

Yes, yes, but Stan was separate from George. Was he? He was separate from every other man, but was he separate from George? I don't know. How can I know?

I left the office early the day we met. He came to me straight after his oral examination. Inside the entrance of the dark bar that is the core of Cambridge doings, we reached out to kiss one another's cheeks, and then we both said, almost simultaneously, "Hello, doctor." And then we burst into laughter.

Don't cry now, Alice. You have to think now. The crying has all been done. I go upstairs to find the box of tissues and bring them downstairs to be near me on the couch.

What am I crying about? What, indeed. Because we hadn't seen one another in seven years and yet we both had exactly the same idea at exactly the same time that exactly those words with which we used to greet one another in graduate school would be the perfect ones to say. That's what I miss: that intuitive responsiveness we had to each other. Being with him was being at home in a way that no home I ever had was home: he was where I belonged.

Then why, why, why didn't he ever take me in?

I must stay on good terms with the Stamford people. I check my file to see how long ago I promised I'd write them something about that unreadable report. More than three weeks. I sigh, and write to tell them that I'll do something about it after the holidays. I drop the letter at the post office when I pick up my mail.

I open the envelope from Radcliffe as we walk. I'm almost afraid to unfold the letter, but it *is* here, in my hand. I only postpone something difficult by not looking at it this minute. I read it swiftly, and then read it again to take it all in. Where is the reprimand I expected? Not here. She's not at all annoyed by my turning down the offer from the Anglican college. She explains her policy of letting everyone available learn of everything available, because she feels she has no right to judge for us what might interest any of us.

"Hey!" I skip my way down to the sand. How extraordinary! I spoke openly to her, and in exchange she spoke openly to me.

On the sand, I slow down to a walk, and then I stop. That's her job. She's simply being courteous and helpful.

I look at the form letter stapled to hers. Radcliffe women are to apply for jobs through the Harvard office from now on, now that Radcliffe is legally part of Harvard. What a pity. I've just learned how to deal with this woman, and now I have to start all over again with someone else. Well. I'll stop off to see them all when I go to Cambridge on my way to New York.

Before I open June's letter, I look at the blue water, roughed up to whitecaps by the wind. I'm glad I wrote to Radcliffe as I did. Even if I hadn't gotten this reply. Or is it that writing as I did is the very thing that got me this reply? Astonishing. Suppose it was. Even so, the only reason for writing as I did was to write what was true. What little I know of what's true. Her reply then falls into the category of unlooked-for gains.

Logos is already down to the water's edge when I slit open June's letter. I watch the gulls rise into the air at his approach and then I turn to the neat handwriting on the thin buff paper. She can't have me there at Christmas. I fly through the rest of the pages: ". . . not really any room . . . Christmas is for children, anyway."

Christmas here. No. No, I'll think of someone else in Cambridge to go to. Who? No one. Maybe having Logos there last time was too much for her. Her cat had to hide from him. Maybe I'm just very boring, going around and around this old circle.

God damn it. *"God damn it!"*

I crumple the letter into a ball and stuff it into my pocket.

"Logos!" I pivot around and take great strides up the cobblestone hill, my hands in my pockets, my head down, not even looking to see whether Logos is with me. I don't care. I have to stay here for Christmas. There's no place else to go.

The cool, dark, smoky first taste of the bourbon becomes a fence between the ugly news and what to do until I leave for the New York meetings. Seven days. They will never end.

It occurs to me that I've been waiting ever since I came here. Waiting for what? Someone to find me? Something to begin? But no one has come and nothing has begun. Like the man in Henry James' short story who had the feeling that something extraordinary was in store for him and who, for thirty years, discussed it with a woman whom he never married but who willingly talked about it with him for all that time. Until one day, when he was very old, he understood that the thing that set him apart from other men was that nothing whatever would happen to him.

Like me. I've walked around the periphery but I've never gotten in. Waiting: for someone to come out and show me what it is to be a human being? For someone to take me inside where it's warm?

But it could only have been a couple of days at June's, and then I'd be out on the world again, looking for the next haven. I've spent almost two months here telling myself every day that I'm alone, that there's no one anywhere in the world who is connected to me. But I'm still lying to myself, because I haven't believed it. Now I have to start believing it.

I pour another glass of bourbon. Tomorrow. I can't look at it anymore today. Today I'm going to drink myself to sleep.

19

I've been waiting ever since I can remember. The only difference between James' man and me is that I've discovered at thirty-seven what took him till sixty to learn: that nothing, nothing, nothing is going to happen.

All the men. The degree. The years of bending over books. Teaching. The theater. All the hours of talk. Nothing? Nothing compared with the thing I've been waiting for. Which is?

I take up my coat and hat, and pull on my boots. Logos goes down the driveway and chooses our direction.

The tide is beginning to come in. We have an hour before it will drive us back to the dunes. I let Logos romp where he pleases.

Larry.

The Sunday people came down to our beach at Malibu during low tide and walked out to the big rock where they sat all day, fishing. When the tide started to come in, late in the afternoon, they showed no signs of noticing. I kept looking toward them as I lay on the sand reading. "Don't you think we should let them know the tide is coming in?"

"Little mother, stop worrying. You can't fish without knowing when the tide is coming in."

"Maybe they don't know how strong the tide is here."

"Maybe they don't know this is Sunday." He screwed up his face in the imitation of me that always made me laugh and headed up the stairway to his house on stilts that overhung the sand. On the stairs he stopped to talk to someone. I went back to my book. Fifteen minutes later he was still talking, and a wind was moving the tide in even faster.

"Larry," I called to him. "Tell them about the tide."

He looked out at the water, then shrugged to Barbara and came back down the stairs to placate his demanding female. He strolled down to the water's edge and made a megaphone of his hands to shout to the people. They waved back; they couldn't hear. He came to sit next to me on the sand, but he kept watching them. A hundred feet or so of water would separate the big rock from the beach when the tide was in. "They'll be all right," he said, more to his own worry than to me. His inclination was to let other people handle their own problems; mine was to spare them pain. In a few minutes, he went down to call to them again. There was a lot of shouting, and then I saw the people gathering their equipment together. Larry walked toward me very fast, stripping off his sweatshirt in one gesture, removing his watch for me to hold.

"They can't swim," he said. He turned, and in two steps was in the water, swimming. He brought them in, hanging to his back, one by one: the man's wife first, his son, his father, the man last. By the time he went back for the man, I couldn't believe he'd have enough breath. Larry swam-carried him, then took them all up to his place, giving them towels, sweatshirts, pants. By then, they could begin to laugh. Then suddenly he said, "You left your gear out there." From the windows we could see the fishing poles on the rock. No one said a word. He swam back out one more time and retrieved them, and soon the people went on their way.

"I'm a little tired, yes," he said, grinning, but in half an hour he was ready to go somewhere again: a drive, out to dinner, visiting—I don't remember.

I hear Dr. Kant's words echo: "You wanted him to rescue you, too."

"From what?"

"You tell me."

He was a good man, kind, generous. He could make me laugh. He knew so many people in a place where I knew almost no one. And they liked him, they welcomed him. But I hated the way they laughed at him when he was drunk. He seemed not to know that they were laughing at something other than the stories he was telling.

One whole year. What did we talk about all that time? He knew I wouldn't stay: I had told him about Stan. Yet I cried the whole day I was packing my things to come east for a third year at Harvard. Why?

The tide reaches almost to my boots. I call Logos and we cross the dunes. Logos leads me to the wooden stairway with the two broken steps halfway up. I start to climb behind him.

I always expect to be slapped when I fall in love. I'm holding one hand out to give something, but I'm keeping the other hand close to my face, ready to protect myself from being struck. Pushed away. From having the thing I'm giving thrown back at me. No one will take the thing I'm giving. Simply take it.

Will love me, even though he knows me.

I sit on the top step of the stairway and look out over the water. No, that's not it. Larry knew me and loved me anyway. He knew all the terrible things I do, just to have my own way. He merely teased me about them. I lectured him, but he teased me.

Yet instead of loving him, I loved Stan. All the time I was with Larry, I was waiting for a chance to be with Stan. As soon as there was the remotest possibility that Stan might be available, I was off and running. Running after him. To be slapped.

Holy Christ, it will be forever beyond me.

The afternoon drags toward sunset. I try to read. Nothing can catch my attention. If there were only somewhere I could go to rest. What a joke. I have access to an entire summer resort, and I'm wishing I could go somewhere else. I *am* in a place where I can rest, but resting is not an option open to me.

I pace off the living room. Why have the men I've loved left me? I'm no closer to understanding it than I was after each breakup. Something's wrong with me that makes them go away, and I can't see it. I've torn it apart, I've stared at it close up, but it keeps escaping me.

Try another ploy. If it's so close to me that I can't see it by looking at it directly, I can try to look at it wrong-end-to. Instead of thinking about the men who have left me, I could think about the ones *I've* left. Why I went to them in the first place. Like Stan, or George, they must have held out a promise to me of something. What was it?

Why, for example, did I stay so long with Larry? He loved me. He wanted to take care of me. I was safe with him. Until I understood that his drinking was undoing whatever security he was able to give me while he was sober.

Evan. That lasted two years. The only way I could break it off was to apply for a fellowship to study in France. I remember the day Radcliffe told me I could go. Their letter came in the same mail with the first letter telling me that Daddy was sick, that he had stayed home from work, that he'd need an operation. I called Ohio to get the details but no one seemed to know very much. I was terrified that he wouldn't have a good doctor. I spent the afternoon on the phone: calling my doctor to get his recommendations about Ohio doctors, calling one of them, calling Weck, calling the airport.

Evan came by with red roses to celebrate my fellowship. He didn't really expect me to go to Europe, but then he didn't know how much I had been counting on the fellowship to extricate myself from him.

I went to my father the next day. When I returned a week later, the rose petals had all fallen off, forming a circle around the base of the jar I had stuck them into between phone calls that day.

Waiting for what? The question stays with me through the day, weighting my thoughts like a strip of lead encircling my forehead.

> Home is where, when you go there,
> They have to take you in.

There's no such place. Home is wherever I happen to live. Like Stan's story about filling out some forms to get the fellowship funds for his summer in Austria.

"Where is your home?" the administrator asked.

Stan gave him the address of the graduate dormitory.

"No," said the man. "Where does your family live?"

"Oh," said Stan. "My family lives in Sacramento. I thought you wanted to know where my home is."

"I do," said the man. "Where in Sacramento?"

"No," said Stan. "My home is here in Cambridge."

"Listen," and the man's tone became very firm. "Where would you want the body sent?"

"Oh," said Stan, and I could hear the special soft note he must have used. "Is that what you call home?"

A place to stay. Not just to go to, but to be able to stay without having to move. I think of Lotte, who, at the end of our first Radcliffe year, had her name and address printed on stationery.

"I envy your having that," I said.

She looked at me curiously. "But you could have it, too. It doesn't cost very much."

"I suppose not. But you know that you're going to live here long enough to order that stationery and to use it up."

"Well, not so long. Probably only this year and next."

"But Lotte, that's very long."

Two months later she was engaged.

"See, Timmie, I won't use it up after all."

I laughed with her. "Maybe I should order some to challenge fate."

Not just a place, but a person to be there with me. No, he himself would be the home. No matter how often we might have to move, I'd be taking my home with me. Yes. That's home: an unbreakable connection with a man who would never go away from me.

We. Another word I try so hard to use and can't.

Where did I leave Joyce Cary's *A House of Children?* Upstairs. I bring it down, and, sitting on the couch, flick back to the early pages. The memoir of his childhood that the boy, Evelyn, narrates is peopled by "we," implying a context of utter security for his growing up. I'm reading of foreign customs in a foreign language. When Evelyn says "we," he speaks from a center whose stability he never needs to question. "We": he and his father; he and his brother; he and his cousin; he and four of his cousins; he and ten of his cousins. Almost never "I": "we." Even when the child says "I," he trails long lines of his connections with all the others.

I've always been "I": separate. Particularly separate from the members of my family. Except Daddy. Yet even he seemed remote from that warring household. "We" implies someone who will stand behind you no matter what; someone who has a right to your loyalty, no price attached, and who will give you his or hers on the same basis.

I see. That's what kept me climbing into beds all these years, ready for the next man, the next time. It was the possibility that he might become a "we" with me.

I'm not crying very hard. It's not a strange reason for people to go to bed together: seeking human warmth. But, oh, it's so brief. And afterward the cold sets in and raises the stakes so high for the next time.

I should provision myself with books. And a bottle: it will be my Christmas present to myself. And groceries for five more days. Six, counting today.

Six days of dragging this body around, feeding it, resting it. And then? And then I go to New York to ask philosophers I don't know for a job that I don't even know I want. And then? And then I come back here to do this again. But I can't stay here. I'll be out of money in a month. And it's too much to have to bear.

But I can't start something new because I don't know what to start. Oh, let me out!

Yes, out: into town, at least. Swiftly collecting my wallet, boots, coat, I am startled by knocking on the door. No car in front of the house. Or in the driveway. I slide quietly around the table, and from that acute angle I see Ralph.

"Hello. Come in. Where's your car?" We shake hands.

"I walked. I came by way of Shimmo and Polpis."

"Where's that? Sit down. Will you have coffee?" Am I pleased or annoyed to have him here?

"I don't drink coffee."

"Oh, yes, I forgot." I pour myself a cup, searching for something to say. We sit at the little table.

"Shimmo is very beautiful. Haven't you been all the way around the island yet?"

"No, I stay out here, except to do my shopping. In fact, I was just going into town. Do you want a lift?"

He shakes his head. "No, I want to be on foot today. I came to say good-bye. The people I'm staying with are going to Washington for Christmas, and I'm going with them."

Even he won't be here. I thank him for sending me a Christmas card. He is pleased to see it propped on the windowsill with some others.

"I've brought you a present. Nothing much, but I thought you ought to have some, in case you haven't tried it." He pulls a glass jar out of his jacket pocket and places it on the table. The label reads BEACH PLUM JAM.

I'm touched. "Let's have some right now."

"No, it's for you."

I thank him, and then remember I wanted to talk to him after all. "I was going to call you to ask your advice about my puppy. I have to go to New York for a few days, and I can't take him with me. I thought maybe you'd know someone who would take care of him for me." I was hoping *he* would.

He looks at me scornfully. "Put him in the SPCA."

"Why do you say it like that?"

"The SPCA won't play with him the way you do, but he'll be safe there. They'll feed him the way he should be fed, and they'll put him outside in a run a couple of times a day, and for the rest of the time he'll be safe in a cage."

"A cage? Are you serious? This puppy has had the full run of Siasconset and three miles of beach ever since we've been here. He can't go into a cage."

"But in a cage, no car will run over him. He won't get into a fight with another dog. He won't turn over trash cans and eat garbage. If you'd start thinking about him as a dog, you'd save yourself and him a lot of grief. I never saw a woman who didn't ruin a dog." He reaches for his jacket and then for the handle of the door.

"Wait, Ralph. What did I do?"

"You didn't do anything. I have to go. I have to help these people pack. We're leaving in the morning."

"But you're mad at me. That's no way to give someone a Christmas present." Why do I even want to persuade him out of his mood?

He zips up his jacket and stands with his hands in the pockets at his chest. "You're right. Merry Christmas. And good luck."

We shake hands. "Come over when you get back. You can show me the island."

"Go see it yourself. Nothing's stopping you. I probably won't come back. Not for a long time, anyway."

"Oh." What does it matter?

"Yes, I'll probably stay and work in Washington. These people can get me a job while I go back to school."

"It sounds fine. Good luck to you, then, too."

He stands in the doorway for a moment, and then he's gone. How many thousands of people have I met and parted from? They're wherever I go. Wandering, like me. Talk to them once, twice, a dozen times, and then we each go our way. Write once in a while for a few months, then never write, never hear from them again. And there's always another one at the next place.

But is there anything else? Won't there ever be anything else?

I think the librarians had higher hopes for me than fiction and dog books when I first introduced myself. The pile of books I check out today is high: ten. Two for each day until I leave: one to read, one to find worthless. The librarian looks at me curiously as she stamps them for me. She thinks it strange that someone would be reading books at Christmastime. Oh, lady, so do I.

After breakfast I lie down on the couch and read. I know I shouldn't. In half an hour I slam the book shut and throw it on the floor. Okay. I'll think. About?

What I'm waiting for. Why I've spent so much time with men I knew weren't right for me. Why I still want to marry Stan. Or is it George?

Maybe if I just say it over and over again, out loud, I'll hear how ridiculous it is: I don't know which of two men I want to marry when neither of them has ever asked me, nor likely ever will.

Why not? What's wrong with me? Am I not smart? Thoughtful of their needs? Attractive? A storyteller to amuse them? What haven't I done for them that they might not even have known they wanted done for them, in bed or out? That's giving, isn't it? That's what the thing between a man and a woman is supposed to be, isn't it?

Supposed to. What is this "supposed to"? Another rule. But this one is mine. I've worked it out over the years. Haven't I? Isn't it mine?

The day hurts so much more when the sun beats into this room in the morning than when the day is gray. The mere fact of the sunshine promises something that I can never get my hands on. When the morning is gray, there's no hope anyway.

"Come here, Sweet Puppy." Logos, not quite asleep, stretches, then slowly gets to his feet and ambles over to me. "I've been no friend to you these past few days." I rub his ears. He closes his eyes and shoves his head closer for me to reach that one deep place that's the source of one special pleasured groan. A dog's life: you eat and sleep and get your ears rubbed and your belly scratched; you get taken for long walks; you can chase the gulls, dig huge holes in the sand, run after sticks that a friend throws for you. And, if pressed, you probably could do most of that for yourself.

Could I do that? Live a life of eating and sleeping and running after a stick that I throw myself? Maybe that's all there is.

Why did I spend two years with a man that I can't even bring myself to think about now? Or one year with a man that I can think of only if I remember how unafraid he was of so many things that frightened me? At least there was something I respected about Larry. With Evan, after the beginning, there was nothing. Two years.

I lean back on the railing of the bench that suspends me over the sand, thrusting me out toward the water, yet above it and distant.

Two of the worst years in a decade of bad years. Stan married and gone. All the people who had entered Harvard with me being given fellowships and grants and awards, but none for me. Jean newly married, involved in a fresh life, both she and her husband polite about Evan but firm in not wanting to spend time with him. Marilyn gone to Boston; it could have been a day's drive away, for all we saw of one another. Friends gone; Stan gone; work a frustration, an empty way to fill endless days.

A shudder sweeps through me. It's not this morning: it was six years ago. Why did I stay with him? There was no one else.

Why did I stay?

Strange to see nothing at all on an expanse of water as broad as I'm looking at now. The gulls must have found the wake of a fishing boat to follow. No person on the entire line of the beach. It must be two miles that I can see in either direction from my perch. From here even the waves don't seem to roar. No one. Nothing. So utterly, totally, unbelievably quiet, and I the only living being in sight.

No, Logos is here. I reach down to stroke the tawny fur.

He held me while I cried.

I catch my throat to stop the words. While I cried. Dear God, how I cried. Some mornings it would take me an hour with cold wash-cloths to bring down the swelling of my eyelids. But nothing could uproot the terror that carried within it other terrors adhering to-gether, waiting only for a chance to burst out, one after the other, as the hours of each day plodded on. Toward a night without sleep; or with nightmares, if sleep; and with tears, no matter which. If I could have cried only when I got into bed, I might have rescued some sleep from the night. But I'd sleep, then wake up at three o'clock and cry until dawn, then sleep an hour before the day had to begin. Or I'd sleep the night and wake up at five, and cry until I had to begin working with the cold compresses in order to look human by the time I had to leave the house.

And he held me. Whenever he was there, whenever we weren't screaming our detestation of each other, thereby adding one more thing to cry about: that even being with him was futile. Who else would have me? How could I know unless I broke it off with him, then, that day, that minute? But would anyone else hold me?

I sit forward abruptly. Larry held me, too. And Jurgen. And Jack. And Tony. I clasp my head to keep it from whirling away. My thoughts fly back through years of men. Not just the ones I stayed with at length. The casual ones, too. And George, even George. Even the men who mattered to me. They all gave me that: they held me while I cried.

And what, please, what, oh what, was I crying about? Different things. There are surely a lot of different things to cry about when you're me.

Aren't there? There's the fact that I didn't know whether I was a good actress. Or smart enough for philosophy. Or beautiful.

Why did I have to *cry,* though? I *had* to cry.

My heart is pounding now so strongly that I wrap my arms around myself to keep it in. I had to cry. I would get drunk so I could tell the man about the terrors that haunted me. So I could cry. So he would hold me.

Oh. Not that they held me while I cried, but that I cried so they would hold me. And once they did, I knew they would from then on.

Hold me? Cry so they would hold me? What does that have to do with loving a man? That's what a mother does to a child.

No.

I stand at the railing and hold on with both hands. And push. And try to lift it up so I can bang it down. *"No!"* I howl the sound and kick the post, and Logos backs away, then runs down the stairs, his tail between his legs. *"No!"* I stare after him even as I scream. I know my face is frozen into place; my throat is torn by the voice that can't come out for all the tears that get in its way. I bang the wood until my hand stops feeling anything at all, and then I sit down.

How do I live through the next minute? And now the next. And after that? Time has stopped being continuous. It opens up into little holes that I fall into, then climb out of, only to fall into the next.

I went to bed with men, looking for her to hold me. I was an actress and then a philosopher, to get her to look at me.

My head is cracking open. Unless I'm very careful, I may not be able to hold it together until I get home. Until I get to where I live.

20

Now I know what I came here to find out. There's nothing further to learn. Or do.

Thirty-seven years of being blind. Deaf. Marking time on the same spot. A little girl looking for her mother to hold her. Everything else is fraud.

I lie quietly until I realize that the room is growing lighter.

Well, I've slept my sleep. I'll get up now. I forget why.

I stay in my robe to make coffee. I try to remember why I should dress. The coffee filters through while I lean against the sink to find an answer. The coffeepot grows cold before I look for a cup, and I strike a match to light the flame under the pot. Each motion requires my most concentrated attention, yet when I complete it I wonder what I've just done. The coffee boils before I notice that I'm still standing next to the stove.

The reheated coffee tastes vile, but when I think of making a fresh pot, I stay in the little wooden chair and drink the cupful I've poured. When the cup is empty, I push it away and stay at the table.

She is the extraordinary thing I've been waiting for.

I look out on the gray day. Logos lies asleep near my chair. He knows already that we'll be quiet for a long time.

She should have loved me. How unlovable could I have been? She made me feel that I had to deserve her love, and that I never did. So of course I was too worthless to deserve anyone else's. Of course I was always looking to some indeterminate but very severe standard that I had to meet in everything I attempted.

If she had loved me, all the things I dislike about her wouldn't have mattered. But I made myself forget that she didn't love me, and I spent my growing-up years fighting her on every level and every issue. I used to hate her for all the things she is as a person. Now I see I hated her because she didn't love me.

What remains, then? She's still that person I dislike. There's simply no point in hating her anymore. No point in having anything at all to do with her. She couldn't love me. I can't sit cross-legged. Irreducible facts, both. Too bad that a little girl can't understand that.

In a way, my life has been one unified whole, after all. I've thought of myself as being a different person depending upon what I was doing, who was talking to me, where I was. A different person to each man; different when I talk to a teacher from when I talk to a friend; different depending upon whether I'm walking through the snow or walking into an expensive restaurant. Yet all the fragments of that life have been tied into one bundle by one single strand that held me together without my knowing it: to find some way of getting her to love me. It's a way of being whole that nullifies thirty-seven years.

Yesterday, today, from now on, I cut the cord. The cord. Of course.

See what happens when I cut it. All the little pieces that were stuck to it fall away, revealing what it's been holding together: nothing. Empty, hollow, nothing.

Is it possible to replace it with what I want?

Oh, creature, who is this "I" that I speak of? The only "I" there is is a little girl, kept a dwarf for thirty years by a need that has only to be said out loud to be discarded. I grew up all around it, festering around a core that I didn't know existed. To remove the core is to remove the whole growth that it supported. I'm now cut back to the bare ground.

I don't know how to want: my wantings have been guided by that core. There is no Me unpoisoned by that need.

I wander into the living room and find my book on the couch. I lie down to read. Half a dozen times throughout the morning I change my position. My stomach grumbles to be fed. I read again. Sometime during the afternoon I put on some clothes and take Logos for a walk down the road to the field on the corner, then turn around and come back to the house again.

How can I think of going to New York to look for a teaching job? It's all I can do to find reasons to eat, to dress, to get out of bed. I can't imagine what reasons could get me on a plane, could let me ask a lot of people who have never helped me before to help me now. To help me do what? Find a job that will give me money to keep me fed and dressed. But that's not enough to get me out of bed each day. First I have to find a reason for doing that.

Have to? What can that mean?

Logos scrambles out from under the bed and sits looking at me, head cocked, puzzled at my silence and immobility. He comes over to me and sticks his nose under the covers, looking for my hand. He takes it, placing his teeth very lightly on my skin and, moving backward, starts to pull me with him. This morning I throw back the covers without a word and take him to the outside door.

What to do with this day?

When Logos is ready to come in I go back upstairs, raise the bedroom shades, stuff some pillows at my back, and sit up in bed drinking coffee, looking out at the moor.

Thirty-seven years old and ignorant. A rotten end for someone who wants to know and understand. Or so I've said. I've also said a lot of other things that I've found not to be true. Or rather, each time I find out what I mean by all the things I've said, I find at the same time that they're not true.

I haven't really lived this life that's lasted thirty-seven years. I've only played at living it, pretending I've been alive, saying and doing things to let other people believe I'm alive. But the joke's on me. Because now that I've stopped playing the game, there isn't anything real to take its place. I'm not even capable of recognizing what I'd be looking at if I were to come upon something that wasn't a game.

Ignorant: without a basis for judging the importance of any action, mine or anyone else's. Worse than ignorant: without a clue about how to begin finding a basis.

I think back to rereading Burckhardt's *Renaissance* in Berkeley last summer. I wanted to see whether the sections on the education of women had withstood all the years since high school when I chose them to guide the course of my own education. To be taught, as men were taught, whatever there was to be learned; to speak on equal terms with any person; to read everything of value ever written; to see everything beautiful ever made; to be at home anywhere in the world. To do away with all barriers that looking and listening and understanding could remove.

God knows I tore away anything that threatened to confine me. Even at fifteen, when my mother's highest goal for me was to become a dental assistant and marry a nice Jewish boy, my best friend was a gentile.

Swallowing some coffee, I suddenly choke on a giggle, remembering Jack's offer the day after I got my degree: "Listen. I know some boys. I'll call them up and tell them I have a nice Jewish doctor for them to meet."

But I had to break down the barrier that being Jewish meant to me. "You don't *look* Jewish." It used to be my reward from some new friend whom I had finally decided to "tell." Not looking Jewish let me be with people who might have chosen not to be with me, if they had known; it also kept me wondering what they'd do if they ever found out. I never brought the subject up, and I knew a thousand ways to avoid answering the direct question.

And then I, poor twenty-year-old, lost Geoffrey because of it. Not that he himself was anti-Semitic. Oh, no. I had told him and he had kept on dating me, anyway, hadn't he? Told him? I confessed it to him, and stood waiting for him to walk away. He didn't walk away; he even helped me keep the secret. I was grateful to him until the day he told me it was over, as we sat in the bar at the officers' club. "They've found out about you now," he said. How did "they" find out? I don't remember now. But it would be too much of a strain on me, he said, to be among them, now that they knew.

Months of crying later, I got the thing straight. It wasn't the loss of the glorious man; it wasn't even the injustice of losing him for something I didn't believe in. It was that he wasn't a glorious man if that was his reason for leaving me.

After that I used not-looking-Jewish as a political weapon. I could lead people into saying all the hateful things they believed about Jews and then turn to them, smiling, to say: "But of course I'm Jewish." Or so I used to do, when winning that kind of argument mattered.

It's difficult to remember that it ever mattered. Religion isn't a problem to me. So far as religious belief is concerned, I have none; so far as identification with a group is concerned, I belong nowhere.

So the religious barriers have been dissolved. And the color barriers. And the intellectual barriers. And, even though I have no money, there are no social barriers to me.

Oh, yes, Burckhardt. The surprise, then, of rereading those pages twenty years later and discovering that I had forgotten what purpose that kind of education had for fifteenth-century Italian women: not glory for themselves, but to render them suitable companions for Renaissance men. It was the wrong point to forget. I had been looking for the glory for myself.

One more mistake: to have misconstrued the purpose of my entire education. Not that the mistake matters. It was a fraud, in any case, now that I know that all I ever wanted was to have my mother love me. That all I ever wanted from a man was to have him hold me while I cried, and that what I was crying about was that he wasn't my mother.

I get out of bed and wash my face and brush my teeth and put my clothes on. It's ten already. I've used up an hour and a half. There are only twelve hours left to get through before I can even think of getting back to bed again.

I read. We walk. I don't pick up my mail: I can't bear hearing Mr. Morris wish me Merry Christmas, or to have to say it to him.

At three I stand in the middle of the living room, equally distant from all my sources of diversion. I could call someone. Who? I could read. No, I can't stay with the pages. I could write a letter. Isn't there someone I can connect with, someone I can pretend is sitting across the table from me and listening as I talk?

"Pretend!" I shout, "No more pretending!"

Logos lifts his head from his paws, watching me where he lies at the fireplace. I can't even play with him.

I can have a drink. I pour enough bourbon to cover the ice, and then, when I'm sure it has the edge of a chill, I take one long swallow until I feel it in the depths of my chest. Yes, this will move the day along till night.

Why should Christmas Eve mean anything to me? It's been twelve years since we had the apartment in Chicago, and we had it for only three years. Or was it four? But Laurel and Pat made Christmas Eve into something having to do with human warmth, and I've thought of it that way ever since.

Another long swallow leaves only the ice clinking in the glass, still unmelted. I bring the bottle into the living room, gloss the ice with bourbon again, and place the bottle on the lamp table next to the couch.

It hasn't *been* that way since. Look at all the Christmas Eves in between. Last year in San Francisco, wandering the streets with the boy who drove me there, trying to find a restaurant open, ending up at last in a New Yorky delicatessen, eating hot pastrami. And the Christmas Eve before that? In New York, alone in Shirley's apartment while she was off skiing in Kitzbühel. And before that, alone in my apartment in Cambridge, my Christmas tree made of gold and silver ribbons pasted onto the wall in the shape of branches, a tree admired by Marvin, newly met, who wouldn't be in Cambridge for the holidays. And before that? The railroad station in Munich, eating a bowl of soup at a table crowded with laborers on their way home.

I lean back and try to remember more. All the way to 1958, and still no fellow feeling. The years before that jumble together. Cambridge, New York, Chicago—what difference does it make? I was alone. Christmas Eve is a time for being with families, or with people you love or who love you. Therefore, I'm alone.

The liquor warms my chest and belly. Is there anything for dinner? Maybe. I can't bring it to mind right now. I'm busy trying to think about . . . what? Oh, yes, I know: Why should Christmas Eve be so important to an agnostic, reared as a Jew only in external ways, who has been sitting by herself for the last I don't know how many years? It isn't that I've missed being with Pat and Laurel themselves. Pat and I haven't been friends all this time, and although I kept in touch with Laurel for a time after she married, it was only last summer that I looked her up again.

But something about the *quality* of that time we were together, or of the idea itself, got to me. That's what I miss. That's what I try to reinstate, wherever I am, when this time of year approaches.

The only reason I'm crying now is that I've been pouring bourbon down my throat. I get up to find the box of tissues, and then decide to stay on my feet. I drink again, and dry the tears. Which do not stop.

Go on and cry. It's one more Christmas Eve to be gotten through. Like all the others that are yet to come.

"No!" I get down on my knees and strike the floor. "No. No. No. No. I can't stand it anymore!" I lay my head on the cushion of the chair next to the fireplace, and bring my arms up to cradle my head, to close my ears off from what I'm saying, to shut my eyes against what I see: Christmas Eves to come, a thirty-year, forty-year chain of them, empty, like this one. Not a chain of unconnected Christmas Eves, but an endless chain of days. Christmas Eves are only one day in each group of 365 empty days. Not only Christmas Eve, but all the other days, too, will be like this day.

Why must it go on?

I bring my head up slowly from the cushion. This is the shadowy thought that's been skipping around the circumference of all my thinking for these two months. I've merely said it out loud at last. I climb to my feet and take two steps to the mantel, where I lean, facing the center of the room, Logos nearby watching.

Thirty more years of having no one who matters to me. Thirty years of days in which I can't feel anything going on inside me, in which I'd always wonder whether the response I was making to a situation was genuine or whether it was one more piece of acting. Thirty years of not knowing what I want to do, because I don't know how to want, what wanting is. Thirty years of getting in and out of men's beds unsatisfied, with no one man who belongs to me.

To die is only to stop breathing. There's neither something to be afraid of after my last breath nor something to hope for.

Like what I leave behind: nothing, no one. I haven't been doing important work that would forever remain unfinished. Nor will any person's life be unhappier for my death. Even Daddy can't mourn for me. Daddy: no one loves him as I do, and no one loves me as he does. As he used to, before. Two months after he and I are gone, who will remember that either of us had lived?

So I've reached a neutral point: it makes no difference whether I live or die. I'm afraid of nothing that lies ahead of me, and I leave nothing behind me. No more counting pennies, asking someone to put me up until I get money, waiting for some man, wondering whether I'm smart or beautiful. No more asking anyone for anything at all.

I sit down on the couch, head back, hands clasped loosely on my lap. To have thought myself so big, to have found myself so small. To be nothing: to be qualified to do nothing, to be capable of doing nothing, to be needed for doing nothing, to want to do nothing.

The light outside has started to dim. There is no sound in the living room, except Logos' breathing and mine. Logos. I'll think of someone to give him to. Ralph. Someone.

I walk to the door to let Logos out and stand watching the darkness gather, letting the cold air hit me to keep me awake until he returns. I could just go into the garage, close the door behind me, get into the car, and turn on the ignition. No one ever comes here or phones. It would be a long time before anyone I know would think of looking for me. As though I need confirmation that I won't be missed.

Later. I'm very tired now.

When Logos comes back into the unlighted house, I stumble against him in the kitchen, reach out to find the doorway, let my hand guide me around the corner of the long table against the living-room wall, then follow that edge to its end, where I head up the stairs, Logos clacking behind me, and lie across my bed. I'll rest here for a little while.

I open my eyes in the darkened room. Am I alive? Logos moves as I rear up on the bed to turn on the light. Two o'clock. Shielding my eyes, I see that I'm fully dressed. I wash my face and brush my teeth. I didn't eat last night. Is it worth feeding this body?

I make some hot cocoa, and find a bowl of tuna salad in the refrigerator. My first meal on Christmas Day, 1962. Or my last, ever.

I've crossed a bridge unlike any other. I'm no longer among the living but among those who are about to die. From this side I can look back at what it was to be alive. All those people whose approval I sought: none of them is here now. The half-dozen people I've thought of as my friends: not here either. I'm looking my own death in the face, and there's no one to stand here with me. Alone dying, as I was alone living.

From this side, how can it matter what anyone else thinks? From this side, how can it matter what I look like? From this side, how can anything at all matter?

Is now the time, then?

Is it?

21

The morning is overcast and cold. I turn my chair to face the wall of windows. Yes, the ground I covered yesterday was bourbon-soaked, but no, none of it was false. There are two things worth having: a work that would absorb me and a man to love who would love me. I have neither one.

If I live, what would the life I'd have to live from now on be like?

I was able to tolerate all my little jobs because they didn't really matter; they were only to keep me fed and sheltered while I studied acting or worked for my degree. Ignore the fact that my purposes were fraudulent. I believed in them at the time; they kept me working, more or less, toward something that seemed worth doing. But what will it be like now that I know I have nothing to work for, nothing that would give point to the next job and the job that would inevitably come after that? It's been bad enough to get through the days thinking I was doing something important. What will it be like if the job is all there is, if I'm earning money only to stay alive?

And men. What will it be like to be with a man when I know that I as myself am not involved with him as himself, but that I as a female am involved with him only in his maleness? I don't even know how to *be* with a man. At thirty-seven, how can I learn?

The forecast for living.

Have I left anything out?

I tilt my chair backward, my hands clasped behind my head. I am aware of a lucidity I have never before possessed. Crying or smashing my fist against something seems irrelevant. Only thinking seems right to do. I have only to decide whether my life is to continue or whether it is to end.

But suppose there's something worth having that I haven't considered.

I wish I could present the whole course of my reasoning to someone very smart. Someone who knows philosophy, so that he won't waste time on pieties. One hour with someone who knows how to listen, and then I could be sure I haven't left something out.

No, that's asking for someone to be Socrates to me. I never knew such a person while I was studying philosophy. What makes me think I could find one now?

Abe.

My feet come down to the floor. I learned what teaching was by watching him conduct his seminars at UCLA. He wanted his students to know what they themselves thought: I watched him draw it out of them. I could almost see them stop showing him how smart they were and start trying really to answer his questions. He and the student became a single mind at work on the same problem. And he had the same kind of interchange with all of them, not just the bright ones.

He's my reason for going to the New York meetings. He always attends. He'll let me talk to him about this.

I could see Mo, too. He isn't incisive, like Abe, but he has his eye on what's important. Even though he's a clinical psychologist.

Yes, between the two of them, I'll find out where the flaws are in my thinking. If they'll see me.

Logos runs the length of the fairway and then, since I'm so far behind, runs back to be with me again. We reach the circular wooden bench and I sit, my back to the clubhouse, looking out over the course.

Am I going to Abe and Mo as authorities? No, they'll serve as checks on my thinking, that's all. By saying it out loud to them, I myself will hear how it sounds. Because they're different men, each of them will find something different to point out to me. If I've made a really big mistake, both of them will see it. They can't change what I already understand, but they might be able to show me that I haven't properly assessed its relevance.

"Logos!" He's not to be seen. I start toward the clubhouse to find him, then walk faster, calling him all the way. I run across the paved road, then stop at the edge of the fairway. A man clutching a golf club stands fifty feet away, staring down at Logos, who is sniffing his shoes.

"Hello," I call out. I get to see a human being on Christmas Day after all.

He barely glances at me. All his attention is concentrated on Logos. "Is this your dog?"

"Yes." I'm puzzled by the intensity of his question.

"Please get him away from me. Please. I'm afraid of dogs."

I'm twenty feet away from the man, but now I walk fast. "He's only a puppy."

"It doesn't matter. Please take him away."

The man is almost wrapped up in his own arms, clasping his body to shield himself from the threat. His face is pale, and I'm close enough now to see perspiration on his upper lip. I reach down to catch hold of Logos' collar and drag him back toward me, away from the man.

His hand shakes as he wipes his face with his handkerchief. "A dog bit me three years ago, and I've been afraid of them ever since. I know I shouldn't be, but I can't control it." He tells me the story and I watch his face as he talks. I see that he's apologizing for showing his fear to me, a woman, and for being afraid of what is obviously a puppy. I start to question him about the details of the incident, but he plainly wishes me gone and my puppy with me.

My hand still on Logos' collar, I start to move away from the man. "We'll go in this direction." I let go of the collar at the same moment that I start running toward the lighthouse. The puppy is after me instantly. He builds up his speed and shoots past me on the road. I turn to wave to the man, but he is already absorbed in his game again. I have restored peace on his bit of earth, and to him, goodwill.

"Hey, Logos!" He slows down and looks back at me. "Let's go this way." I swing around on the road and start toward the path that leads in front of all the houses that line the bluff. We've been out so long, and we haven't seen the ocean yet.

I throw off my coat and hat and feel my cold face with my cold hands. I sit in the kitchen chair, taking off my boots. The phone rings. I stop with one boot off to listen to the unfamiliar sound, and then I race up the stairs. I grab the receiver and sit on the bed in one motion. "Hello?"

"Hello, Dr. Koller."

No friend, then. The voice is thin and young, a girl, very far away. I feel my stomach cave in on my disappointment. "Yes, this is Dr. Koller. Who's calling?"

"I shouldn't have expected you to recognize my voice. It's Stephanie."

Dear God, that a child I befriended in Santa Barbara last year is the only person in the world to have thought of me today. "Stephanie! Are you at home?"

"Yes, my parents are gone for a while. I told them I was going to call you and that I'd pay for it out of my allowance."

"You'll be paying for it for a long time. You shouldn't have done it. How did you find me? It's like something I'd do."

She laughs with pleasure. "Being like you is the greatest compliment I can get."

How can I tell this little girl that being like me is something to be avoided? She doesn't know that she wishes I were her mother. But Stephanie, the only mother you can have is the one who wasn't able to care you existed at the very time when that was what you needed to know.

"Are you working there, Alice? What are you doing there?"

Suddenly I'm glad for the human connection, however frail, and I talk to the child for the few minutes that I know will please her without being too expensive for her.

"My dad will be at the New York meetings. Are you going? Talk to him so he can tell me how you look and what you're doing."

Astonishing. "Will Abe be with him, do you think?"

"Yes, they're going together."

"Stephanie, hang up now. Thank you for thinking of me."

I place the receiver back on its cradle and sit on the edge of the bed. Abe will be there. I have the one piece of news I needed to know. Merry Christmas, Stephanie.

Throughout a day of errands, I think of myself as on leave from what I must still decide. It keeps me wondering about the purposes of each of my actions. Why am I bothering to shop for just the right scarf for the blue sweater? Why did I fix the hem of the green skirt this morning? It cuts my words to one-tenth of the quantity I ordinarily use in my encounters with clerks: in the grocery store, in the clothing shop, in the drugstore, at the gas station, at the airport where I pick up my ticket for tomorrow. Saying only what I need to say teaches me that until today I've been playing the Gracious Buyer role, acting even on Nantucket. But I don't have to show these people, or anyone else, anything whatever. I simply remember myself as I was yesterday morning: alone, prepared to die. I find myself measuring everything I say or do today against the clarity of that hour, and I come upon a strange quietness within me when I compare these motions with that stillness, these sounds with that silence.

I write my will, in the form of a letter to Randall, making him my executor. I surprise myself by writing two pages of instructions for him. It's easy to distribute my few pieces of furniture still stored in New York, my books, my clothes. In setting it out for Randall to understand I use a care I didn't know I had. I give him Logos: he's the only person I know who can afford to keep the puppy and who would also be good to him.

I address an envelope to Randall and fold the pages inside, and then I clear my desk so that the envelope is the only thing lying in sight. It will be the first thing to be seen by anyone entering this room, in case something happens to me on the plane to New York or back. And if I make that trip without an accident, this envelope is ready in case I want it later on.

Through the rest of the evening I'm aware of the envelope lying on the desk. It becomes a focus for a strange new knowledge that I don't remember having before: I've set my life in order, and I don't doubt that Randall will arrange things exactly as I've requested. From now on, anything can happen.

Awake to a wild sound: the alarm clock. Logos scrambles out from under my bed, ears back and quivering. I fumble to shut off the low-pitched buzz, and then I'm out of bed, my arms around the puppy, now sitting, head cocked, puzzled at the abrupt silence from the intruder he never heard before. I tumble him onto the floor to scratch his belly.

Today I leave him for the first time. Today I have to put him into someone else's care. Have to. That means there's something else I'm doing that takes priority over keeping Logos near me. I lean over him and place my face against his chest.

I race him downstairs and let him outside.

Walking on the wet sand at the edge of low tide, I think of what I'll be doing by noon: walking on New York sidewalks, wearing shoes with heels, wearing a skirt, wearing makeup, talking to people I know, being in crowds. There will be the dirt on the streets, the sickening smells, the millions of people who are always between you and wherever you want to go. But here I can stand in the complete silence of this shore. Complete human silence, anyway. Gulls ride the waves a little distance out, and the waves themselves slap gently down.

Logos stands before me, uttering tiny barks. I stoop and rub his ears. "You're right. There's time to think of New York when I'm there. Find me a stick."

His tail begins to wag violently, he throws his paws against my legs to touch base, then he whirls and runs off to search for some prize from the sea. He finds a stick, and although I stand waiting for him to bring it to me to throw, he keeps it in his mouth and flashes back and forth on the sand, eying me as he passes. I know his game: I'm to chase him for the stick. It's a game I never win. This morning I play it anyway. I run him until he drops the stick, sides heaving, and falls onto the sand to rest. I try not to think of the cage that will confine him for all the days I'm gone.

I look at my watch. Time to go home. The watch feels heavy on my wrist. I haven't worn it since we went to Cambridge, and before that, since the first morning I forgot to put it on. Twice now this morning timepieces have dictated what action I shall take.

At the top of the long wooden stairway I stop to look back at the water and the brilliant sky guarding my desolate shore.

All the way home I memorize the look of Logos: the way he moves, the way his fur lies, the melting of his golden eyes whenever he turns his beautiful head in my direction.

At the SPCA office I give Mr. Lema the list of things I want the vet to check while Logos stays there. Then I hand him Logos' leash.

"We'll give him the best seat in the house," Mr. Lema says, and immediately he turns to lead Logos into the room where the cages are stacked one on top of another. Logos, watching me, plants his legs, amazed that I'm not taking him with me. He stands staring at me. All of a sudden he makes one great leap toward me, but Mr. Lema pulls the leash in the other direction. I'm almost out the door, not able to watch, but I turn when I hear Logos protest. I go back inside, past the examining table, into the kennel room. Mr. Lema is lifting Logos off the floor to put him into a cage.

I touch the puppy's head and look at him very hard. "Logos," I say, and then swallow my throat. "Logos, I'll be back."

And then I turn and run. In my car, it's almost impossible to fit the key into the ignition.

22

I hesitate at the edge of the hotel's high-ceilinged mezzanine, then move past pairs and small groups of people, avoiding the thicker clusters in the center, aiming toward the registration tables that line the far wall. People call out greetings to one another; they laugh, they talk. The sounds and movement coalesce into an overarching roar that draws me more closely into the silence I carry within me. Unless I'm watchful, I may lose hold of my connection with it. The game here holds a special danger for me.

"Alice! How are you?"

The man and I shake hands. What *is* his name? I try to place him while he talks. He hasn't seen me since the New Haven meetings. Two years ago. The night I met George.

"Is it so long?" The registration line moves up a few steps.

He's teaching, likes his job, is here only to hear a few papers, see some friends. "How about you, Alice? What are you doing?"

How fast it comes. *Must* I answer that question no matter who asks? I want not to lie. "I'm not doing anything. I thought I might look over the teaching possibilities."

"There's an opening at Hawaii, I know."

Another island. I grin. "Thanks for the news."

By the time I fill out a registration card, my unremembered colleague is talking to someone else. The man behind the desk slips my card into a small file box. "Is that how I find out whether my friends are here?"

"Help yourself." The man shoves the box toward me.

Abe is not registered. I flick through the cards again: George is here; Stan is not. For an instant I close my eyes. What am I doing looking for them? It's Abe I'm here to see. They don't exist.

I slide the box back to the man and turn away. The scatter of men and women in groups, on the stairways, entering and leaving through corridors: What has this to do with me?

I return to the registration desk. "Where are the people who know about jobs?"

The man grins. "Look around you."

"I mean the official people."

"To your right and up that stairway."

The path I carve is slow. I glance into some faces as I pass; semifamiliar ones smile back. I can return a nod or raise an arm to wave without stopping my forward movement. Please don't let me see too many people I know, not at once, not right now when I've just arrived.

A tall and boyish-looking man comes toward me grinning. "Alice!"

"Jan!" We put our arms around each other. "Is Anne with you?" It's good to see him.

"She's here but she's with our millstone up in the room. We take turns guarding her. Kaja won't stay with the baby-sitter the hotel got for us. She screamed for an hour when we tried to leave her this morning." But he seems unmoved.

"They're well, Anne and the baby?"

"Kaja's three now. Not exactly a baby. More like a headache. Yes, they're fine. We lost you last year."

"I lost myself. Are you still at New Hampshire?"

"But not for long. Where are you? Still at that contract research place outside Boston making a fortune?"

"They fired me last July. The man I was working for made a pass that I turned down. Old story. Then I worked in New York for a while. I'm not working now. Not teaching, anyway." It's hard to say what I'm doing, no matter who asks. "Jan, come with me while I check into the job openings."

We link arms and walk up the stairway. People stand ten-deep outside the door. Jan leads me into the room and plants me at a desk. "You start here. I'll see you outside."

A woman hands me a card to fill out. Another damned questionnaire. What did I expect? I look around for a place to write. Portable bulletin boards are propped on tables against the walls. Neat rows of cards tacked to the boards list the details of each job: advantages and requirements, the name of the person to contact and where he can be found nearby. I'm actually considering going to some of these people. Asking them for a job. Talking and listening closely. Trying to convince them to hire me. Please, sir, can I have some more?

"Are you through?" Jan is next to me again.

"I haven't started. I have to fill out this card."

"Do it over here." Jan guides me to an unoccupied spot on the edge of someone's desk. "It's almost two o'clock. Are you going to the philosophy of science session?"

"Nothing else looked very likely."

"Then hurry. Joel is waiting outside. We'll all go together. He knows where all the jobs are, even the ones that aren't listed."

I bend over the card. Name, address, present place of employment. I close my eyes and see Logos running ahead of me on the sand. And then I start filling in the blanks.

As many people stay in their seats talking at the end of the meeting as get up to join the swarm moving out the door.

Jan rises. "Time to relieve Anne."

I look at him. Shall I ask him or shall I wait to let him tell me? Fraud: I want to know, and so I have to pay for it. "Have you seen George yet?"

"Oh, yes, we had lunch together." He hesitates. "Elizabeth is with him."

I make a sound that I think might be a laugh. "So nothing much has changed." Not even me: I'm trying to make Jan think that I don't care.

"He'll probably be at the smoker tonight. I hope to bring Anne. You'll be there?"

I nod, and he's gone.

On the way through the milling crowd, Joel fills me in on a list of openings. I only half listen. Elizabeth is here. How will I see George alone?

"Alice!"

"Alex!" We shake hands. "You take California with you wherever you go."

"What's wrong with this shirt?" He doubles his chin to look down at the wild pattern.

"Don't let anybody tell you. Is Abe with you?"

"Yes, he's here somewhere." He looks around.

Find him for me now.

Alex turns back to me. "I have a letter for you from my daughter. I'll bring it to the smoker tonight. You have a real fan in Stephanie."

"Alex." I want to tell him that his daughter is looking for someone to replace the mother she can't get near. I study his face. "Alex, I've just discovered that we each get only one chance to have a mother."

"What?" He leans toward me, confused.

No, it's not fair. Either I say it all or I shut up. "It would take too long to explain, Alex. Will you do me a favor? Will you tell Abe I want to talk to him?"

"What do you want to talk to me about?"

Abe stands in front of me, bearded, grinning behind the black-rimmed glasses that always seem too large for his face.

I reach out both my hands to him. "I can't tell you how glad I am to see you." I want to sit him down, here, now, and start talking. In this moment I know how much I've longed to talk to someone who knows how to listen.

"You look gorgeous, Alice, as always. Don't you get older like the rest of us?"

"Only inside. Abe, do you know that I still remember how you conducted the seminars you invited me to attend when I was in Los Angeles? That was nine years ago."

He's pleased, but he teases me. "Do you mean you're interested in me only professionally?"

Another time I might have teased back. "Listen. I learned what teaching can be from watching you. You weren't telling your students what thinking was: you were showing them."

He hugs me, laughing. "I'm glad to see you, too!" He turns to Alex. "Let's take her to dinner with us tonight." Alex nods. "We'll meet you here, on this spot. At six-thirty. Are you busy then?"

"No. But Abe, I want to *talk* to you. I want you to listen to me the way you listen to your students. I'm thinking about something, and I want to be sure that I know what I mean."

He touches my arm lightly. "We'll talk. If the crowd gets too big at dinner, we'll find another time."

He and Alex wave and move off together. I watch him go. Candy is being taken from my mouth.

I use part of the two hours before dinner to look into the jobs at Hawaii. The recruiter senses my ambivalence, and both of us quickly bring the interview to an end. I wander across the mezzanine, restless for human interchange. I want to stock up on people extravagantly before I go back to my silence. I want to laugh with them, to listen, to talk. A man of medium height strides by.

"Henry!" I scurry around the knots of people and touch his sleeve.

He turns. *"Kleine!"* He holds open his arms. We embrace, laughing. "Are you still out there in the Atlantic? Hmmm? We've got to get you back." He drags on his cigarette, remembering our lunch last month in Cambridge.

"Back to what?" I smile, but Henry knows what I'm saying.

He looks at me closely. "Haven't worked it all out yet, hmmm?"

"Almost, Henry. Listen. Let's go to a party. Do you know anyone who's having a party?"

"I'm having a party. Right now."

"You're not!"

"I *am*. I'm just on my way to buy more booze. Go on up to my room and you'll find a dozen people finishing off my liquor. Tell you what. You be my hostess. Now go on. I'll be there in ten minutes." He tells me the room number.

I need no urging. Up the elevator, down long corridors, I knock on a door that opens to laughter and ice in glasses and talk that I haven't heard for a long, long time.

There is no time to change before meeting Abe. Alex hails a cab, tells the driver the name of a Syrian restaurant in the Village, then hands me an envelope.

"Here's the letter from Stephanie. I'm supposed to find out your dog's name. And your address."

"Oh, Alex, I'm not sure how long I'll be there. Tell her I'll write when I'm settled somewhere."

I read the letter in the feeble light cast by streetlamps as our cabby bumps us along, then I join the gossip of who is here, and who not, of who is with whom but shouldn't be, of who is not with whom but should; of who is going to what university, of where a job will open by next fall.

We are eight at dinner. The talk is fast and rich and funny, and Abe most often is its source. There neither is, nor do I try to make, an opportunity to talk alone with him. I'm caught up in something festive, and he'll be here as long as I. And, too, he said we'd find another time.

They drop me at my hotel. I want to change out of the clothes I've worn since morning. Was I on Nantucket only this morning? I wash my face, make up my eyes and mouth, suspend long earrings from my ears, and button myself into the plain wool dress that covers me from chin to knees.

My hand is on the doorknob. I'm dressed for a party. I locate myself sitting in silence, thinking, far away. What am I doing? I'm going to see George. Well. As long as I know. But George doesn't exist. True, in one sense. But George used to listen when I talked. I need to have him listen to this. To listen, and find the flaws, and ask me questions I haven't thought of yet.

And is that all you want, Alice? Are you sure that's all?

I stand in the doorway long minutes before a path appears through the thicknesses of human beings. The noise batters at my ears, the smoke catches at my throat and narrows my eyes while I search the faces jammed around me.

There he is. Not far away, but many bodies in between. The crush allows me time to think. He ducks his head to listen to someone, his face half turned away from me. He nods, then laughs. I'll wait until he sees me. And then? No guarantee he'll come to me. My throat tightens. Ah, that's familiar. Who could tell that I'm watching a lover and not someone I fear? No one who pays attention only to my bodily response.

The crowd moves me toward him. Hands holding lighted cigarettes and glasses of beer constitute lesser obstacles than my own racing thoughts. What will I say? What will he say to me? Suppose Elizabeth is one of the people standing near him?

The crowd undulates ahead of me, turning George to face in my direction. He looks at me for a moment, and then he smiles. I wave. He turns away.

I stop as best I can. Is that his message: "Don't come to me"? But he doesn't know what I've been doing. I have to tell him. I have to know what he's like, too, now that I can see him.

I reach him. "George," I say, and then I stare. His right arm hangs in a sling, his hand encased in a cast visible from the end of his sleeve. "George, what happened to you?" How young, but now how tired he looks.

"I had an accident." He takes a puff of his cigarette and exhales it quickly. "How are you?"

"I didn't think you did it purposely. Tell me about it."

He's told it many times already. "I was driving alone in the mountains. The road curved around to the right and I didn't. The car rolled off the road. I was thrown clear, but I landed on my arm and broke it. I was unconscious for a little while, but then I simply lay there for hours until near dawn, when another car came along and the driver found me." Punctuated by many exhales.

"Does it hurt you now?" There's something strange in his whole manner. I watch his face, unable to name the thing.

"Mostly a nuisance. It takes so long to do anything. I can almost dress myself now. Occasionally there's a twinge. But it's apparently mending well, and the cast should come off when I go back to Colorado."

"How long were you in the hospital?" The play of the look on his face absorbs me.

"Too long."

He looks down at me, attending now to me. "You're looking very good, as usual. What are you doing these days?"

At that instant I understand the look. "George, you're angry that I didn't come to the hospital while you were there."

His eyes widen, and then he laughs shortly. "Smart girl."

I have more. "You wouldn't write to tell me; you know I had no way of knowing; but you think I should have been there anyway." I'm very sure.

His smile is wary. "How did you know?"

I think a moment. "Your manner, your tone implied that something was my fault. And that's the only part of it that you can make my fault." I am as startled as he. "And, anyway, we always knew what we each were thinking." No, that's not true: there was Elizabeth.

He grins but will not meet my eyes. "I'm going to find some place to sit down." He turns away, toward the chairs that probably line the wall behind all the standing people. I watch his back.

I can't just follow him. Yes, I know how tired he looks, but I'm here, too. I turn in another direction. The human swarm has a will of its own, and a path is molded for me even without my complicity.

So George carried on the same silent conversations with me, lying on his hospital bed, that I carried on with him, walking along the shores of Nantucket. I *did* matter to him two years ago: I must matter to him now. But then he has to say so. The question is: Will he say so in time?

"Alice!"

I shake hands with the man who first hired me to teach philosophy. "Have you been well, Professor Burch?" I ask. His ruddy face looks ill and aging. His hair was not so white five years ago. Five years. The spring before my fellowship to France.

"You know, they'll never forget you at Tufts." He's hugely pleased to say so.

"I'm not sure what you mean." I think of the day I walked into my ethics class, prepared to show my students how to read a closely reasoned piece of philosophy. I found adults standing along the sides and rear of the room, and I decided on the instant that, whoever they were, they were going to have to listen, too. At the end of the hour, I discovered they were parents, there for a yearly visiting day. And I had subjected them to the logical difficulties Augustine encountered in jointly defending God's omniscience and human free will. Did they remember that?

"Why, the trustees voted to give the teaching fellows a raise."

"I didn't know!" In the noise of the room, my laugh sounds only in my throat.

Henry comes up behind Mr. Burch and throws one arm around his shoulder. "What did she do at Tufts, George? Will it ever be the same again?" He raises his eyebrows high and drops them quickly to underscore his joke.

Mr. Burch turns to Henry. "Why, she wrote a letter to the board of trustees telling them that the teaching fellows were grossly underpaid. She used as an argument the fact that she had eight years of higher education, but that as a teaching fellow she was earning only about four times as much as she had earned at her very first job. Selling toys, I think."

"How do you remember all those facts, Mr. Burch?"

"They were the basis for the raise. The teaching fellows throughout the university know the story, not just the ones in the philosophy department."

Someone comes up to talk with him, and from the side someone turns Henry away. For a moment free space exists around me. Think of that. Five years ago an action of mine was effective. What else have I done that I don't know about?

I join Jan and Anne at a table. "Jan, you didn't tell me George broke his arm."

"I didn't? I guess I thought everybody knew."

Anne smiles. "You know Jan. I never hear the gossip from him. It's always old by the time other people get around to telling me. He hears it and forgets it, all at the same moment. For instance, he hasn't even told me what you're doing, Alice."

"Anne, I haven't told him myself. I'm not doing anything. In philosophy, I mean. I'm on Nantucket. I rented a house there for a while, to try to think about some things. I've been there since November."

Anne makes a little screaming sound. "On Nantucket in the winter? There's nothing to do!"

The walks along the ocean, morning and afternoon. Sunset, sunrise, moonrise. The cross-rip. The smell of the air. The silence. The way the fogs come in suddenly, and then vanish, leaving a brilliant sunlight in their wake. "Yes, that's true. There's nothing to do."

"Anne's aunt has a house there," Jan offers. "Tell Alice where it is."

"Well, Jan, she's not there in the winter. No one's there at this time of the year. Who are the people you talk to?"

Talk. Yes, Anne remembers how I had to talk. It was my tragedy, she said. "Alice, if you could just not need other people so badly, you could get some work done. And that would be good, for you and for philosophy." Was that only last year?

"Well, I see the postmaster once a day when I pick up my mail." I grin, ticking off the people. "I see the dog warden every now and then, when something is wrong with my puppy."

"When did you get a dog?"

"When I went to Nantucket. To protect me. There turns out to be no one to be protected from. Once a week I go into town to buy groceries. I stop at the A&P, and the hardware store, and the drugstore, and the liquor store, and the library. Other than that, I don't lay eyes on human beings from one day to the next, let alone talk to them."

Anne looks at me in disbelief. "How long will you be there?"

I shrug. Maybe in a week I won't be anywhere.

Now Jan is listening too. "But what are you *doing* there? Getting your thesis ready to publish?"

I laugh. "My God, no. Who'd want to read that? Jan, I've been trying to understand what I've been doing with my life." I look at him. Can I say it now to him?

"Hey, Alice!" A man leans across the table to me.

"Hello, Rufus." Merely recognizing someone from Mitre flips my stomach.

"Are you still working in New York?"

"No, I'm not." He doesn't seem to notice that I don't want to talk to him.

"Well, I'm certainly glad to see you here. You should be doing something in philosophy. I'm scouting for a teaching job myself. There seem to be a lot of openings this year."

He's being too nice. What does he want from me? "I hear there are."

"Listen, Alice, I didn't get a chance to tell you before you left, but I was very sorry that you had to go."

I look at him hard. "Of course I left under a cloud."

"Only if you think so. Everybody knows why Hal fired you, and everybody thinks that it was a stinking thing for him to do. It was too bad that he had power in the company and you didn't."

I'm surprised. "How did my side of the story get around?"

He smiles, and I can't mistake that he's simply being friendly. "Well, you left some good friends there. And everybody knows that Hal shouldn't have that kind of authority. We all try to work around him, to keep out of his way."

"I'm glad to forget the whole thing. Good luck in your search." I say good-bye, smiling.

I turn back to Jan and Anne. Someone talking to them has their deep attention. I fill my glass again, and take it with me. I follow whichever direction provides a path. Strange to learn that people knew all along how Hal had abused his authority. What else will I discover by saying what I mean?

I circulate among the people who have crisscrossed my life for eleven years. I move from group to group; sometimes a group forms around me. The evening approaches a middle point and I haven't yet talked with George. How do I arrange it? No, that's my old way. I must go to him myself and tell him.

I pick my way through other groups to where he stands listening politely, not talking. He doesn't see me coming. I touch the sleeve of his good arm. "George, come have a beer with me."

He glances at his watch, and instantly I imagine Elizabeth waiting for him somewhere.

"Willingly." He smiles. Courteous, distant. I shake aside the thought.

We find a table nearby, but it has neither beer nor unused glasses on it.

"You stay here. I'll get a pitcher of beer." He starts to rise, but I get up faster.

"No, you have only one good arm. I'll get it."

He's standing anyway. "My good arm is my carrying arm." He is gone.

My thoughts fly through all the ways there are to start what I want to say. I want him to come back to Nantucket with me. What can I say that would make it sound like a good idea to him?

Henry sits down next to me and puts his hand on my shoulder. "*Kleine,* you're the most popular girl here."

"Can you think of anyone more deserving?" I manage a smile. How will I talk to George?

"By God, when you put it like that!" He starts to laugh. I see him in bold relief throughout my graduate years: the only teacher who tried to help me along all the stages toward the degree, the only one who found jobs for me, the only one who gave me a clue about how to write my thesis. A friend, by any standard. Erratic, yes, but he cared what happened to me.

"Henry, you know you're very unreliable. But when you take it into your head to do something for someone, you really do do it. No matter what."

He grins. "I do, don't I?"

George sets the pitcher down on the table and slides a chair over next to me. Henry leans across me to tease George about his cast. I push my chair back a little to let the talk run more easily between them. Henry begins a story, using his impeccable imitations of some of the members of our department. I start to laugh, and so does

George, and this in turn fuels Henry. He embroiders the story until we're laughing at every phrase, helplessly and totally, yet Henry will not stop, nor can we.

From nowhere Stan is standing next to Henry. "You're having the best time of anybody in the room." He smiles. "How are you, Henry?" They shake hands. He leans toward me. "Alice, you look marvelous. What color is your dress, anyway? One red sleeve, one orange?"

I stand, turning a full circle to show him the dress. "Mostly red. Some orange, a little green." I smile into his face, and he into mine. The same thing in me goes out to him as it always does. It never diminishes: it's always at high pitch. Ten years.

Henry offers Stan a beer. "No, I can stay only a minute." He sits down on the other side of Henry.

And now we are four.

Henry introduces Stan and George. They reach across me to shake hands, murmuring that they have heard of one another. For a moment we are all silent, and then Henry starts to talk again.

Why is Henry here? I want to talk to Stan. I mean, to George.

Something starts to swirl within me, and I shoot up out of my chair.

Three startled faces look up at me. I have something to say, but at this moment I don't know what it is. "Excuse me" comes out. That lets me move away into the crowd. But why away? Back there are three I know, two I love. That's why I have to go. Half of me belongs to each of them. Torn in half, jointly shared: oh, let me go away.

I shove my way past people, breathless from my effort and my flight. The mezzanine is almost empty. Where am I going? I look around at stairways, elevators, corridors. Where? I want to see no one. I want to see:

Myself.

I run into the ladies' lounge and stand straight up against the full-length mirror at the far end of the room. I look at my face. Is that what it looks like to be me? I stare at my image for a very long minute. I am one person after all. It will be all right to go back to that table now.

The men stand when I return. "Did you put the cat out?" Henry asks, lifting and lowering his eyebrows. I'm unsure of his joke. George helps me out: "You could only have put the cat out in the time you were gone."

Yes, I fled.

They resume their conversation. I lean back in my chair, looking at them one by one. Stanley. Henry. George. I know them all. The standpoint from which I now look at them is very solid, very stable. In a little while, I join their talk.

I undress for bed. No puppy drags my shoe into another room, insists on going out one more time before we settle down for the night, crawls beneath my bed, displays for me his regular breathing under my mattress. The room has empty spaces that only he can fill.

I get under the covers. A blessing to be alone again. The throng of people since this morning passes before my mind's eye. I think of the successful ones, established with tenure appointments at important universities, writing books and articles, delivering endowed lectures. Others, like me, inhabit the fringes. Qualified by virtue of possessing the degree, yet never receiving the endorsement of those who have the power to hand us on to the desirable jobs. Somehow, these faces stay with me longer. They look the way I've felt: baffled, hurt, expecting slights, ready to fight back.

I sit up in bed abruptly. If I see that in them, others must have seen it in me. All the years that I've spent pretending, trying to make people think I was everything but what I was: I didn't fool them! The whole point of the pretense was exactly that, to fool *them*. But *I'm* the one who's been fooled, thinking that I've fooled them. How much work, how much wasted time, when all along other people must have recognized that I was trying to fool them.

I shiver involuntarily. They couldn't have avoided seeing what I was doing.

How does that change what I'm here to do? It doesn't. It merely gives me one more reason to say what I feel like saying, or to say nothing if nothing strikes me as worth saying. No, not a reason: a reminder that I have no alternative to trying to see the world as it appears to me. If I live.

I settle my body into my sleeping position, but something won't let me fall asleep. What's not in place? I've locked the door; I've left a call for morning. Ah. Good night, Sweet Puppy.

23

The morning interviews with department chairmen are without enthusiasm on either of our parts. My qualifications are questionable. Of the five semesters since I received my degree, I've taught during only one; I've written no articles; my thesis hasn't been published; and, with the exception of Henry, none of the members of my graduate department will give me strong recommendations. A race began a long time ago, and I, unaware that it was a race, have not been running strongly; yet now the results are being made known, and I can only stand helplessly by, because to cry "Foul!" would merely announce that the foul was by my own hand.

I wander through the lobby. The interviews were oppressive. How do I shake off the coating they laid on me? Yet it was my doing. I sat there saying the expected things in the expected ways. Have I learned nothing at all on Nantucket that I can put to use? Is it the case that my alternatives are either to play the game their way or not to play the game at all? That if I want a job teaching philosophy I have to have good references, a good publication record, a gapless history of teaching? Or else stop looking for a teaching job?

Damn them: they're making me apologize for myself. That's it. I'm oppressed because I feel apologetic, and I feel apologetic because I'm trying to follow their rules and can't. They don't want somebody to teach philosophy: they want somebody who fits their requirements. But there are teachers, and there are requirement-meeters. I know how to reach students, to make them talk to me about their concerns, to thrust philosophy into their lives so that it uproots unfounded beliefs and gives them an instrument for exploring and comparing the adequacies of beliefs they haven't yet examined. Picture putting that on a job application. Listen to what that sounds like to a sober administrator responsible to a university president for the faculty he hires.

Maybe if I burned to do philosophy, I might have said all this to someone this morning. But I don't burn, for philosophy or anything else. And that must be apparent, now that I know how visible my motives are. I'm here talking about jobs only to line one up, just in case. In case I live, I'll need a job.

I have a sudden image of Logos closed into a heavy wire cage since yesterday morning, confused, not knowing where I am. I stand abruptly, walk down the stairs to the revolving door, and push myself outside. I have to smell fresh air, even if it's New York air.

I return through the revolving door and, at the foot of the stairs, nearly collide with the first of half a dozen men coming down.

"Hello, Professor Quine." I can say hello.

The imposing man in the center of the group stops, and the others stand just behind him. I say hello to each of them: I know them all.

"Alice. We haven't had news of you for a while. I think Donald mentioned that he had heard from you." He smiles. Warmly, for him.

Through him I learned what intellectual elegance is. "Yes, I wrote him. I hope you've been well."

"Very well. Where have you been teaching?"

Oh, no. Not with these others listening. "Well, I was out in California last year."

He smiles, encouraging me. "And where are you now?" He listens.

I look at the men surrounding him almost as a bodyguard. A certain impatience lines their faces. They listen.

I listen, too, but to something ancient and heavy trying to drag me along with it. I look at him and smile. "I'm staying in a house on Nantucket, reading and writing. Getting some things clear."

He nods. "I didn't know people lived there during the winter."

"There aren't too many people at my end of the island. Sometimes three or four days go by without my talking to anyone except the postmaster when I pick up my mail."

"What a waste."

Of what? "My words aren't so important that someone has to hear them."

One of the men breaks in. "Alice, would you like to have lunch with us?"

I understand their impatience then. They have successfully captured Quine to have lunch with them, and I, being of no importance, am impeding their plan. The invitation is pure formality. "Thank you, but I have an appointment."

The others start down the stairs again, stepping around me, but Quine reaches out his hand. "Good luck, Alice." I thank him.

He goes his way. I watch him for a moment, and then I ascend the very stairway on which I spoke the truth to someone in authority for the first time in my life.

I slip into the two o'clock meeting late and stand in the back of the room, my eyes sliding across the rows to find an empty chair. None. I lean against the wall with others, listening. A sentence, a paragraph. My thoughts rebel against the speaker. I force myself to listen. But that means I'm bored! I bite my lip to stop the giggle. Out the door, across the lobby, I almost skip. The only things I *have* to do are things that are necessary steps to what I *want* to do, or to what I *choose* to do. A talk that bores me *can't* be something I have to listen to. Not now. Not ever.

I'm outside on the sidewalk facing Macy's. Ten dollars in my purse for two days' meals won't take me far. But there's no charge for walking in the aisles. I roam through the store's abundance. What can I buy?

A tall wide cabinet filled with spice bottles catches my attention. I lift out a bottle of dillweed from its shelf. For George.

"Sixty-nine cents plus tax. Seventy-two cents, please."

Seventy-two cents will buy me his grin. He'll read the label and know that I remember his dill-tomato passion. Not green tomatoes, canned by mechanical manufacturing processes, but ripe ones, canned by his mother's hand.

"Ripe?" I asked him once. "You mean red ripe?"

"Yes, red. What other color are ripe tomatoes?"

"But George, they'd get too soggy in the brine."

"That shows how much you know."

"I concede my ignorance of canning." But it was a dare. I phoned the wife of a Ukrainian minister to find a recipe as close as I could get to one his mother must have used. But the woman's English was execrable, and although I repeated each ingredient after her, something seemed wrong when I read over her instructions and I abandoned the whole plan.

I return to the hotel, eager for my joke. Groups of people stand talking in the upper lobby. Height and sling set George apart.

"I have a present for you." I try to keep my laughter in.

"For me?" He takes the small brown bag, draws out the bottle, and reads the label aloud. I wait on the edge of my glee.

"It should be 'Dull Weed,' " he says.

"What?" The bubble inside me deflates and is gone.

"Dull, like me." He smiles ruefully. "You still haven't told me what you're doing."

"I want to. Can we go somewhere for a drink?"

He glances at his watch. "I'm sorry. I don't have time. Tell me here."

I look him full in the face. "I know Elizabeth is with you. I'm not going to entice you away from her. But George, there are so many things I understand now that I didn't used to understand. I want to tell you about them."

"Well, that's marvelous."

How did it come to this? I'm pleading with him. My calmness breaks apart, and I speak sharply. "Don't you want to talk with me?"

Something flickers across his face. "Briefly."

I stare at him. I feel my face flushing. "Good-bye, George." I turn away from him. Unaccountably I turn back. "This really is good-bye."

I walk as swiftly as I can. I stop to gossip with two men I know; we laugh; we discuss the meetings. George still stands where I left him. Double damn him. Serve him right. I keep on talking as George begins to move across the room, stopped by people as he goes.

A man is telling me about the opening in his department. "Send me your *curriculum vitae*. And your references. We won't decide until March. But if you can wait until then, I think you'd find us very . . ." He outlines the advantages of his college. With the little attention I now possess, I listen. But look around. George is gone.

It's over. All and absolutely over.

"I will, Peter. I'll write you next week. I'd like to know sooner than March, but of course I understand."

We shake hands. I put on my coat and walk the long cold block to my hotel.

I lie across my bed. The second evening in New York and still no talk with Abe. No talk with George now, either.

Nor anything else with George. He was certainly true to form: ungenerous, suspicious, making me do the asking.

I sit up against the pillow. But if I had to do the asking, then I shouldn't have asked at all. I was bursting to tell George about Nantucket, and so it kept escaping me that he wasn't bursting to hear. About Nantucket or anything else. It's really very simple: George doesn't care about me. Whether he cares about anyone else can't be my concern in any way, can't occupy my thoughts ever again.

Why don't I see these things while they're happening? I catch some clues, but somehow they don't get *to* me in time. They're out of reach, on the far rim of my awareness. A delay factor intervenes before the clues about what's going on finally register with me. I suppose that's a gain. Up to now they've almost never registered at all. How do I learn to allow for that delay? Is it anything that can be learned? Whatever emotional awareness is, it's definitely not immediacy. Not with me.

Abe is not to be seen in the upper lobby. Or the mezzanine. The few people who might know where he is haven't seen him since noon. I phone his room. Not in. I'll look in one last place. A man stops me at the door. It costs $7.50 to enter the cocktail party, including the banquet afterward.

"I'm only looking for a friend." The man lets me pass.

People are sitting quietly at the round banquet tables. I skim the room. He isn't here. I escape into the hallway and walk straight into Abe. "I've been looking for you all day!" I almost crow.

"Then come on, let's have a drink. All of us are going to the bar, then out somewhere for dinner. Come along." He loops his arm through mine, and I become part of his small group. The evening takes an upward turn. The fragments of the last hour fall away, and now the time condenses into focus. I'll talk with Abe. Now, finally, I can talk with Abe.

When I finish, Abe sighs and shakes his head sadly. "People are like little children. They cry when somebody takes their candy away."

I'm puzzled. "What does that have to do with anything I've said?"

"Well, you're not as young as you were, and you haven't got a good job. And you're unhappy about those things."

"Abe! How can you distill that out of what I've been telling you? I'm not crying about anything. I simply think that all the years I've lived up to now have been a waste. Because I've been behaving like a five-year-old trying to make my mother put her arms around me."

"That's what I mean: crying when the candy is taken away."

"But, Abe, I'm not crying about it. I'm not even asking you to evaluate what's already happened. I *know* it's all a total loss. I'm asking you only what reasons people have for staying alive. It seems to me that there are only two. Either you have a person who's very close to you, so that each of you matters more to the other than anyone else does. Or you have some work that absorbs your thought and uses your talent and training. Of course, best is both."

"Of course, those are extremes."

"I'm talking about extreme things. And I'm looking around for any other reasons besides those. If you know some third reason, or fourth, or tenth, tell me. I'm not asking you to help me judge the past, or even to help me decide what to do from now on. I'm only asking you to tell me what other alternatives there are, in case I've missed them. Maybe you know something that I don't know. Maybe there's something else to consider, something else worth waiting for. To me it doesn't look as though there is. That makes the decision simple." I smile. "In one sense."

The other people at our table are getting to their feet, putting on their coats. I rise, too. "Abe, I'm sorry. I took all your time. You didn't have a chance to talk with your friends."

He helps me into my coat. "They seem to have gotten along without me. Anyway, you needed me more than they did."

I smile at him. "That's true." We're the last to leave.

He takes my arm as we go out the door. "You haven't talked to anyone for a long time, have you?"

"As you know."

"Don't let it be so long next time."

"Abe, it's not something I've had any choice about."

I try to bring Logos' image to mind before I fall asleep.

If there's some third alternative, Abe doesn't know it. If there's not, he was evading saying so to me. Is it possible I wasn't clear enough about what I expected from him? On the other hand, who am I to him that he should think carefully about a problem of mine, simply because I asked him to?

Late in the dark afternoon I stand outside the meeting room of the final session. The man coming toward me to talk may have a job open next fall, but I'm not supposed to let him know that I know. I pick up my coat and my single piece of luggage, and we leave the hotel for a nearby bar.

Our table is a short distance from an open fire. I'm given the privilege of facing it. I let the man carry the thread of the talk, waiting for him to close in on the job. I listen, watching the fire almost as often as I watch his face.

"But if you had your choice of how to spend your life, without having to worry about the money, which would you do: sit quietly at home reading and writing, or be out among young people teaching?"

The question is so close to ones I'm brooding over that I'm silent for a long moment. He's asking me what I want to do. I can't tell him that I don't know what wanting is. I drink some of my bourbon to delay.

"Come, now, which is it?" He sits back in his chair, smiling encouragement.

"Will you believe that your question is one that I've been thinking a great deal about lately, and that if I can't answer you, it's only because I can't answer myself?" It's like pushing a stone uphill to say what I think.

"Well, your inclination must go one way rather than another." He lifts his glass and waits for me to speak.

Alex's warning plays back. This man is exceedingly clever, and I must be exceedingly careful to match him. But if I could answer his question, I'd be a long way toward what I need to know. "You know, it's so quiet on Nantucket that one day, walking near the lighthouse, the only sound I could hear was the flag flapping in the breeze."

He smiles and says nothing.

"I'm getting so used to that silence that being back in New York is like being subjected to an onslaught on my senses."

He laughs shortly. "A lot of New Yorkers feel the same way."

I look into the fire again. With a little more time, I might be able to elicit my own reply.

"So, then, it's the quiet fireside and writing by yourself that you prefer."

It's difficult for me to answer, and difficult for me to tell him that it's difficult to answer. And then what happens to the job he might offer me here, away from silence and fresh air? "I suppose it is. Yes, probably that kind of life is closer to what I'm comfortable doing. And yet, I'm not completely sure."

He looks at his watch. "I'm going to have to run to catch my train. Can I put you into a cab?" He pays the check while I put on my coat.

We stand on the slushy sidewalk. "My bus stops at this corner.

Don't bother to wait." I take my luggage from him just as the bus brakes in front of us.

He hands me aboard. "Good to see you, Alice. I'll be in touch with you if we have an opening soon." He's gone.

Oh, yes: the opening. I toss my coins into the fare box and find a seat. I talked myself out of it. If I could have said, straight out, that I like teaching, he might have started to talk about the job. Instead, I allowed myself to believe that he was interested in the windings of my private thought. I should have asked myself *why* he was so interested. Since he's not my friend, there *is* no reason for him to be interested in me for my own sake. His interest extended only to the point of considering me a potential member of his department. Nothing wrong with that, except that I didn't happen to notice it in time.

Looking through the dirty window at the dirty streets, I involuntarily shake my head to mock myself.

"The whole thing is nutty! Plain, ordinary nutty!"

I watch Mo pace the length of his large living room, then turn and pace it again. "I'm waiting for you to stop calling me names and start trying to answer my question." I sip my drink.

"It *is* nutty. People just don't do such things."

I laugh. Mo stops in front of me. "What's so funny?"

"That's the last line of *A Doll's House*."

"That's just what I mean, damn it. You're considering the possibility of suicide, but you talk about it as though you were trying to decide between apples and oranges for dessert. And you hear my remarks as lines from plays."

"Oh, come on, Mo. I know a lot of plays. Why wouldn't I recognize a line when I hear it? So far as my coolness is concerned, you think that I'd be more serious if I were crying or pulling my hair or incoherent, don't you?"

He stands looking down at me. "I suppose so, yes."

"Look, Mo, I didn't come to talk to you because you're a psychologist. I came to you because a year ago when I lived in New York, feeding and clothing and housing myself only by draining my will, it got through to me, indistinctly, but it got through, that you had a lot of common sense. By the time I reached the present point, trying to decide whether to live, I realized I wanted certain people to check out my thinking, to make sure I hadn't missed anything. You're one of three people that I wanted to talk to. The philosophical meetings are only the occasion, not the reason, for my being here."

"What did the other two say?"

"One wouldn't talk to me. The other avoided answering me directly."

He sits down on the couch next to me. "That leaves it up to me."

"No. It was never 'up to' the other two, either. It's my decision, for my reasons. But I'm slowly being confirmed in my belief that there are no reasons other than the ones I've told you. So I don't really expect you to add something new. Although if anyone I know can, you can."

"I'm flattered." He is silent, puffing his pipe. Then: "There are probably more people who are alive without thinking about it than there are people who are alive for one of your 'good reasons.'"

"I don't doubt it. But I have to *know* what I'm doing. And why."

He punches the pillow between us. "What's so damned important about knowing? Why can't you just *be?* Look at you. You have your Ph.D. from Harvard; you're an attractive woman; you look ten years younger than you are; you're charming and interesting; you could do anything you wanted to do. Instead you stare at your navel and talk about suicide. Because—" He turns to me angrily. "I forget why. Remind me of why."

I look at him steadily. Maybe I made a mistake talking to Mo. "In the first place, you have a Ph.D. too. So you're not in a very good position to sneer at my wanting to know. In the second place, all those things you said are things about the outside of me. Inside there's nothing. I'm either incapable of feeling or, if I do feel, I don't know how to recognize what I feel when I feel it."

"That's nonsense. I don't believe it."

"That's because you *do* feel. I told you that I've just discovered that I never learned how to recognize feelings. The question is, what use is my life to me when I have no way of discovering what's important to me, so that I can't possibly know how to look for it?"

"My God." Mo gets up and walks into the kitchen. I hear dishes and pots rattling. I join him and stand watching him prepare a pot of coffee.

"I'll cut the cheesecake. Where's a knife?"

He reaches into a drawer and hands me one. "I don't know whether I should put dangerous weapons into your hands."

I take it, grinning. "I wouldn't do anything here. You might try to stop me."

He makes no reply, but continues measuring out the coffee.

"Hey, Mo." I walk over to him and make him look up at me. "That's a joke."

"Of all the things you're saying, I don't know what's a joke and what's real. Do you?"

"Of course I do. But you're forgetting that I might decide to live anyway, even knowing that I have no good reason for living. I'd just never forget that I had no good reason. And, do you know, I have a peculiar sense of something very strange—I might even call it 'security'—knowing that I can give up my life at any moment, without loss to myself or to the world. It's this not being afraid to think of my own death that you see as my lack of seriousness about it. Maybe it's the people who gnash their teeth who are still afraid."

He looks at me, and I know that now, finally, he understands what I'm saying.

Over coffee, we talk of his work and of people we both know. I accept his offer to take me home, and in the cab we are both silent all the way.

24

I settle myself into the same corner seat I've occupied each time I've ridden the ferry. I'm weary of traveling. By the time I get home, it will have taken me twenty-four hours, thanks to the snow that closed the Nantucket airport. I count the conveyances: cab in New York to limousine; limousine to airport; plane to Boston; Marie's car to Marblehead, and then to the bus this morning at dawn; bus to Boston subway; transfer to another subway; intercity bus to Woods Hole; boat to Nantucket; cab to my car at the airport; my car home.

I watch the harbor fall slowly behind us. Three times now I've kept my eyes on that single house on the point of land that reaches farthest out into the water at Woods Hole. Will I see it one more time coming back?

Three hours stretch ahead of me, to be broken only by the stop at Martha's Vineyard. Logos isn't here to interrupt my train of thought, purposely or simply by catching my attention. I smile, thinking of the times I've found myself looking down at him asleep near my desk where I sat trying to think my way through some maze or other.

Something about his fur wouldn't look right, and I'd get down on the floor to run my fingers through it, checking for any bare spots on his skin. Or he'd seem not to be breathing, and I'd lay my ear against his chest to listen to his heart. Or I'd watch his paws move in his sleep; perhaps he was dreaming of the run we had had in the morning. Sometimes the sight of his relaxed body touched me merely because of the trust that it implied. Two or three times I tried to sketch him as he lay with his back up against the fireplace.

My hands ache to touch him again. See: he's a distraction even in his absence. No, I can't think here. I'll wait until I get home.

The door of the SPCA is locked. I batter at it, and all the dogs inside protest. I run down the porch stairs and follow the walk around to the side of the small building. Enclosed in separate outdoor runs are two dogs, muddy, dirty, gazing at me in surprise, then barking. The farthest one is Logos. I look at him dumbfounded.

I run back along the walk, up the stairway, and bang on the door again, rattling the knob. Mr. Lema opens the door.

"I've come to pick up my dog. The German shepherd puppy." I am skirting the edges of politeness. He lets me in. "I'll pay for him first. How much do I owe you?" I scribble out the check, waiting to fill in the amount.

He finds his record books. Long minutes go by before he replies. "Seven days. Ten-fifty, please."

I hand him the check. He is so *slow*. He enters the check in his book, files it, finds his keys, and gets up from his chair. I follow him into the back room where the cages are stacked. A radio is playing trashy music loudly. He walks over to one of the cages.

"No," I say, almost spitting the words. "He's outside." Will you for the love of God hurry?

He passes me, flicking keys to find the right one as he walks through the doorway. He opens Logos' run. Looking only at the man, the puppy crouches low before him, not moving, even though the door is open. Mr. Lema gets in the run behind Logos and urges him toward me. I stand in the doorway, almost bursting to hold him, waiting for him to jump up on me, not caring about the mud that hangs from his fur. Logos skitters the few steps to reach me, and then, inexplicably, he cringes at my feet. Mr. Lema is two steps behind.

I look up at him angrily. "Why is he doing this?"

Mr. Lema looks down at the puppy on the wet muddy floor. "Well, he's glad to see you."

"This isn't what he does when he's glad to see me. What have you done to him?"

Mr. Lema enters the doorway and instantly Logos cringes lower, then runs over to his cage and scurries in through the open door.

"Logos!" I shout. "Come here."

The puppy starts to crawl out of his cage, his tail thumping on the floor. Then he looks at Mr. Lema and crawls back. I run to the cage and grab his collar. "Come on, Logos. Come with me." He comes with me only because I have hold of him, but he keeps turning his head toward Mr. Lema. I take him out through the waiting room and open the door. I have no leash.

"Logos! This way!" I race him to the waiting cab, hoping he'll follow, and hold the door open for him. The driver looks pointedly at the muddy mess Logos drips on the back seat and floor, but I don't care. The car rolls toward the airport.

"Logos." I start to pet him. He ducks his head and looks out the side window. "Logos, it's me." His interest lies only in what he sees outside.

The driver pulls up to my car at the airport. Its wheels are buried in two days of snow. The driver looks at me impassively as I pay him; I can't ask him for help.

Someone in the airport must have a shovel. It's offered, along with a pair of hands to dig me out. I hustle Logos into the car and toss my luggage in after him. The miraculous little car with its automatic choke starts at the first try. Logos sniffs his way through all the familiar smells of the car.

Exhausted, I reach for the gearshift. Logos is suddenly interested in my hand. He sniffs, licks my wrist, and sniffs again. He looks up at me, then all at once he knows me. He croons, he cries, he rests his paws on my chest, he licks my cheeks and nose and eyes and chin. And when the tears begin, he licks them too. For all of twenty seconds, he lets me keep my arms around him. I find some tissues in my purse, and in a little while I have something to say: "Logos, let's go home."

The house echoes my sounds as I go through the rooms on my way upstairs, the emptiness itself responding to my presence. I stay only long enough to change into slacks, find my boots, and turn up the heat. Then Logos and I are out the door and running.

He flies ahead, and I laugh with gasping sounds to watch him go. He reaches the road before I realize how fast he's moving, and I yell his name to stop him from crossing without my being there. I stoop to pick up a chunk of icy snow.

"Hey, Logos, look what I've got!" I hold it high for him to see. He turns in time, and as he looks, I sling the ice back in the direction from which we came. Immediately he turns to chase it, shooting past me, making up in these few seconds for seven days of confinement in a wire cage. I keep him active until I can reach the road myself to see whether a car is coming. I break into a jog-trot the last few feet of the way to the bluff.

We make our way down the long low slope onto the wide stretch of dune grass, and Logos leads the way straight to the water. He starts to dig the moment he hits the wet sand, then dances to another spot and digs again, where, perhaps after all, the thing he's seeking lies.

I'm glad enough to watch him. In the cold, I gulp the salt air. How fast can I exchange the New York breath I carry within me for this clean fresh ocean air? I find a snowdrift soft enough to use for snowballs and fling one downwind for Logos to chase. I want to run him hard, to overflow his awareness with good things, to make him forget what happened to him while I was gone.

I stick my hands into my pockets, ducking my head into my collar, and walk next to Logos' tracks on the sand. What did I accomplish, going to New York? Images of the people I saw and talked with pass before me, but the array comes too swiftly and its parts are unrelated. No, it's too soon. I haven't really landed here yet.

I glance at my watch: I haven't even taken off my watch. I have to get into town to buy food before the stores close. Pick up the mail.

I keep Logos chasing sticks most of the way home. He falls onto the rug with a sigh and is asleep before I find a pencil to make out my grocery list. I stand in front of the open refrigerator trying to remember what I need. The phone rings. For a moment, I'm still in New York where phones and human beings using them are ordinary parts of the day. And then the strangeness strikes me. I pick up the receiver, almost not daring to say hello.

"Dr. Koller, is that you?" A New England voice, an older man, familiar somehow.

"Yes. Who is this?"

"Mr. Morris, at the post office. We've been very worried about you. No one has seen you walking with your dog since before Christmas, and we thought maybe something had happened to you."

Then people do see me here. "I went off the island right after Christmas, Mr. Morris. I knew you'd save my mail, and so I didn't bother to tell you I was going."

"Well, I've been calling you every day. My wife said you might have gone away for the holidays, but I wanted to be sure. I even went over to your house last week to see whether you might be there in some sort of trouble."

I hold the phone away and look at it. He would have found me if I had closed myself into the garage. "That was very thoughtful of you. You're very kind, and I appreciate your thinking of me. I do thank you." The words say exactly what I mean, and yet they are such formulas that he'll think I'm being only polite.

"It was no trouble at all. If there's ever anything I can do, you shouldn't think twice about calling me. We know that you're out here without anyone, and sometimes people just need someone for something."

"Thank you for that, too. I'll be over for my mail in a little while. Happy New Year to you."

When we hang up, I sit with my chin in my hands. I imagine Mr. Morris dialing my number every day, getting into his car and driving over here, peering into my windows, looking into the garage, listening for Logos, for any living sounds at all, discussing what might have happened to me with his wife. Some vagrant thought about my connection with this community stays just out of reach. It's so novel an idea that I have to let it escape me now, for lack of the proper net to snare it in.

25

My growing puppy reaches his paws onto my bed to lick my face in morning greeting. No matter how I squirm, laughing, to get out of his way, he follows me, and then in one smooth movement, leaps onto the bed.

"Hey, what are you doing up here? Get down!"

The command is new and puzzling, but my tone of voice is hardly stern. He's trying to decipher me. I grab the covers and lift them high, dumping him onto the floor.

"That's what 'get down' means, you clown." And then I'm out of bed with him. To begin a day that I've been working my way toward for a very long time.

The sunless day neutralizes the world I look out upon. The moor, the road, the row of houses, the water tower, the beach and ocean I can't see from here are more congenial to me gray, I think, than lighted by a brilliant sun.

Is there anything to stay me from taking my life? Stan, coming here and saying, "I want you for what you are, no matter what you've been or done." Heady stuff. But I am a creature who stopped short thirty years ago. Stan knows me only as that display that was my life. Nothing about me interested him beyond the merest temporary possession.

I think of Marvin, telling me how he decided finally to marry. "She went out to California, and said that's where she'd be if I wanted her, without games and forever. And so I thought about it awhile, and then I got on a plane and brought her back." What man I've ever wanted would have done that for me: gotten on a plane to bring me back? I've never dared to take the chance of finding out. My move was always to make myself available.

I rest my head in my hands. What would it be like to say, "These are my terms. If you want me, it will have to be on this basis"? And on top of it, to go away, letting the man decide for himself.

Why am I thinking of Stan at all? I've said I love him, but I don't know what loving a man is. I probably have to discard the two dozen beliefs I've been mouthing about loving. And yet, if not Stan, then no one.

I shake my head. What kind of balance sheet am I drawing up? How can it be anything more than a debating point, knowing whether I've loved Stan? He doesn't love me, and never did. And never will. And never will, Alice, and never will. Like me and oysters: I just don't happen to like them. Not that there's anything wrong with oysters.

Not that there's anything wrong with me.

I sit up quietly in my chair. The fact that Stan doesn't love me doesn't *necessarily* mean that there's something wrong with me. There is, in fact, something wrong with me: I don't know how to use my own evidence for choosing what I want; I don't know what honest wanting is. But it's not likely that Stan knew that; it's not even likely that he thought about me long enough to have figured out what was wrong with me.

I'm struggling with an idea that won't let itself be viewed right side up. What, please, am I trying to say?

I walk around the room, I stoop to pet Logos until he groans his protest at being disturbed in his sleep. I go into the kitchen for more coffee. I circle around the idea as I circle these rooms.

I have it. Stan's not loving me wasn't *my* fault. There was nothing at all I could *do* to make him love me. He simply didn't. Doesn't. Can't, in the only sense that is relevant: he isn't able to, just as a blind man isn't able to see. No matter how visible I try to make myself, a blind man can't see me. No matter how lovable I try to make myself, someone who doesn't love me can't be made to. But it's not something lacking in *me:* it's that there's nothing in him that responds to me in a loving way. And it has nothing to do with whether I'm fouled up or perfectly sound.

But I've thought of loving as something I had to deserve. My little-girl solution to my little-girl problem. And now I see that people either love each other or they don't. What, exactly, loving consists in, I'm not sure. I have to think about it. I'd have to know what it would be like to deal with a man as himself, rather than as a potential source of motherly love.

Suppose I've deceived myself even about Stan. And yet, in spite of all my pretending, I think I probably loved him. I'd be sure only if I were to spend time with him again someday, to see how he looks to me without the filter through which I've been looking at everything and everyone.

The dim chance of beginning something with Stan again someday? That's no reason for staying alive.

Daddy.

But Daddy lies worsening, cared for like a thing, fed intravenously because he won't eat. He isn't able to care about staying alive himself. How can he care about keeping me alive?

Logos pushes my hands away from my face to lick my tears. I cry into his fur, my arms around his neck. He lets me hold him briefly, then backs away. I find some tissues in my pocket and use them up. The tears do not stop.

Even before he was sick, I'd cry whenever he did things for me. The time he clipped a check for ten dollars to his letter, saying:

"Don't tell anyone. Just spend it for something you'd like." I cry even now, remembering. The time I announced my engagement to Randall: "I'm sure he's a fine boy. I liked him when you brought him here. If you think he'll make you happy, go ahead and marry him." The time I wanted to go to Goodman: "If you want to study acting, it's okay with me. I'll try to help you as much as I can." Or to Radcliffe; or to Texas; or to Chicago. Always the same: "If you think it will make you happy, go ahead."

It's not possible to have tears still left in me. Why do I cry for his *loving* me? I have it all upside down. I should be crying if he didn't love me, not because he did. Does. Would, if he could.

What more perfect evidence can there be that I understand nothing about feelings: that I cry when someone loves me?

And why wasn't his loving me enough? Why didn't my father's love free me to grow out of my childhood? Why did I so desperately need my mother's? Maybe because it wasn't there.

I go outside with Logos to feel the cold air on my face. Each thing I come upon strengthens my reasons not to live.

There are my friends. Are they a reason? Jean. Marilyn. Etel. Joyce. Maybe Weck. If I have friends, these are the ones. How do I know? I tried, or found it worth trying, to explain to them what I'm doing here. The others, the people I couldn't tell about this, fell away so painlessly. I was using them, I think, as I used my men. The temporary warmth to get in out of the cold, the illusion of having someone to talk to, a place to go to share a meal. A home, again. Oh, I should have had a sign on me warning people of the danger.

I get up from the couch and look out the front window. Maybe I wore one, after all. If I was the only person I fooled, maybe other people had their own way of seeing what I wanted from them.

Even my friends. But can I go to the phone right now and say, "Jean (or Etel, or Joyce), I'm thinking of committing suicide. So far I have no reason not to. Is there some reason you can think of? And will you come and talk with me?"

I flick the curtain back to its place, and turn away from the snow-covered lawn. How could Jean leave Toronto, leave one little boy and one infant? Her husband wouldn't let her come. No, that's not fair. Both of them were very good to me, trying to help me get over Mike. They invited me to share their matchless cooking; they opened their house to me when my own company became intolerable. For Jean to come here is a lot to ask.

And yet, that's what I'm looking for: someone to whom I'm worth a major inconvenience.

I think them over, one by one. Each of them has done for me things that were uncomfortable for them, and only because I asked it of them or seemed to need it. And would do them again. But none of them would come here. They'd talk twenty dollars' worth of long-distance time to me, but not one of them would offer her undivided attention to what I'm thinking about, if I were to say I needed her right now. They'd think I'm drunk, or depressed. Or that it's one more wild play I wrote for myself.

I sigh. From what they know of me, I understand how they'd think those things. I've used up their sympathy for my crises. I understand, in one sense; but in another, I don't. I *am* seeking an extreme sign: I have to know that someone cares enough about me to disrupt her life for a short time to discuss mine with me.

And yet, once here, what could any of them say? "Come and live with us"? "Near us"? No. They have their own households, their own friends, their own preoccupations, their own lives. They wouldn't want me to die, but they really can offer me nothing to live for.

I understand. I understand.

Logos lies asleep beneath the desk. His legs twitch slightly and, even as I watch, they begin to make the circling movements that imitate running. His eyes blink open and shut, and sudden low cries issue from his partly open mouth, even though he's fast asleep. I sit on the floor to pet him. "Don't cry, Sweet Puppy." What menace is he running from? Under my hands his feet slow down, then stop. He sighs a long inward groan, opens his eyes briefly, reminds himself of me, stretches, and falls asleep again, quietly.

I take my hand away and sit looking at him. How often would I have gotten out of bed in the morning if I hadn't had to let him out? Would I have explored the beach so extensively and regularly if I hadn't wanted to give him a good walk? Would I have maintained any sort of human existence here at all if I hadn't had to keep fulfilling his needs for food and water and exercise and elimination?

I'm connected to him as I am to no human being. He lets me touch him, hold him, play with him. He makes me laugh. He puts up with my taking care of him: brushing his fur, examining his paws or his ears, giving him medicine. He gives me a creature to care for.

He gives me someone to talk to. The mere hearing of my own voice is a relief from the inward pressure. Maybe loneliness is so intolerable because human beings are able to talk, and once they begin, they can't *not* talk. But talking requires a living being to listen, and a person by herself can't be both talker and listener. Something restrains people from talking out loud to themselves, anyway. The times I've done it here, the voiced words slipped out by themselves. They startled me as I heard them, so I'd go back to the silent dialogue. A second person, as a separate being, acts as an absorber of some sort. Logos gives me that: someone independent of me to whom I may address words. Words for him, not for me: talking to him about what I've unwound of myself would have been like talking out loud to myself. The words I direct to him are words about his concerns, and each new one widens the range of his responsiveness to me.

I scratch his belly lightly. The very tip of his tail moves feebly to thank me.

He's always here. He never goes away. He never threatens to go away. But more than that: he wants to be with me. He never sleeps in the kitchen while I'm at my desk; he's always near my feet. And when he sleeps, I see him open one eye from time to time to check that I'm still here. As though I could leave the room without his knowing it. I have only to slide back my chair, to take one step on the rug, to put down my pencil, to open a drawer for paper, and he's awake instantly, ready to come with me wherever I might go, whether from this room to the kitchen and back or for a three-mile walk along the ocean. He's here, and with me, and nothing short of my giving him away could ever make him leave me.

But I'm not so loyal. I can think of giving him away. Can I? Can I imagine him at Randall's house? Randall's wife and little girls playing with him, taking care of him?

I close my eyes and situate him in that household without me. My eyes fly open: there is an empty place in me to find him gone. I tear out a branch of my own being to think of giving him away. He belongs to me.

Involuntarily my mouth falls open. Not some unattainable person, but this puppy who is here with me now. I say his name aloud in my astonishment.

"Logos!"

He's wide awake and on his feet, shaking himself in a series of motions, ready now for the walk we haven't had today.

"Logos."

He trots to the doorway, then turns, impatient that I'm not following on his heels. I remain sitting on the floor, watching everything he does. How well I know him. As he knows me. He is *familiar*. But always new. He's part of my life. To give up my life is to give up him. It's easy enough to give up people who were never mine, but can I give up him?

I study the curving line of the shore, the separation of sand and water cleanly marked by the narrow white edge of low tide. There is very little wind, the day is brilliant, the horizon seems within reach. It is fantastically beautiful here.

I shake my head to make the pieces of my interior kaleidoscope slide from pattern to pattern.

I've accomplished nothing in two different attempts at a career. No relationship I've ever had with a man was genuine. I missed out on being equipped with the most basic tools for living a life: purposes and wantings and feelings are beyond my comprehension. Can I think of my life as valuable to me, even though it doesn't matter to anyone else?

Valuable. I visualize the word. It carries no meaning for me.

Wait. It's true that I've accomplished nothing in the eyes of people that I've let judge me. But suppose I use my own eyes. Suppose I take myself as my judge. That doesn't transform my failure into accomplishment, but it lets me see what the failure was: I failed because the things I set myself to do weren't things I *chose* to do. There was no real "I" to do the choosing. That hollow creature led by a child's heart, fighting rearguard actions all over the place to prevent anyone from noticing: I've torn it all away. And look what's left: this small shuddering self.

And yet I know some few things. I love Logos: I must have him with me. I can't think of myself without him. This ocean matters to me: my free access to it, the silence and the beauty, the vastness of the view.

Suppose I start with these things. And with the idea that other things may join with these. I don't know now what they'll be. Or when they'll come to me. Or whether there will be anything else at all.

But I start with these. They are all the self I have. But they are mine.

26

I awaken to an unfamiliar weight on my covers: Logos lies curled in a circle at the foot of the bed. In the moment I raise my head to look, he is upon me, licking my face, jumping over me from side to side to get a better purchase.

"Enough!" I sputter the word and try to form more, but instead I start to giggle at the persistent way he follows my head through all my movements of trying to avoid his tongue. Even he, finally, has to take a deep breath.

"You are on my bed." I note the fact plainly. He takes no action, except to underwrite his claim by settling his rear solidly on my knees and staring back. I bring my knees up quickly. He tumbles to the floor. But instantly he's back again and lying down, his chin flat on the covers between his paws. I smile at the intensity of his look. He's gauging my availability for further games.

I am awake one day beyond my time. Have I decided to live? I think I've only not decided not to. If I live, my life will have to be all mine, not anyone else's. No one else saved it, if saving it is what I'm doing, and no one else can take its measure. I haven't very much to go on, but I'll find my own way by myself, not by anyone else's version of what I can or cannot do. I don't know yet what I want to do, but when I find it out, I'll do it. Whether I'll do it well, whether I have the talent for it: these questions won't arise. "Is this the thing I want to do?" There's the point on which my pressure won't relent.

In the meantime, there are these days from waking to sleeping. Each one of them makes up my life. Each one of them must give me the same sense of whatever-it-is that being with Logos gives me, that walking along the ocean gives me. Closeness. Fitting me. Belonging.

Yes, from now on, I'll shape my day to make each thing in it fill me.

I start to carve a pat of butter for my toast, then draw back my knife. From now on I'll buy sweet butter. I don't have to wait for special occasions to use it, because from now on my whole existence is a special occasion.

I kick the sand as I walk, turning a small circle to keep Logos in view. Far behind me he barks at the gulls who had thought to have an undisturbed morning rest on the shore.

I shall measure everything I do against my knowledge that I can die. Not just that I'm flesh and shall therefore one day die, but that I, by my own hand, can choose the day. Of each thing that I do, I shall now ask, "Is this thing I'm doing worth being alive for?" The very doing is what matters. Even when I choose some future good toward which these present minutes point, I won't let there be hours that I only tolerate. I won't ever again put up with unthinking habit or being bored, or ugliness in things or persons. I have nothing important to do, but I have no time to waste marking time. Each thing I touch or see or smell or taste or hear during my day must give me the sense of something good in the doing. The list I wrote out last month was only one page long, poor list. I'll never be able to put together such a list again, because everything I do would have to be on it.

Nor are there things to wait for, except things that I myself set in motion now. Waiting? Why, the stupendous thing I used to wait for was something that was going to be done *to* me, or *for* me: to be initiated by someone else, independently of my choice. But there isn't a someone else to make things happen to me: I'm the only person who can do what I decide needs to be done. And besides, there is no *reason* for anyone else to do anything at all for me, particularly something as glorious as that thing I expected.

So on two counts waiting is irrelevant. Nothing to wait for, because I'll initiate what happens to me. Nothing to wait for, because these minutes now passing *are* my life. They are the minutes in which my living is to be done. Whatever I do, I'll do in my own time, and *I* will do it.

"Hey, Logos!" I pick up a piece of driftwood and throw it as far as I can. Logos appears from behind a dune to fly after it. "Bring it!" I cup my hands to my mouth to make my biggest sound, and although Logos hears me, it doesn't happen to be the game he wants to play.

I stand, watching the whitecaps form and roll into shore.

I don't have to wait to get married to have a home: I'll make my own. Oh, I know what that house will look like. I know the shapes and textures and colors that will fill it. Each thing in it will interest my own eye. Like Paris, designed to provide a view wherever you stand. My house will be my living museum.

I don't have to wait for someone to give me a sense of continuity: I'll carry my continuity within myself. I'll belong wherever I am. I'll institute my own permanence.

I find myself smiling.

After breakfast I take my book to the couch and lie reading all morning. At noon I take Logos for a long unthinking walk and return so hungry that I combine lunch and dinner at three in the afternoon. Logos falls asleep, and I return to my book until the fading light makes me notice that the day is gone. I tumble with Logos on the floor, toss the ball for him to bring back to me, test some of the obedience training I tried to teach him weeks ago, then take him outside.

Night here is both black and brilliant. My eyes are drawn upward, not only by the brightness of the stars, but also by the darkness against which they're set: the cloudless backdrop of the sky itself, and the unlighted night here on the ground. The stars are so clear and distinct that they could be Cartesian ideas. I look and wonder, noting certain relationships among them, but I'm unable to say more names than "Big Dipper."

Seven miles from here a hundred years ago, Maria Mitchell's father helped her put together an observatory, which the family deeded to the public at her death. What was a respectable young lady to do with her evenings that long ago? Play the piano for her father, read until her eyes smarted from the whale-oil lamp, and then, on her way to bed, look outside and upward. And if some matron asked her, when she grew older and remained a spinster, why she had devoted herself to studying the sky, she probably said, as Hillary said of Everest, it was simply there. Or perhaps even: I wanted to.

Such a luxurious day this has been. When did I last spend such a day? Not in grown-up memory. There was always something that had to be done, or done faster. As though unknown hands were shoving me forward. Yes, that's what the pressure was: I had to hurry without really knowing what it was I was hurrying to do. Maybe I can use that sense of *having* to hurry as a sign that I'm being propelled into doing something I haven't *chosen* to do.

Because that's what's different now: the urgency attached to everything has disappeared. There are no longer things I *must* do: there are only things I'll choose to do. And when I don't come upon them easily, I can at least avoid what isn't my own by attending to that sign.

We return to the house. On my way upstairs, I find myself smiling. Twice now in the last two days I've found myself smiling. I shake my head in disbelief. I stretch, anticipating the fullness of the sleep that will cap it all.

I have a peculiar sense of newness. I'm not sure what it is. I have the feeling that the words that come to me are new. Ridiculous. What do I mean?

I remember comparing notes with Mike one day. Most of the things we said seemed to us like lines in a play, as though we had memorized them, or planned them in advance. We told each other that we knew we had to break out of the script, yet it may even have been part of the script for us to say so. The sense of newness now is that the script is gone. I *find* myself thinking. I find myself talking. My words don't follow a prearranged pattern. They surprise me, even as I speak or think. Their unexpectedness catches my own attention, and, examining them, I discover what I *mean* to say.

I know what it is: I'm not being tested any longer. I've stopped submitting myself to an unending examination that I keep failing, question by question, letting the accretion of terror from past failures foredoom the next failure and therefore further terror. That's gone, that perduring sense of catastrophe, both present and impending. In its place is a sense of exploring, of tentativeness, almost of daring. I, who am such a coward: think of it. The question has stopped being whether I shall fail or succeed. Now it's merely whether the thing I'm doing is new or interesting. I can even make mistakes and *call* them "mistakes," instead of immediately considering them calamities.

Will I ever learn what loving is, and hating, and being angry, so that I can call them by name, too? Will I learn about them one at a time? Or is there some general capacity for feeling which, if I can ever find the way to come upon it, will show me to myself as sensitive to separate feelings on appropriate occasions? I didn't know how to talk about such things when I wrote my thesis, and it's still beyond me.

I reach down to scratch Logos' ears. He opens his eyes briefly, sighs, and falls asleep again. My education in these matters may be so long delayed that I, now entering middle age, may not learn about loving in time to have children of my own. Logos may take me as close to being a mother as I'll ever be.

I'll leave here at the end of January. I'm ready to go. I understand Thoreau now. The private business he went to Walden to transact was probably what I've been doing. But he never says why he went there, nor yet why he left. He says only that he left the woods for as good a reason as he went.

And yet, even if he had articulated his most private thinking, I couldn't have used it as an example for my own proceeding. Even if he had said only that he had smashed apart his being, without telling me how, I wouldn't have understood. Not till afterward, till I had done the thing myself. But before I came here, I didn't know that, and so I hoped to learn from him.

What sort of knowledge is this, that it can't be taught either by specific example or by abstract precepts? I think it's that knowledge Socrates meant when he said that virtue is knowledge but that it can't be taught. It can't be taught, but it can be learned. You have only to set yourself to be both teacher and learner at the same time. What you learn is something true of yourself alone. The reason no one else can teach it to you is that anyone else who has such knowledge knows only something which is true of himself, of herself, alone, too. Should it be called "knowledge" at all, then, since it concerns what is unique, as every self is?

I break off the thought abruptly. I know what I understand of myself up to now, but I can't know what else is still to come. I'm premature to start correcting Socrates.

27

Maybe teaching has the edge. Something about philosophy (I don't know what) may have attached itself to me beneath that exoskeleton that I bore.

Still, even if one of the teaching jobs comes through, it won't begin until September. I'll have to get some money between now and then. I could go straight from here to whatever town the university is in and get any sort of job until my teaching pay begins.

I quiver slightly, shaking off a sensation I cannot name. It's such a different way to look at things. Is this what it's like to see?

I draft three brief letters to the men I met in New York, informing them that my background file is available from Harvard. Two other openings will require longer letters, applications in themselves. But they'll need the Harvard information, too.

I fish through the new disarray on my desk for the instructions about filling out the Harvard questionnaire. I know why I hate questionnaires: they're pieces of treachery. Touch any part of all the neat printing and blank spaces, and something abominable wriggles out. Here: "Address." But in order to write down your address, you have to be living somewhere, and where do *I* live? They give me a space for both a temporary and a permanent address, but what do I do when all I have are temporary ones?

Well, I'll give them my Siasconset address. And for the permanent one, I'll think of someone who will let me receive mail at her house for a while. Who? I start to write in June's Cambridge address, but then stop. Mail addressed to me there would automatically be forwarded by the post office to whatever address I gave when I moved away from that apartment two years ago.

The old reaches up to drag me down again on the very page where I'm trying to start out fresh. I have to try to free myself from it. Maybe all I can do is realize that the traps are there, and try to avoid them. Until, if ever, I won't need to ask anyone for anything at all.

I glance quickly through the rest of the form. Each question turns me inside out at the thought of preparing an answer. References. Who will speak for me? Henry. But I need five others. How shall I find five men who have taught me or hired me, and who will also write letters of recommendation that will help me rather than stand in my way? I rest my head in my arms on my typewriter. One by one I discard the highly respectable men I know. I've dealt badly with all of them. Not because they were who they were, but because I was who I was.

Must I write them each a letter, explaining what I now understand? Why should they believe me? There's no reason for them to give me an opportunity to undo the way I've behaved. I can't even tell them I'm committed to philosophy and to teaching, so I can't tell them the truth even now. Because I have to have food and shelter and clothing. For those things, it seems I have to continue to lie. For this little while, anyway. At least I'm lying only to them.

My own past is trying to lock me in again. I will *not* let it. How could any of these men have known that I was running for my life? They probably saw me as running away from whatever promise I had made to them. And condemned me. Rightly.

I sit back in my chair. I'm exhausted merely considering going back into that world. The doors may already be closed against me, by my own hand.

I slip the form into the typewriter again. Did I think it would be simple?

The gray day gives me no clue about the passage of time, but Logos knows that he's been lying still long enough to deserve a walk. He takes my hand in his mouth and gently pulls. I let him lead me to the back door, and I hold it open for him. He starts to go out, then stops, looking up at me, his tail wagging tentatively.

"Tell you what. You go out, and I'll be right there." I hold the door open again. He views the situation differently. His eyes still on me, he backs into the kitchen, to be wherever I am. It's too late to get my letters into the outgoing mail. I still have two to recopy.

"You win." I slip on my boots and my hat. It's not easy, with a large puppy leaping up against the door and crying out his joy.

If the teaching jobs don't come through in time, I'll find some job near one of my friends.

Strange. From one day to the next, I've stopped thinking of them as people to whom my life has to matter in some essential way. I'm the one to whom my life must matter. I can hardly ask of my friends something that I don't yet know whether I can ask of myself.

Can I live near Joyce? No, too near my family. And we haven't been close recently. Our lives are too different. I think perhaps she alone might have tried to come here if I had asked. But I couldn't have asked her. Her little boy's illness requires her presence there.

Etel. No, we don't hold up when we see one another regularly. Etel is for a long talk that's better when it's rare.

Jean. Yes, a good idea. Or Marilyn. I'll write them both.

No, I'll call Marilyn right now. Her letter from the hospital was dated—where is it?—December 28. How long before new mothers take their babies home? It's the sort of fact I'll probably never confirm firsthand.

I can write Jean the letter I couldn't write Etel a month ago. Now I understand beginning, middle, and end. I write it in outline, promising to fill in the details when we see each other. I ask her to poke around the University of Toronto for a job for me, and for an inexpensive apartment where I can live with Logos. In case I decide to go to Toronto until a teaching job comes through.

The letter makes a thick handful with the others, and when I drop them into the outgoing mail and head for the beach, I have a sense of unfamiliar lightness.

The letters I've just sent off mark my pursuit of all the available possibilities. Each of them can start a new path for me. It will be a week at the earliest before I receive a reply from anyone. Now I can only wait.

I inhale the salt air. The tide is in. The sea is silver. We've been three days without the sun.

My sense of being unconnected to anyone is turning back on me and becoming something else. Something I'm not sure yet that I understand.

I am disburdened. That's it. Free: not obliged, not required, not compelled to do anything. Free: no longer condemned to keep repeating the disasters of the past.

The nun who stopped to ask me directions on the Berkeley campus last year. Her black robes being blown by the wind entered my peripheral vision as I lay reading on the sloping ground, and I looked up. There were so few students wandering around that Saturday, cold and portending rain, that perhaps I would have paused to examine any passerby. But as she climbed the winding path, I realized that it was her own movements, not the wind, that were making her robes whip and flow around her. She was walking, not mincing. Her stride was long but graceful. It was the walk of Indians. I knew what it felt like: I had read about that walk as a little girl and I had taken it for my own. She was showing me what it looked like.

By the time she was a dozen steps away, I must have been smiling, because she smiled at me and waved, then continued up the hill toward one of the buildings. The motion of her hand was as fluent as her walk, so much a part of one unified organism that any tutored actress would have envied her. I turned back to my book, but then I heard footsteps on the grass behind me and there she stood, looking down at me, her hands clasped loosely in one more easy gesture. I started to get to my feet to reply to her question about where a certain building was, but she raised one hand to stop me, and then as quickly returned her hand to what must have been a position of rest for her. I stood, anyway. I wanted to be able to help her, but I didn't know the campus too well myself.

"There's an information office in that building." I pointed toward Sproul Hall. "But I'm not sure whether it's open on Saturday afternoon."

She smiled at me again, thanked me, raised her hand a little higher than the gesture that had told me not to disturb myself, and said, "God bless you." She spoke directly to me, as though she were imprinting the words on my mind. And then, in the same astonishing harmony, her body moving without hindrance, moving with its garments rather than in opposition to them, she started up the hill again.

I stood looking after her until she was out of sight. She was the only person I had ever seen who was free. She moved so naturally because inside she was also graced. When she blessed me, I understood that she was giving me something of what constituted the core of her being. It was something that was at once so personal and yet so impersonal that I almost ran after her to ask her to explain to me how that could be.

If I had met her now instead of then, I think I would have stopped her before she turned away, to talk to her about who she was, and why she had become a nun, and whether what I understood of her was how she saw herself. But that afternoon as she walked away, I felt myself in another world from hers. I was waiting for replies to all my letters asking about jobs; I was seeing Stan almost every day, waiting for him to look at me and see me and say, "Stay here with me"; I was living in a dreary hotel on money I had borrowed from Etel, from Weck, from whoever could spare me something to keep me fed until I got a job.

I wouldn't have known then how to speak to her. She would have been only one more person whose help I was asking for.

I know why I think of her now. Things have been feeling new to me for the past several days, and she, in spite of her acquiescence to the authority her robes symbolized, remains in my memory as some exemplar of independence. No, not quite. Of genuineness: although she accepted the authority of the Church, it was she who chose it, and her choice freed her. How do I know? It was the quality that came across to me.

In the distance I can see the high fence that announces federal property. I look around for Logos. I know why I don't often come this way: the fencing places a limit on how far I may go. I see Logos busy digging far away, the unrelieved flatness of the beach presenting no obstruction between us. I walk toward him, and together we scramble up the low bank that separates the beach from the road. The houses here are smaller and closer together than those that line the bluff, but these too give the same impression of having grown where they happened to have been planted.

At a sharp angle to the paved road I find the road that leads the long way into the Siasconset Road. I save this way home for leisurely days, of which there will be more until I leave than there have been up to now. I slow my steps, amused. What do I mean? I mean that the torturing work is over, that the thinking I'll do from now on is of a sort so new that I don't yet know what it will be like to set myself to it.

What makes me think it's something I can set myself to do?

The routine of my day fits me like an old sweater: comfortable, easy to move with, room enough to stretch. Awake when I finish sleeping; meals when I'm hungry; outdoors when I want to feel or smell fresh air; reading when it beckons me; Logos sandwiched in among it all for playing, for fun, for a living being.

I'm beginning to be able to rank things in order of importance. Before, I responded to everything at peak pitch, without gradations of intensity. I see now why people thought I was theatrical. I always played to reach the last row in the balcony.

Because I had no gauge within me. The standard for any performance of mine, on stage or off, existed in other people's eyes. Now I seem to be growing a gauge of my own. Still fragile, still very small, but mine.

Crudely shaped milestones, set out more than a hundred years ago, mark the seven-mile road from Nantucket to Siasconset, ending at the flagpole in front of the post office. I leave Logos in the car behind bags of groceries, and hop out to pick up my mail: Etel and something from Harvard. I stick the letters into my pocket, turn into my driveway, unload the packages, and drive the car into the garage. I hold the back door open for Logos to precede me, but he stands outside, legs planted firmly, barking me a long story about how he's played my game by letting me shop and pick up mail, and now it's his turn.

"Okay. Wait till I put away the food that goes into the refrigerator."

It's not soon enough for him.

"Okay, okay." I keep up a chatter of persuading words as I store the perishables, and we're on our way.

I slow down, reading Etel's scrawl on three sides of a notepaper carrying an Egyptian print on its cover. She thinks I should join the Peace Corps. I resent the suggestion. Not just because the Peace Corps means wandering for two more years, but because it's irrelevant to what I've been thinking about. Well, how could she know? I haven't been able to write her a good letter since I've been here.

Logos is leading me down the road to the golf course, but a long walk can be only a hope today: the sun is very low on the horizon.

I suddenly remember the Harvard letter and slit it open. Routine, as I thought. They've received the forms I filled out. They'll type them and send them where I requested. They enclosed recommendation blanks to be sent to the three new references I listed. I start to stuff the letter back into my pocket, and then I reread it closely.

"Oh, no!" On the empty road, I cry out. Logos looks back at me, then turns and runs with me, flying ahead to the house. I rush upstairs to the phone and sit next to it, my hand trembling on the receiver. How could she have misunderstood my letter? I've got to stop her from sending out those old references. Before I dial the operator, I try to plan my speech. I must be cool, not angry. I must be clear, not garbled.

The operator has the woman on the line before I've fully caught my breath from my run. "I'm calling to ask whether you've had time to finish typing the forms I sent you."

"Why, yes, we sent them out just this afternoon."

I hold my hand over the receiver and bite my lip before I speak. My words come falling out anyway. "But it never occurred to me that my old Radcliffe references were transferred to your office. I thought my whole file would be new."

The woman doesn't understand what I'm trying to say. How do I tell her that when that bastard Hal fired me he read me one of my references but wouldn't tell me whose it was, and that the reference spoke more about my irresponsibility than about my mind? How do I tell her that she has gotten me off to a new start by dragging me back into uncertainties and apologies? How do I tell her to throw away that reference whose author I don't know? How do I find out who wrote it so that I, trusting him, don't ask him to write one for me again?

"We thought we were helping you by getting your forms and references out as quickly as we could. But we seem to have done something to upset you. Please tell me what it is, and perhaps we can undo it."

I try to swallow my tears, but even I hear them in my voice. "You see, inadvertently I discovered that one of my references is detrimental to me, but I don't know which one."

She is silent. I'm silent, too, hoping for some miracle: she'll remove the letter from the outgoing mail and tear it up.

"I'm sorry that there's been this misunderstanding. I'll withdraw your old references from your files, and send you three more new reference blanks. That will give you six new recommendations. It's the only thing we can do now."

When I hang up I lie back on the bed. Good-bye to the job where she sent the old references. I fling my body to the other side. How will I ever be sure that I haven't included the betrayer among the new set of six? Maybe I can't go back into teaching, after all. Not if that record will trail me for the rest of my days.

Here I sit, singing in the wilderness. Well and good, so long as I stay here. But my first footstep back into the world where I'm to live the life I've just begun to take into my own hands lands me smack in the middle of the same black mess. I've torn away the old causes, which lay in myself, but I can't tear away the old consequences, which will continue to lie in places like the Radcliffe files and in the opinions of men who have the power to give or withhold my jobs.

I sigh a long sigh. And I was going to teach only to give myself the time to see what I want to do. No, I haven't worked this out yet at all.

I head straight for my desk after breakfast. It takes me the morning to write six letters requesting references for the Harvard file. I get up from my chair, pace the room, sit, go out into the kitchen, sit down again, play with Logos outside, and come back to my desk one last time. By noon it occurs to me that I don't want to write to these men. I'm asking for their help, and I now find asking for help difficult to do. Worse: I'm asking *these* men, who know me as I was. And yet, what am I now except a woman who, as the fruit of thirty-seven years, knows only that I love my puppy and walking along the ocean?

I copy out three of the letters and enclose the Harvard forms. The other letters can wait until the rest of the forms arrive.

Logos and I go out the door, he so unexpectedly that in the driveway he's still shaking himself awake. I stand for a moment in the sunlight, holding my face up to allow the weak winter warmth to bake out the last unpleasantness from my morning's work. Then we walk very fast to the post office, more to get the letters out of my hands and thoughts than to make the outgoing mail. It happens that I do both.

28

The Kennel Club registration blank for Logos finally arrives. I read the letter from my landlady on my way to the beach, then stick it into my pocket. Something about it puzzles me, but I don't know what. And then I see. She should have been angry. I defaulted on my offer to keep her house open until spring, and now she has the cost and bother of closing it for the rest of the winter. She has a right to be angry, but she isn't. Or rather, it comes through only in little ways, almost as an aside. She wants to avoid displeasing me. How curious. Why should she care?

It's like my own sidewinding way of dealing with something difficult: appease it, because if you say what you mean, all hell will break loose. All hell: my mother's raging, screaming fury.

I have to sit down.

I'll keep finding her in my life anyway, won't I? So that's why I never became angry: to avoid the anger that was always at her disposal and that always won. Another little-girl lesson learned too well. And yet, I screamed back at her. I close my eyes to close out the years of battles. Perhaps I started screaming back when I gave up the hope of getting her attention any other way. And later, growing up, I deliberately decided not to be angry, to keep from being like her in any way. I've done such a good job of it that even I don't know when I'm angry. So I stay unangry with other people because I still believe that otherwise they'll go away. As she did, by raving at me.

Think of the times George did something I didn't like. I'd become silent, and then try to persuade him not to do it. Even the day he told me about Elizabeth over the phone, I discovered that I couldn't speak, and so I simply hung up the receiver. But, oh, the price I paid to make him stay.

I get up from the sand and brush off my coat. I have to say what I mean. I *have* to. If, in the process, someone goes away, why, then, he was no friend in the first place.

Where did that come from? I grin. It's one of the things I find myself saying.

It will be a long time before I touch a man again. I think I haven't often *liked* the men I've made love with. Maybe allowing myself time to find out whether I like the next man can spare me an unnecessary involvement in advance.

I smile. What's a necessary involvement? Why, it's one that I don't need but that I want. I don't mean sexual wanting. I know what that feels like: an engine inside me starts chugging and then leads me by the nose, never fast enough, to a man's arms. Used to lead me. I know now that my being drawn to a man is the best reason of all for never seeing him again, because the thing in him that draws me is something I no longer need. Perhaps I'll never be drawn that way again. Perhaps I'll be suspicious of anything that seems too urgent.

I could install some sort of brake on myself, in case I'm tempted again. Say, by asking myself what the man might be like afterward. There's a difference between male and female sexuality: done and done, for the man; still ebbing, for the woman. And that's a difference of kind, not of degree. That's why a man can always be at least sexually satisfied, whatever else he gets from an encounter. It's why a woman can't be sexually satisfied unless she also has some affection for the man. I suppose that a man's satisfaction increases in direct proportion to his fondness for the woman, but for him the only question is how intense his pleasure will be. For her, the question is whether there will be satisfaction at all.

I suddenly understand that the idea of female chastity is psychologically sound. It's a way of enshrining the difference in sexuality so that male and female have equal advantages. It's a way of giving the woman time to discover what sort of person her companion is, to learn whether a valuable relationship can be built with him. If she can only tell herself to bide her time, not for the purpose of bestowing herself, of doing the man a favor, but for the purpose of coming to know what sort of person he is.

But he may choose to pout at waiting. Or he may threaten to go elsewhere. Well, then, he's telling the woman what he'll be like afterward: spoiled, childish, insensitive to her. And that's signal enough for any woman. If she can hear it.

Because if it starts in bed, the likelihood is that it will end there. A man goes away when he uses up his sexual interest in a woman, if he has no incentive to search for other interests to share with her.

I don't mean that a woman's sexuality is moral, and that a man's is not. A man's sexual wanting of a woman is honest, and to that extent moral, at the time she falls into bed with him. But his desire for water is also honest at the time that he drinks. If the woman quenches his thirst in the hope of becoming his friend later on, she fails to recognize that for a man sexuality can be two things, while for her it can be one only. For a man, a woman can be either a vessel or a friend; for a woman, unless a man is her friend, sex is merely a temporary connection.

Chastity is a way of arming a woman in case her runaway body inclines her to believe that her sexuality is like a man's: that she can pop in and out of bed, just as he does, and with the same gain. Or worse, that his sexuality is like hers: that if he takes her to bed, he thereby commits himself to her.

So it's simply irrelevant to condemn a man for taking a woman to bed and then wandering away from her. If the woman is willing, if the water is free, he beds her, he drinks. Because his sexuality can be separate from himself. But a woman's sexuality is an inextricable part of herself. Chastity is a discipline she can impose upon herself to guarantee, as far as guaranteeing is possible, that her single-faceted sexuality will be gratified by a man who has two facets at his disposal wherewith to treat her.

But the whole thing has been turned on its head. The psychological importance of chastity for females has been transposed into a rule of conduct for us. No matter that sooner or later we break the rule and feel guilty about it. Yet sexuality has almost nothing to do with morality in this narrow sense. Moral questions arise only when the man or woman contemplating an encounter is connected in some special way to someone else. The moral question is: Will this encounter undercut, betray, destroy, or even weaken, that other commitment? The answer depends upon the nature of *that* commitment, not upon *this* encounter.

Chastity can preserve a woman's *psychological* purity, not some narrowly conceived moral purity. When some third person isn't involved, the scope of morality in relation to sex is so broad that it really concerns what it is to be a person. And that's exactly what psy-

chological purity is about: Can you, without pretending to yourself
or to him, be whoever you are and let him be whoever he is and
thereby gratify your sexuality? A woman damages herself psychologically if she can't be at her ease sexually. She can't be at ease sexually unless she trusts the man, she can't trust him unless she knows
him, and she can't know him unless she gives herself time to know
him. That's what chastity can do: give her time.

Historically, men imposed chastity on women to keep women
"clean." But the mistake was theirs, in thinking that female sexuality
has two aspects. And yet, some women must have understood that
chastity was to their psychological advantage, accepted it for that
reason, and passed the knowledge on to their daughters.

A strange business. In order to understand how to be true to herself, which is the only sort of chastity that matters, a woman must
first be what men call "unchaste." Unless it's possible to explain all
this to a virgin. And why not? You begin by doing away with all the
little do's and don'ts of sex, and you stand back to give the child
room to grow into the self she can become. Then chastity for her
won't have anything to do with the number of men she makes love
with: it will have to do only with whether she, knowing herself, has
shared something valuable with another person who is also her
friend.

The sky in the east reflects the red of the setting sun. My body is
stiff and cold from sitting on the sand. Logos stretches, too, and we
walk slowly home.

The pieces of my ideas about sexuality yesterday at the beach surprise me by the way they fit together. They seemed transparent:
nothing screened me from them. I pursued them to their end and
found them sound. But that's brand new: throwing off any inclination to look outside myself for confirmation of my own beliefs.

All the years I spent reading and trying to learn how to think may
not have been a total loss. Perhaps what I freely believe lies buried in
my mind beneath the weight of other people's standards, and I have
only to try to tear away whatever is foreign in order to bring my own
beliefs to light.

Think how many times before yesterday I tried to understand what
it is to be a woman. Impossible to count them. I've thought about it
more than any other single thing, but it forever eluded me. Because I
had to use other people's starting-points. Even Dr. Kant's idea wasn't
right for me. I abandoned it at the first sign of difficulty with George.

But yesterday I pulled together all the ideas about sex that I could never quite give up, even though almost nothing in my experience justified my holding on to them.

Like: it's important to be honest with a man. True. I just didn't know what "being honest" meant. I thought it had to do with telling the man everything I had done in the past. But (why didn't I notice it before?) that's treating my life as something that requires confession, and treating the man as someone having the power—no, the right—to grant absolution. That's not what being honest is. I'm honest when I refuse to deceive myself or the man about my feelings, in any situation in which feelings are essentially involved. I haven't been honest with men, then, because my responses have almost never been genuine. With friends, with work, with anything at all. I don't know how I'm going to learn to find out what I feel. Until I do, I won't look for a man to be involved with. I won't deceive myself into believing that some man standing attractively before me has something to give me, or I to give him.

And then that other idea that you can't be a woman until you're first a person. I could only insist on it before.

"What do you think being a woman is?" I can still hear the scorn in that psychiatrist's voice, the one before Dr. Kant. He wanted me to believe that first I was a sexual being, and only after that, if ever, could I be a person. What else could he, a Freudian, believe? But he was a man, and so was Freud. Maybe Freud is right, for men. But a man who wants to understand a woman's sexuality ought to look closely at what sex is like for him when he's with a woman he loves.

I said to that psychiatrist, "You have to be a person before you can be a woman. Being a person has to do with being generous and thoughtful and kind and gentle." I was wrong, but not for his reason. I was wrong because being a person has to do with generosity and kindness only secondarily to being honest with myself. Suppose my generosity is the means I used to get someone to give me something. Suppose my kindness is my way of ignoring my own anger. Suppose my thoughtfulness is my way of manipulating other people's lives. Those are exactly the deceptive purposes I've been tearing away here. I'm no person yet. But I know that until I know the person I am, I'll be no woman either. I'll be no woman because I won't take on a man until I can be honest with both of us.

Does that mean that it will take a man to show me my womanliness, but that I can show myself my personhood? Perhaps that's what it will be for me, since I'm so late in coming to understand. Or perhaps by the time I come to know myself, I'll find myself a womanly person, and merely most womanly of all in the presence of a man.

I feel naked and very small. But new. Nothing ever again has to be the way it was. If I can only hold back the world until I can catch up with my own unclad response to it.

29

One by one, the letters in my mail cut off potential routes away from Nantucket. The likeliest job opening is out: they have to delay choosing their candidate until certain administrative matters are dealt with. Living near Marilyn or Jean is out: Marilyn is off to Mexico next month, and permission for Americans to work in Canada is difficult to come by.

The Harvard envelope can wait until we get home. Walking the long blocks, my thoughts move on square wheels. Absently, forgetting that I decided otherwise, I slit open the Harvard envelope and find a letter enclosed with the reference forms. The woman has read all my old references and doesn't see how any of them can harm me. "In all honesty" she thinks they'll help me in my candidacy for any job.

I stop in the middle of crossing the road. Someone is lying to me: she, to cover over her misreading of my instructions, or that bastard who fired me, to destroy my confidence in my own references.

I kick the stones along the gravel road. What do I do about all this? The very place that's a source of teaching jobs for me may also be the place that undercuts my every attempt to get one. A chill runs through me and I shudder it away. This is the same old world. I'm deluding myself to think that I can be different from what I was, in relation to it.

An hour, a drink, I wait for the confusion to assume some usable shape. On my desk, bills still unopened from yesterday. Maybe I should pay some of them now.

The checks for two months' phone and electricity and for three months of the local newspaper leave my balance at $27.79. Shall I break into the California savings account? Not yet. That $600 will melt away once I start on it.

I lean back in my chair. I have to get some money very fast.

The Stamford company. I'll write an analysis of their report. No, it would take too long. I'll talk to them about it. I'll tell them that I don't have time to write something for them, but that if they want to come here, or if they want me to go there, expenses paid, I'll discuss with them what needs to be done.

I sit down at the typewriter, grinning, and write the letter in minutes. I seal it into its envelope and put it next to my keys. I'll take it to the post office first thing in the morning, and then get to work on the report. It will be at least Tuesday before I can look for a reply. Unless they phone.

I lift my glass and toast the room. How incredible to deal with a problem in its own terms. No monstrous cloud of problems tags in the wake of this one, magnifying and making complex what isn't complex at all. Difficult, yes, but simple in the sense of being single, of being one problem only. Well, we shall see whether my solution is a match for it.

I skim the pages of the report and find that my marginal notes go as far as page eighteen. I start mid-page, but in two sentences I see that I've forgotten what the early pages covered. I turn back to the beginning and read the first page, and then, baffled, read it again. The third time through, I slam it down on my desk and go into the kitchen for a cup of coffee.

Think of it like this: if it were comprehensible, they wouldn't pay me fifty dollars a day to make it so.

I carry my cup back to my desk. Suppose I try to put myself in this man's place. When he wrote this, there was something he was trying to say. He himself can't say it. But scattered among all these words are some clues. I can try to unravel it for him, at least to the point of asking him whether such-and-such is what he means, and if it is, then the way to say it is thus-and-thus.

I pick up my pen to wade in again. I've done exactly this for students in my courses. For far less than fifty dollars a day.

I keep a record of the hours I spend on the report, covering its pages with notes and underlinings and arrows indicating which paragraphs are to be moved to other sections. I return to it several times before the day ends. Sometimes I close it in despair. But it offers an intellectual exercise that I'm surprised to find absorbing.

I discover a restlessness to be gone. Perhaps my preparations are long since completed. I'm not content to move through my accustomed day. I cut short the morning walk and we drive into town. We amble up one side of Main Street and down the other: Logos eager to explore, even with the leash's restraint; I peering into shop windows. To the library, next, for a new stack of books. Back in the car I crisscross the town along the narrow cobblestoned streets. I become a tourist. I park in front of Nantucket's three-hundred-year-old house. From my car I look at it speculatively. If there's an admission charge, I won't be able to go in. I turn the ignition key, and drive home at twenty miles an hour.

I'm waiting again. The difference is that I'm waiting for specific events. I've submitted myself as employable, and now it's up to others to accept or decline my offer.

I read long after lunch, but then I want to be moving, active. An hour remains until the afternoon mail is due. I stick my book into my coat pocket and head for the beach by way of the long paved road. Walking, I read. From time to time, check to see that Logos doesn't stray into someone's yard, or that my feet aren't leading me off the road. Once, looking up, I see three schoolgirls coming toward me from far away. The next time I look, I can almost discern their faces.

And then, before I know it, I hear their words from the opposite side of the road. I smile at them and go back to my book. Abruptly they become silent. And then I hear their giggles in irregular chorus, and ". . . with her dog . . ." and ". . . she's always. . . ." I look back at them. They've stopped. Their eyes meet mine.

I know immediately that they've seen me before, that they've heard me discussed. People may not have been in the streets for me to see, but they've been in their houses, and they've seen me walk by. I'm the town curiosity, and it's only now, looking into the faces of these children, that I find it out. They want to talk to me, but they're not sure whether they should. I don't help them decide. I go back to my book, and continue down the road at my slow pace.

My concentration refuses to settle on the page. What new thing just happened? In a dozen steps I understand: I've just encountered public opinion and discounted it. I've ceased caring how I look to other people or what they say about me. I've stopped letting faceless groups demand my adherence to imaginary standards. "They" cannot be with me while I die; therefore "they" have no right to set rules for me while I live.

I could invite someone here. Someone for whom this island would be a vacation; someone whose hospitality I've never been able to repay.

"Laurel, would you like to come out here next weekend? There's nothing to do, but it's very beautiful. The light is spectacular; no one bumps garbage cans at five in the morning; and the fresh air will put you to sleep. How about it?"

"It sounds too good, Tim, but something might be on for the weekend. If not, I'd love to come. Can I call you as late as Thursday?"

"Or five minutes before you step on the plane. Try to come."

"I will. I'll call you in a few days."

In the middle of Tuesday afternoon the Stamford people phone. The man with whom I've been corresponding will come here to talk with me tomorrow. He'll drive to Massachusetts and catch a plane from one of the shore towns. Yes, I'll reserve a room for him in Nantucket.

I hang up, clapping my hands and shouting. Logos comes running as if I had summoned him, a ball in his mouth, ready to play. I wrestle with him on the floor instead. "Logos, we're going to have some money, real green money. Yes, we are, we are."

The two hotels open during the winter are booked for tomorrow. One clerk suggests a guest house in the town. I settle the reservation there immediately, and come away from the phone grinning. This is how you get something you want. First, you figure out who has it; then you figure out what its possessor needs and whether *you* have *that*. Then you're in a bargaining position.

How plainly simple. Not the getting, but the thinking about getting. Yet before, I thought that the only way to get what I wanted was to ask for it, or to let it be known that I wanted it. And that I'd get it if the person liked me; otherwise, not. It never occurred to me to consider that something was expected of me in return. What kind of idiot does that make me? A practical idiot: an idiot for all practical purposes. I wince at the parade of people who must have been baffled by their dealings with me.

I walk downstairs to my desk to find the report. I start to make some notes to get my ideas in order for the discussion tomorrow, but my thoughts keep recurring to the very new way I've been thinking in the last few days. How do I *know* that getting something requires that I understand the reasons a person might have for giving it to me? Or know that I'd better look closely at what someone expects in return before I take what he offers me?

I shake my head. It's a strange other world. Wait, that's it. I inhabit a natural world of causes and effects, which I understand well enough; but I also inhabit a social world of persons having purposes, which I'm only starting to understand.

I'm just becoming able to separate out the human beings from the trees in the general landscape. But what lets me do it?

The edges of a reply tease their way into my thinking, but the idea is still too shapeless for me to reach. I give it up for now and turn my attention to the report that is my new source of food and shelter.

Ugo tells me how to type out my bill to his company. The figures on the page are so fat and round that I smile to see them holding one another up in their fullness: $350. For the assorted four days' worth of hours I've spent reading and scribbling on the pages of this report, for the brief talk last evening and for all day today, and then for one day thrown in for the pot. I take the page out of the typewriter, keep one copy, sign the original, and hand it to Ugo.

He folds it into his pocket. "I'll have this taken care of as soon as I get back, and you'll have the check in a few days."

Over a drink he talks further about his plans for employing me. "I know I can persuade Len to hire you. If I can't get you thirteen thousand dollars a year, will you settle for twelve thousand?"

I look at him, contracting my eyebrows to keep the laughter inside me. He interprets the scowl as disappointment. "All right, then, I'll try to make it something in between. Would you consider that?"

I let the question hang. He knows whether the amount is too little or just enough, and soon or later, in some way or other, he'll let me know which.

"Let me take your report back to my office."

"But these are only notes to myself. Half the words are my own abbreviations."

He insists. My misgivings find no voice. I hand him the report. "I really don't think it will be much use to you."

"I know you want to leave here by the end of the month, so I'll write you a letter making a formal offer as soon as I get back."

A silence begins to settle in the room, and then the phone rings. I excuse myself and fly up the stairs, removing the phone from its hook gratefully.

"Timmie, I'll be there on the six o'clock plane tomorrow. Do you still want me to come?"

"Laurel! Of course. I'll be waiting for you at the airport. I'm really glad you're coming."

"So am I. See you tomorrow."

I hang up, unexpectedly pleased. Instantly I remember the difficulty simmering in the living room. I delay a few minutes longer to consider it. Just be careful, Alice.

When I go downstairs, Ugo is standing a few steps from the entryway. He looks at me steadily.

I find the words I want to say as I hear my voice saying them. "You're a married man with children, and I may be working for you soon."

His hands brush my words away. "What has that got to do with it?"

"From your point of view, nothing. From my point of view, it's the whole story."

I drive him into Nantucket, Logos in his usual place beside me, Ugo in back, and drop him at the guest house. I concentrate on finding my way through the streets of the town, unfamiliar now with streetlights and darkness, and then swing out into the Siasconset Road.

It felt strange yesterday to have someone else walking along the shore with me. I, who lived my life in the reflection of other people's eyes, seem now to have lost all sense of what I look like to them. Half a dozen times yesterday I turned to look at Ugo and found a look of surprise on his face. He wasn't used to hearing provocative ideas, he said, let alone from a woman who remained womanly. A line? I shrug. Perhaps it matters whether a man means what he says only when the man himself matters.

Anyway, I was only being the one person I am, instead of playing different roles with different people: the seductress with a man; the humble student with a teacher; the rebel, only sometimes silent, with administrators; the sophisticate in the city; the tomboy on walks around Cambridge at night. I was what others expected me to be.

Yet, even now, I try to have no silences during conversation. The actress picking up cues, keeping the lines coming, not missing a beat in the dialogue. Half of the words I've uttered in my life have probably been some sort of stuffing: to fill the void, to be polite, to be agreeable. I kept trying to fight that yesterday. I seem almost to have taken a vow not to say anything until I can say what I mean. That leaves stretches of unaccustomed silence while I consider my thoughts. But then when I hear the words I find myself finally saying, the sense of newness fills me again and repays me for the difficult work. Or when I force myself to weigh what someone says to me, I discover, incredulously, that I can say the truth politely and not worry about its agreeableness at all.

Logos is digging a deep hole nearby.

"What would you like, Sweet Puppy?"

Immediately his mouth holds a stick. He places it at my feet and then backs away, poised to run. A lesson in how to make your meaning clear. I toss the stick very far and watch him run. He's back before I can take up the thread of my thought. I toss it again, then half a dozen times more, until he's content to lie next to me, panting to catch his breath. I stroke his head. "You're first, even though you didn't have my undivided attention yesterday."

We head for the post office on the way home. There will be time to think about Ugo's job offer after Laurel leaves.

30

I cash a check for twenty dollars at the supermarket. Laurel steps in front of me to pay for our groceries at the check-out counter.

"But, Laurel, you're my guest."

"I'm working, you're not."

We load the bags into the car. "Laurel, I want it to be only a loan. I'm going to get that fat check next week, and as soon as I do, I'll repay you."

"Tim, really, it isn't that much: twelve dollars and some cents."

"You didn't come here prepared to buy my groceries for the week. No, I want to pay you back."

She shrugs. "Okay. Pay me when you can."

I shift into reverse to back out of our parking space, but then I move the stick into neutral again and look at Laurel. "Since I already owe you twelve dollars, how about letting me owe you five more? The bourbon is getting low."

We look at each other and burst into laughter. "You haven't changed, Tim. You're still trying to beat the game."

"If you hadn't called me to come here by the end of this week, I was going to call you. I've been worrying about you. I didn't really know whether you'd do yourself in."

I rest my arm around her shoulder as we walk. "It took me a little while to make up my mind." We are silent, following the curve of the bluff. The narrow path forces us to walk single file.

"What made you decide to live?"

Logos swings around in front of us to take the lead. I nod my head toward him. "He did."

Behind me Laurel stops. "Oh, come now, Tim."

I stop too, and turn to her. "It's true. He belongs to me. No one else does, nothing else does."

"I think you've spent so much time on that puppy that you haven't really dealt with the thing at all. If I were contemplating suicide, my two children wouldn't be enough to stop me, and they belong to me more than Logos could ever belong to you."

"Maybe. But you asked what stopped me, not what might stop you. I don't claim that anything I've come to understand about myself is true for anyone else."

We begin to walk again. The sky is clouding over, the wind is shifting to the north. I glance at Laurel, wrapped in a leather coat, her black fur hat leaving only the face between her eyes and chin visible. "You look warm enough. Are you?"

She nods, and continues walking without speaking.

"Ready to go home? We can take a shortcut through this driveway."

"No, Tim, you go on. I think I'd like to walk along the ocean by myself."

I'm surprised, but I raise my arm to point out the dumpy gray cylinder that constitutes the Siasconset skyline. "See the water tower? Use that as an orientation. I live on that street."

We wave and go our separate ways.

An hour before her plane is due to leave, Laurel starts to pack. The pouring rain has kept us in since noon. Between the bursts of rain, the fog grows thicker. I call the airport to check on her flight. It's canceled.

Laurel looks at me in dismay. "Can I take a boat?"

"The boat left two hours ago, if it left at all. The next thing leaving here is the ten o'clock plane tomorrow morning. If it flies."

"But I've got to be at my job tomorrow!"

"Nantucket is an island, Laurel. This is what it means."

It takes her a while to give in to the geography of the matter, and then she gets on the phone to New York to rearrange her plans. When she comes back downstairs, I have drinks ready for both of us. She settles back on the couch, glass in hand, and sighs. "I'm glad to stay another day. I don't remember when I've slept as well as I've slept here. I've needed this quiet and this freedom. I've needed to have time away from my beautiful little girls, much as I love them. I've needed to get away from the pressure of my job. Oh, I like the job, but there are too many new things that I still have to get used to. Being here gives me some breathing space."

"I've got an idea, Laurel. Let's talk about you."

She looks up at me quickly. "I know I always find a way to bring the conversation around to myself."

I smile. "And I was one of the people who used to tease you most about it. But that was only because I thought we ought to be talking about *me*. One of the benefits to my friends about the thing I've been trying to do here is that I don't have to talk about myself anymore."

She starts to ask me a question, but I cut her off. "If I can be some sort of sounding board for you, I'd be very glad. Start wherever you like. I'm listening." I lean back in my corner of the couch and turn my whole attention to her.

Another day of fog clears long enough to permit the evening plane to land. I wait while Laurel finds a seat next to the window. She waves to me. I watch the plane take off and then I run back to the parking lot where Logos waits in my little car.

We're halfway to Siasconset before I know why I'm grinning. It was good to have Laurel here, but now we have our silence back again.

I know I've had a long sleep, but I'm not ready yet to get out of bed. Even Logos is content merely to go through the gestures of his morning greeting before settling next to me to have a little nap. His back fits exactly against mine, and I, amused to feel a living body next to

me, turn to look at him. Suddenly I grin: his head is on my pillow.
I stretch and look at the clock: 9:00. That's why I'm so hungry.
"Come on, lazy." I throw back the covers, burying Logos under
them. He fights his way out and lands on the floor, shaking himself,
then leads me down the stairs.

Curling into the corner of the sofa, I pick up my own words to
Laurel again. "I don't have to talk about myself anymore." Another
one of those things I find myself saying. What did I mean?

Talking about myself was my way of inviting people to think
about my problems; to help me solve them; to (Jesus!) feel sorry for
me because the knots were so entangled; to reassure me; to compliment me. Oh, most especially that: to tell me how clever and bright
and kind and beautiful and insightful I was.

I realize now that no one will ever again be able to tell me something about myself that I don't already know. Not that I've brought
back to full memory everything I've ever done or every thought I've
ever had, but that I've looked at all the things about myself that used
to make me say, "No, I'm not like that." But I was like that. And
still am. The mere fact of my trying to hide it was enough to make
me look under the denial to discover what it concealed. Now I know
all of it. Now no one can point to any of those things, intending to
surprise me by knowing them. I've torn down the fortifications. The
thing inside doesn't require defending anymore. I don't even have to
think in terms of defense against attacks. I refuse to be attacked, because I agree at the outset that I am not what I've tried to appear to
be.

I don't need to talk about myself any longer because I don't need
people for those old purposes any longer. I certainly don't need people for solving my problems: I fall into thinking about them without
constraint; I find myself handling them in some way that ends up
being comfortable, suited to me. I can even tolerate not resolving
them immediately. I can let them go back to be chewed over a little
longer. I still haven't resolved the problem about my Harvard references, but somehow I have the feeling that I haven't yet explored all
the options connected with it. It will come. I'll work it through.
That's it: the problems are manageable. They don't haunt me, shapeless things without beginnings, their loose ends dripping over everything else I do.

And I don't need anyone to tell me what I'm like, what I do well,
what I ought to try. I know who I am a little bit more each day. I

simply am this or that, so compliments and reassurances are both irrelevant. It's a waste of both our time for me to invite anyone else to evaluate me: no one else can have my vantage point on me.

Not needing people frees me to look at them. To look at them and see them; to listen to them and hear them.

I get to my feet in sudden excitement. But that's what I couldn't do before! I couldn't hear what George or Mike or Stan was saying to me; couldn't see what I myself was doing. Now I'm not looking to other people as mirrors to tell me who I am: I can see my own outlines.

That's why I'm able to see other people: the glass that used to reflect me is now transparent. I know where I end and where other people begin.

I'm dancing around the room. Logos scurries under the desk to regard me watchfully.

How the thing all fits together! I'm no longer eying people as instruments for filling my needs: I fill my own needs. So I can see their needs, their purposes, as separate from mine.

"Fantastic!" Logos comes toward me in the middle of the floor, tail wagging tentatively.

I didn't know what I was saying to Tony or to Dr. Kant when I talked about George, but they heard me. As I can now hear Laurel and Ugo. I hear them because I don't get in my own way. I never understood what other people were doing because my needs made a barrier between me and any other person. But now I've torn away those unfulfillable needs. I deal with problems in this new way that I work out as I go along, and suddenly people themselves stand forth clearly to me in the very space where I used to see only mirrors. Incredible!

I bounce up and down on the couch, clapping my hands. But the outlet is too tame. "Come on, Sweet Puppy!" He flies with me into the kitchen, where I grab my coat and the doorknob at the same time. "We're going to play!"

What do I want to do?

We walk the beach almost to the lighthouse. The images that pop into my mind are poor attempts to give me my own answer. I remember preparing lectures; teaching classes; listening to students discuss philosophy and then themselves in the privacy of my office or in some sunny courtyard nearby; wandering through library stacks, unfailingly appalled by how few of all the existing books I've read; writing my dissertation.

Maybe this is one problem I can't slambang into. Maybe the solution to this will come to me, instead of my going to it. But first I have to let the little steps multiply and then try to consolidate them. I'm inventing my own life, thirty-seven years late. It may be a while before I see and use all the possibilities.

I slow to a standstill in the road, aware of the silence. The shadows tell me the sun is at noon. The sky is brilliant blue and cloudless. I strain to hear a sound, but there is none. No car starting. No plane overhead. No door closing. No branch creaking in the wind. Indeed, no wind. Logos stands watching me and then turns into our driveway. I hear his feet crunching the gravel until he steps onto the lawn. Then the soundlessness resumes. For a long moment I don't take a breath. I want to impress my memory with this silence in the midst of all this brightness.

A thickness of snow lands during the night, and in the morning the sun has the whole outdoors glittering. Logos wants to chase snowballs even before breakfast. When I come back into the house to make coffee, I feel my cheeks tingling and I laugh to see Logos tumbling in the snow. I move my chair around to watch him play while I eat. He burrows his head into the snow, then suddenly leaps up; he lies on his back in it and slithers from side to side; he takes it up in mouthfuls. Why does a land creature want to be so wet, inside and out?

A pickup truck enters the driveway, and Mr. Santos and another man step out. Logos inspects the truck and the men. I go outdoors to greet them. They're here to check on something about the heat.

Standing in the snow watching them, I have a sense of being looselimbed. Only indoor clothes and boots, no gloves, no hat, no coat burden my movements. The feeling makes me want to turn a somersault.

"Logos!" I plunge my bare hands into the snow to make a snowball, and the snow surprises me by not being cold. My hands cradle the lightweight coolness briefly, but Logos takes my stillness as an invitation to grab what I hold. His jump knocks me down, and the men laugh to see me fall. I get to my feet instantly and make four snowballs in a row.

The moment is an abundance of delight: the sun, the snow, my sense of being free. My words spill out: "Oh, isn't this a glorious day!"

Both men look up at me, and Mr. Santos speaks. "If I didn't have to work, I might think so too."

I have no words. In the silence, I stand a long moment while they bend over their work. Their hands are red on the heavy wrenches. They're not wearing gloves, either.

I go to the door and hold it open for the puppy. "I'm leaving in a week, Mr. Santos. I'll call you when I go, and you can start watching the house again. Come on in, Logos." When I close the door, I lean against it.

He's figured me out as someone so rich that I can be here during the winter without a job. I'd never be able to explain to him what I've been doing here. It doesn't use the muscles of your legs or arms or back, so it's not work. He's decided that I'm here doing nothing he can see and therefore doing nothing. That's the nasty note I heard.

And yet I deserved it. I should have seen myself as he must see me: a full-grown woman romping in the snow with a puppy at nine on a January morning. I forget that people here see me and wonder about me. Before, I was too much concerned with people's opinions of me; now I care too little.

No, it's my way now. I'll simply remember that I have no right to expect anyone to share my gladness. Why should that surprise me? I've been learning here not to expect anyone to share the bad things, either.

31

During the morning I pick up yesterday's mail. Another department isn't ready to decide who its new members will be. I may have to take the Stamford job after all.

Have to. I don't like that. I'm trying to learn what my life will be, independently of money. Instead of earning the money and then figuring out what it's for, I want to find out what I *want* to do and then find some way to earn my living doing that. To let the money support my choices, my way of filling my day, rather than arranging my day around someone else's schedule. But I may get lost in my own shuffle between "want to" and "have to." And I won't know what I want to do until I learn what wanting is.

Until then, having-to takes over. No point in turning away: so long as I look it in the face, it's not the old life. So long as I know the purpose it serves, it's still a choice I make. Anyway, I'm uncertain at best about philosophy. So teaching and the Stamford job are both having-to.

I start to weigh teaching against the Stamford job, but there are too many aspects to keep in mind as I walk. When I get home I sit down to my desk and pull a thick pile of blank paper toward me. In longhand I write on the top of the first sheet: "Considerations for Taking Any Job." I set down two items quickly: freedom to do work that interests me; people I'd be working with. The list grows in little spurts to eight items. I'll run through it thinking first of the Stamford job, then a second time thinking of teaching.

I turn a new page to start, and soon my pen is flying as fast as the thoughts I couldn't keep separate on my walk.

The pile of pages of "Considerations" grows. I write a sentence or two whenever a new idea strikes me: in the middle of cooking, coming in from a walk, just before bed.

I bear in mind that I'm considering possibilities only, even though Stamford is likelier than any of the colleges. I ought to receive Ugo's letter any day now. In seven days I am to leave.

Thirteen pages of scribbled reasoning, and when I read it through, the Stamford job emerges as the sensible solution. I'll accept it, then. I'll keep the Harvard lines open. Someone may still offer me a teaching job for September. In the meantime this job will let me pay off debts.

A letter from Stamford is my only mail. I take it from Mr. Morris with a grin. Other people come through the door as I go out, and when one of the men stoops to pet Logos and ask about him, I feel I can afford the time to talk.

I cross the traffic circle and step onto the public path before I slit the envelope. Inside, a blank sheet of paper is wrapped around the check, and that is all. I stop.

What happened to the letter? Has something gone wrong?

I start to walk again, but slowly. Logos is far ahead of me already. No, nothing's wrong. What could be wrong? Ugo was the one convincing me to take the job. No, this is merely the accounting office efficiently processing the check request. Ugo said he'd ask them to hurry it through, and they did.

I look at the check again: $350. It's as real as it can be. I feel a smile beginning. I fold the check carefully into my pocket. Then I break into an easy run to catch up with Logos.

The night-long rain has turned the ground soggy, filling the ruts in the muddy road with yellow water. The thin fog is like a scrim over the landscape, except when a light wind moves it, and the road becomes visible block by block as we walk. It's weather for watching Logos closely. He can move faster than I, but I can know what's coming before he does. Today a car could be upon us almost unheard.

I think of him first automatically. Me, protecting him. It was to be the other way around.

How often I used to ask my friends what their love for their children was like. Why should a mother's love for her child be treated as something so plainly understood that it never has to be described? Only someone like me, to whom the whole idea of motherly love was opaque, would ask. Was it like loving a man, or was it something different? I gave up trying to understand it. I'd wait until I was a mother myself, and in the meantime I was willing to take the word of mothers that it was special.

But now, through Logos, I begin to understand. I can't sort out all the things that make up my loving him, but that I love him is certain. The whole thing sets me to wondering how different my life might have been if, as a child, I had sensed from my mother the feeling I now have for him.

Perhaps loving something is the only starting place there is for making your life your own. Anything: a bird, a collection of porcelain. Or must it be a living thing you love? Perhaps so. Something that permits a growing sense of being connected, a closeness that's in your power to nourish. You want the creature to flourish because you love him, not because it profits you something. I love Logos for his own sake, because he is what he is and I am what I am.

So I'm back to it again: loving isn't something to be deserved. To deserve something, I have to be able to work for it. But I can't work for someone's love, although I can try to earn other things: admiration, respect, perhaps even loyalty. By the same token, someone can't be blamed for not loving me. If I'm not loved when I love, the lack can't be repaired by any action of mine or repented by the person who doesn't love me. It's all right to cry when the thing is over, but after that you have to let your reaching-out wither away by not feeding it. Which I never understood before.

Or am I simply getting around to noticing that loving is something shared, and that one person loving without return is telling herself a story?

The rain begins again lightly as we reach the sand. Far up ahead, some gulls stand in an irregular line on the beach, heads down, facing into the wind. The rain will continue harder, then, rather than let up. I pull my hat down over my ears, and we go back the way we came.

I awaken mourning Daddy.

Stop, oh, stop. Why can't I deal with this as I'm trying to deal with other things? Look at it; set forth the conditions; consider the alternatives; imagine the consequences of each step.

Hopeless. No part of it is in my power. My mother has the legal authority, and she delegates it to her son, her most loved being. My sister has decided not to fight their version of what to do; and, anyway, Memo has a family of her own. I'm only the eldest daughter.

Who will even tell me how he is? Memo would, if she knew, but she gets her story from my mother, who doesn't know how to tell the truth. And the doctor is the very man who pronounced me in perfect health six weeks before I underwent emergency surgery in Cambridge.

My thoughts rake back and forth across the familiar rows: not this, not that, not this, not that. There's no least bad in all of it: there is only bad, bad, bad.

Who would know how he is? I decide finally to call the urologist who performed Daddy's most recent operation. The afternoon is late by the time I reach him. Daddy has just come through new surgery; considering his general condition, he's doing rather well; the doctor expects to keep him in the hospital for a week or so, but only because he's so debilitated. I give the doctor my phone number and ask him to call me in a few days. He hesitates, then informs me that he has been giving his reports to my mother.

"But I want to know, too!" My throat barely lets the words escape.

Another pause. It is his custom to report to one member of the family, who then informs the others. He is sure I can understand that he doesn't have time to discuss his cases with each of the many persons concerned.

"I understand that you're busy, but you have to understand that I must know." I take a deep breath. "I don't trust my mother's explanation. She either doesn't understand what you tell her, or else she doesn't ask you all the questions I want answered." Even I can hear how it sounds: I'm discredited wherever my life touches hers.

The doctor will consider my request. In any event, I am not to worry now. My father is doing well, under the circumstances.

I hang up trembling. I have a vivid image of Daddy lying in the hospital, the look of quiet terror on his face, incapable of understanding what's happening to him. And not even I, not even by holding his hand, can comfort him.

I cry for a very long time. When I get up from the bed, the outdoor light is dimming fast. I take the car and drive to the post office. There is no letter.

Time to begin putting the house in order: waxing floors, cleaning rugs, storing pillows, covering furniture. The vacuum cleaner doesn't work. I call a store that advertises its ability to repair such things.

"Bring it in," the man says. "I'll have to look at it."

Another store like Daddy's. The man behind the counter lifts up the cleaner to examine it. "Now, what's the matter with it?"

"I don't know. I plugged it in, but nothing happened."

He plugs it in and nothing happens. He unscrews something, and then something else. "This is pretty old."

"I suppose it is. It came with the house when my landlady bought it."

The man looks up with interest. "What house?"

"In Siasconset. Burnell Street. There's no number."

"Oh, the Elwell house. Nice house." He pushes and snaps and pulls things again.

All at once I understand the New England custom of identifying a house by the name of the people who built it rather than by those who currently own it. It's a way of insisting on the continuity of the environment and the impermanence of human occupancy.

"I'll tell you one thing this vacuum cleaner needs: vacuum bags." He grins.

"Oh, no." I have to smile, too.

"And an oiling here, here, and there." He points. I look baffled.

He does it for me. I buy wax, rug cleaner, brush and cloths from him in gratitude.

It's too early to stop at the post office to pick up the mail.

Before I start scrubbing the living room rug, I move the furniture off its surface. I dust, mop the surrounding floor, and store chair and couch cushions with mothballs in the upstairs closet. When I get down on my knees to begin, the rug is suddenly mammoth. A one-foot-square patch takes fifteen minutes. I survey the expanse behind me. I may catch the boat on Friday if I do nothing else until then.

I bend to the work and discover with surprise that it pleases me to watch the now cream-colored area begin to encroach upon the dirty gray of the rest of the rug. I settle into a routine of steps: sponging fresh water over the patch to be cleaned, pouring the shampoo on the wetted place, scrubbing it in, adding more water to rinse.

But the satisfaction is not of the lasting sort. I get to my feet, place newspaper under the cleaned area to absorb excess water, and mark off with my eye how I can partition the job to finish it by tomorrow. After that, I have only to wax the floor in my bedroom. I sigh. But it's a way of using up my restlessness to be gone.

The middle of the sunny morning is cold but inviting. I take the short route to the water. Three more days of this beauty, and then I leave. For the house in Connecticut that I can now have, after all.

I remember a summer Sunday morning in New York, just after finishing at *Mademoiselle*. Someone showed up at Laurel's apartment in the Village offering a country drive. I piled in with so many others that we took turns sitting on each other's laps, singing as we left the city behind us, becoming quieter as the houses became fewer. We had no destination in view: we were only getting away from the heat and the concrete for a time.

And then Ginny, driving, let the car slow down and stop. None of us uttered a sound. Ahead, high on a hill, sat a huge white clapboard house, the trees around it shining in the sun. I left the car and stood in the road. No other car, no person, came. In whatever direction I looked, some marvelous white house was sheltered by green and moving boughs.

"Where are we?" I asked. "What is this place?"

Ginny consulted her map. "Connecticut," she said.

What will my house be like? Away from other houses, perhaps surrounded by woods. Too much to expect the sea to be nearby, but I can look for this silence somewhere, this privacy. No neighbor within shot of eye or ear. Room for Logos to run without having to be on a leash.

At thirty-seven, a woman alone: new friendships will be hard to come by. I may be so old by the time I understand what wanting is that I may never marry. What's marrying, anyway? Being able to, wanting to, live your life with a man. Fitting your way of going through each day to his way, so that neither of you is chipped at or intruded upon, so that there is a benison when you meet that isn't present when you're apart. But I'm just now beginning to learn how to live with myself. There are only fragments of my knowing who I am and what I want, and only rarely do I find some of the pieces coalescing. No, I'm not ready to marry, not until I can stand separately as one unified whole being. I won't need the man I marry: I'll only want him.

But what does "wanting" mean when you specifically exclude needing from the idea, and when you're talking only about persons? What things are there to want, not need, from other people? Oh, this idea of wanting has many sides, and it's going to trip me up at all turns.

The tide is in so far that the margin of beach it leaves is too narrow for walking. It's coming in so fast that I can watch it edge its way to the highest point.

"You wanted him to rescue you, too."

"From what, Dr. Kant?"

"You tell me."

From my failures. Marriage would have been a way to legitimize myself: the man I married was to save me from the dishonor of having failed at my career; he was to turn me into an honest woman after all those men. But suppose the man had looked to me to save *him:* marriage as a mutual rescue mission. I'd have ended up the fooler fooled again. At least I carried only my own disaster on my back. I might have spread the agony around, or bent even further under someone else's, if I had married.

No, I'm not in need of rescue any longer. How did I get everything so backwards before? I know: I had no sense of who I was. I was available for a very low price. The man had only to give me a hint that he might someday begin to consider that I might be a woman he could possibly think of loving, at least a little bit. On that hint, I fell at his feet. But now, when I try to think of who they were, those men who preoccupied me year after year, they're indistinguishable from one another. Faces, hands, bodies were different, but as persons I didn't know them. How could I? I neither saw myself nor heard them. I wonder whether any of them *could* have loved me. Were they capable of loving anyone? It wasn't a question I knew how to ask myself. I knew only how to wonder what I could do to persuade them to love me. Any shred of attention would do as a sign that my cause was progressing.

Oh, God, what I put up with for the sake of what I called "loving." My hands veil my eyes. Then quickly I look up again. No need to shudder about it. I can't be that way again. Can't. That doesn't mean I vow not to be. It means that I, what I am so far, am not like that any longer.

I finish half the rug by the time the mail is due. I set myself not to be disappointed if the letter isn't here today. But I am. And apprehensive, watching the days peel away without knowing where they end.

I intersperse cleaning the rug with waxing the upstairs floor, two tedious tasks whose visible results please me doubly: to look upon and to know that I've done it. The rug is more difficult today because the outdoor light is overcast. I need the sunlight to show me the places I've missed. For variety, I begin the minor packing: books, clothes I won't wear before we leave.

Another hour's work on the rug will see it done. Shall I finish before I go for the mail? No, it's not my rule.

I race Logos to the water tower, and then we cross to the wide Siasconset Road bordered by large frame houses well placed on their acreage. Trees, lawn, and shrubbery complement the shape and color of each presiding structure. Will my house be like one of these? No. They're too close together. I'll need ten or twenty acres for Logos to run free.

The Stamford letter is here. And a letter from my sister. I fold her letter into my pocket: no letter from my family ever brings anything but bad news, and I don't want bad news right now. I stand next to the outside door and hold it open for Logos, but Mr. Morris has some things to say to him, and he willingly trots into the office to be petted and played with before he scoots through the door and across the road ahead of me.

I have the envelope open by the time I'm in the street. At the first sentence, I stop walking and stand still, holding my breath to read the rest.

. . . my complete inability to make up my mind about your value to us. . . . If you can open your mind to other matters besides philosophy . . . intellectually more rewarding to deal with whole problems and not just philosophical aspects of them.

I crumple the letter into my pocket and storm down the road. The bastard! Another engineer trying to reshape the philosophy out of me. Lecturing me about *my* closed world! What the hell is a "whole" problem, anyway? I *knew* I shouldn't have let him take my copy of that report. I *knew* he couldn't understand my notes. I *knew,* yet I let him take it.

And how much of his "complete inability" to make up his mind goes back to the fact that I turned down the pass he made? Two men in one year showing me that their fairness extends only to their rejected loins. It's an occupational hazard for a woman.

I'm still swearing at him when I turn off the Siasconset Road into the short block that jogs to become Burnell Street. I *must* take this taste out of my mouth. I reach into my other pocket for Memo's letter and slit it open.

Daddy is on the critical list. Nurses around the clock since Monday.

I run. Logos gets in my way, but I run. We cross the road and enter our street. I'm running on no breath. The pounding in my chest will crack it open. I run to our door, throw it wide, and keep on running up the stairs to the phone. I place the receiver to my ear, my other hand on the dial. Who will know what's happening? Not Memo: she knows only what Mother tells her. I drop the receiver back on its cradle and fall onto the bed to cry.

No don't cry: think. Yes, think: what can I *do?*

I see Daddy on his hospital bed, in pain and confusion.

I have to *do* something.

I rise from the bed and walk down the stairs to the buckets of water and soap. I get down on my knees and pick up my brush and start to scrub the area that remains undone. I do one patch, sponging, wringing cloths, rubbing, blotting excess water. I watch the patch come clean under my hands, and then I begin another. I pick up the soap bottle to pour, and then I put it down.

The young doctor: Memo's friend who examined Daddy when I insisted on an independent opinion of his general condition. I remember his name as I rush up the stairs to call him.

He's out of his office but will call me on his return. I press both hands into the unyielding receiver. "Operator, tell his secretary that it's very, very urgent. Please have him call me as soon as he can. Please." The secretary will give him my message.

I have to hang up. I have to wait.

I go back downstairs to the rug and, scrubbing, rinsing, blotting, I wait. Why did the other doctor say Daddy was coming along well? That was only two days ago. Did I talk to him before or after Memo wrote this letter? Dear God, how can something so important be so completely out of my hands?

I finish the rug. The wet expanse of the floor eliminates the living room as a place to wait. I start up the stairs to my room, turn back down to the kitchen, make a drink, and head upstairs again. I sit propped up against the pillow on my bed and watch the day darken.

I have the receiver off the hook the moment the ring begins. I explain to the young doctor the conflicting stories I now possess. Will he please go to see my father himself and then call to tell me what in all of this is true?

"Alice, you remember what happened the last time I saw your father for you. Your family let me know in no uncertain terms that I was interfering."

"From their point of view, everything I do is interfering. But I have a right to know the truth about my own father. Their way is to tell me only as much as they want me to know. I've given up trying to guess what their purposes might be. Please help me."

Neither of us speaks. He hears me. He offers to call the surgeon for me.

"But two days ago he was the one who told me my father was out of danger."

"Well, his information now will be more recent than your sister's."

I agree to have him call the surgeon. If he himself isn't clear about Daddy's condition after that, he'll stop in Daddy's room when he makes his own rounds at the hospital.

"Today?"

Yes, today. He'll call the surgeon as soon as we hang up. If he doesn't call me back immediately, it's only because the surgeon himself might not be available.

I lie back in my pillows and wait again. An hour. Two hours. The phone rings.

Daddy was on the critical list, but he has been off it since Monday. His general condition is poor. He won't eat or drink; he is fed intravenously. The only thing to be done is to try to get some strength into him. That takes time, and although the surgeon will go off the case in a few more days, the regular physician is certainly capable of trying to bring Daddy's weight to where it should be.

"Ed, isn't there anything I can do?"

"No. You already understand that the debilitation is one of the consequences of the brain damage, and that that itself is irreversible."

"Yes, I understand. The only thing I've ever tried to do is to make it all less fearful for him."

We hang up. I switch on the light on the bedside table. I suddenly remember that I have no job and no place to live.

I call Marblehead for the only person who has room to take me in. "Marie, you came with me the night I got my puppy. You were tired, you didn't want to, but you knew I needed you. I need you now. Can you put up with me and Logos for a while?" I tell her about Ugo's treachery, and about having to wait to hear from Harvard.

She is reluctant. "It would be like two families living in one house. Our house is very big, but we'd all begin to snap at each other in no time."

"Marie, I wish I didn't have to ask you. I'll pay you of course, and then I'll do my best to keep both of us out of your way."

We talk for fifteen minutes before she agrees. She is no happier than I.

32

I lay a path of newspapers across the still-damp rug to my desk. I add and subtract one final time. My money could last three weeks if I were to stay here. But then I'd have to have an immediate source of income. I lean back in my chair. I'll simply bear in mind that I'm imposing on Marie; I'll track down any job Harvard turns up; and just before I go completely broke, I'll take any secretarial job I can find. Settled. Not to be thought about further, only to be done.

I write Laurel about Ugo and send her the seventeen dollars I owe. I write my sister a letter that I discover is angry when I read it over. A poison touches my every interaction with my family; I can free myself of it only by freeing myself of them.

A light snow has fallen during the night, enough to muster a snowball every dozen steps to throw for Logos all the way to the beach. Tomorrow this light, this view, this silence won't be mine. I give myself over to the smell of the sea air, the sound of the gulls calling, the look of their wings as they settle on the water, ride near the shore, then rise up and wheel outward again.

I don't need to condense all this into one parting memory: I have three months of days to remember. And besides, I don't want merely to remember it: I want the quality of this moment to permeate the days of all my life. I will make it so, if it's not. I will let it be so if it is.

I toss a stick for Logos and grin to see him race for it. When will he be as free to run on miles of beach again?

And I, will I be free, back among people again? Will I be able to guard against trying to please them at all costs? I have to remember that sense of being uncomfortable without knowing why. It's a sign that the thing that's happening hasn't yet gotten through to me but that I must avert it until I understand it. Later I discover that the thing is something I don't want to do, like giving Ugo my notes on his report. The mistake was mine for not trusting my own so faintly whirring sense of discomfort.

But what makes me think of guarding? To guard this freedom is to stunt it, and it's now so fragile that I must give it space to grow. The few things that have let me claim them for my own haven't come to me on some arbitrary schedule: they've come unpredictably, because I've done away with all protective coloration. I must be open all the time. Not just here, where I'm safe because I'm alone, but back in the world, where there are people and difficulties. If I once begin to dissemble to someone else, I may end by dissembling to myself again.

I have a sudden image of Szigeti last May at Leverett House. Two or three bowstrings broke as he played, the shreds hanging visible to us all in the small common room. We tried to listen to his music, but everyone's attention kept being drawn to the diversion. In the middle of a phrase he stopped, ripped out the offending shreds, and resumed his performance. How many beats did he miss? How far back into the piece did he go to begin again? I don't remember. I walked home afterward, envying him. Now I know why: he was absolutely clear about the order in which things matter; he was able to call things by their right names.

In the evening the snow begins again. On impulse I decide to take a walk, and Logos, amazed at his good luck, romps out into the road ahead of me. The streetlight near the water tower is too far away to remind me where the ruts are in the black road. I stumble once, then again, while Logos trots easily along, his nose down in the snow. Flakes whirl around the globes of the streetlights, but the wind is very gentle and soon drops entirely. Our footsteps pressing down the snow make the only sound I hear. I pass houses, some dark, some lighted. Now, the night before I leave, I know which curtains have been parted as I walked the town, which windows have remained opaque. We follow the main road to the post office, then down the side street bordering the casino, and back toward the water tower again. Even inhabited, the town is silent.

It's difficult to go into the house and leave the friendly snow outside. I keep my coat and wet gloves on to throw snowballs for as long as Logos cares to chase them.

The instant I awake, I remember that we leave today. I play hide-and-seek on the bed with Logos as though it were another day, not the last, and then I let him out. Will the sun dance in my next kitchen as it does here? I watch Logos roll in the snow while I make coffee, and then go upstairs to dress, strapping my watch onto my wrist. Seven o'clock. The boat leaves at two. Time begins again today. How do I blunt its tyranny? By simply noticing it rather than knuckling to it. I'll notice it for catching boats and trains, but not for the doings that are my own.

I find my landlady's list for closing up the house. What to do first? There, see? It has me by the throat even as I deny it permission.

I drive my car up to the kitchen door and load my cartons of books and belongings into the back seat. The snow makes for uncertain footing, and as I trace a path back and forth from car to house, the snow packs down and adds its slickness to the hazards.

I remove the last carton from the living room. When I return through the doorway on my way upstairs, the effects of my own efficiency stop me. The room has ceased to belong to me. Cushions are gone from couch and chairs. The furniture is back in the positions in which I found it three months ago. My desk is no more: it has become the dining table on the other side of the room. The rug is spotless: no trace of a puppy's growing up or of my daily pacing. It's one more room, shining and smelling fresh, in a house being returned to its owner.

One by one, the other rooms take on this aspect. They all but push me out the door. I throw on my coat and hat and stride across the lawn on the familiar diagonal for the last time, Logos ahead of me as always. I pass the moor, and then the water tower and head directly for the post office.

I write out my new forwarding address on the standard pink form. How many more pink forms will I file in how many more post offices before I have my house? I hand the card to the man at the window, peering around him to try to see the postmaster. "Isn't Mr. Morris here today?"

"No, not today. He retired, you know, January first. He's just been coming in to help out from time to time until I felt ready to take over."

I remember now. "Will you thank him for me for all his courtesies?"

The new postmaster nods. "We're sorry to see you leave. Good luck. Come back again." We shake hands through the window.

I hold open the door for Logos, and when I close it behind us, I'm sorry not to have seen, one last time, the man who construed his job as one requiring thoughtfulness at its very center. His work provided my main line to a world to which I now return.

We round the corner, down the cobblestone hill, past the posts and chain barriers onto the sand. Logos races to the water's edge, barking to make the gulls rise up, then sniffs his way along the beach to discover who passed by since yesterday. The waves are calm: the wind that blew the snow clouds in last night has vanished.

I walk slowly, parallel to the water and looking out at it. This was home for me: to come here any time to walk and think and play and sit and drink the air in perfect freedom. I hereby appropriate it to accompany me wherever I go.

It occurs to me that nothing of my external circumstance has changed in these three months. I have no source of income, and almost no money. I have no place to live: I must rely on someone else's goodwill for a while. I can't point myself with certainty in any direction at all. I have no human beings connected to me. I am without power to help my father.

But from inside, the aspect of it all is different, except for Daddy. What do I mean?

I try to sort out the parts of it and come upon the shapes of ideas new to my repertoire: being alone, burgeoning in it; making my own decisions, insisting on it; uncovering my own authority, reveling in it; seeing other people as beings in their own right, astonished by it.

Logos paws at something in a pile of seaweed: a dead gull, losing its way and its life during the snowy night. I hook my finger around Logos' collar to drag him away, and find almost no space between the collar and his neck.

"But you're growing up." I stoop to examine the fit of the leather. The collar is fastened on the last notch and beginning to rip at the side. We'll get a new one today.

It's time to leave. I stand and look in each direction up the beach. I walk backward slowly across the dunes. When I reach the road, I walk backward again to keep the ocean in sight to the last. Now I know I'm leaving. I turn again and head down the long road to the tasks remaining at the house.

Mr. Santos comes by as I struggle with the sunken garbage can.

"Never mind," he says. "When the ground begins to thaw, I'll take it to the dump for you."

I empty the refrigerator down to two slices of bread and a thick hunk of butter. I smear the butter onto the bread, break it into pieces and place it in the back garden for the birds to find. I pack my luggage into the front seat and prepare a corner of the back for Logos.

Mr. Santos and I shake hands, and then I realize that Logos is gone. I shout his name. I run out to the road, then around the house to the moor side, then into the backyard calling him. He emerges on the garden path, licking his lips.

"What did you eat now?" I try not to imagine the carcass inside him, and then I notice something yellow on the tip of his nose: he ate the bread and butter himself. Now he'll be seasick on the boat.

"Oh, Logos, you're not helping." I settle him into the back seat.

Good-bye, house. I keep it in my rearview mirror until I turn into the long straight road to Nantucket.

I drop my books off at the library, and then drive two blocks to the hardware store. It's not my father coming toward me.

"My puppy needs a new collar." I hand the man the almost broken one to show him its size. He leads me to racks of collars in graduated lengths, plain and studded, red, black, green, tan. I choose one. The man takes up a pair of pliers, and attaches Logos' identification tags to the ring of the new collar. I thank him, pay him, but cannot say good-bye to him at all.

In the car I buckle the plain black collar around Logos' neck. It fits loosely, not nipping in his fur as the old one did. He sits in his corner, all alertness, knowing something different is happening today. I smile to see the big ears quivering, taking it all in.

I buy my ticket and drive my car onto the ferry. I snap the leash on Logos' collar and we run up the stairs. I want to be on deck when we depart; I want to watch the ferry pull away from the dock; I want to know the exact minute that I sever my tie with this island.

The rear deck is thick with people. I start to push my way to the railing, looking down every few steps to keep Logos from being squashed by all the pairs of feet. Then suddenly my leash goes limp: Logos is gone, the collar hanging like a noose from the leash's end.

"Logos!" Dear God, if he falls overboard!

"Here, miss." A man, laughing, lifts the squirming puppy over to me and stoops to hold him by his front legs until I, kneeling, slip the collar on again. I get to my feet and thank the man. People standing on the pier wave and call, and the people surrounding me return the farewell. We leave the land slowly. For a moment I'm not sure that it has happened.

Someone standing next to me speaks to his companion. "We're on our way."

Yes. I think we are.